DISSATISFACTIONS

# MINORITARIAN AESTHETICS

General Editors: Uri McMillan, Sandra Ruiz, Shane Vogel

Minoritarian Aesthetics promotes scholarship that develops a minor position toward aesthetics and an aesthetic stance toward minoritarian experience. The aesthetic—the domain of sensation, beauty, value, taste, (dis)pleasure, and the sublime—instructs not only representations and judgments of the social but the relational bonds that form between objects, subjects, and entities across spatial-temporal domains.

*Deadpan: The Aesthetics of Black Inexpression*
Tina Post

*For Pleasure: Race, Experimentalism, and Aesthetics*
Rachel Jane Carroll

*Dissatisfactions: Queer Latinidad and the Politics of Style*
Joshua Javier Guzmán

# Dissatisfactions

*Queer Latinidad and the
Politics of Style*

Joshua Javier Guzmán

NEW YORK UNIVERSITY PRESS
New York

NEW YORK UNIVERSITY PRESS
New York
www.nyupress.org

© 2024 by New York University
All rights reserved

Library of Congress Cataloging-in-Publication Data
Names: Guzmán, Joshua Javier, author.
Title: Dissatisfactions : queer Latinidad and the politics of style / Joshua Javier Guzmán.
Description: New York : New York University Press, [2024] | Series: Minoritarian aesthetics | Includes bibliographical references and index.
Identifiers: LCCN 2024000919 (print) | LCCN 2024000920 (ebook) | ISBN 9781479812820 (hardback ; alk. paper) | ISBN 9781479812837 (paperback ; alk. paper) | ISBN 9781479812851 (ebook) | ISBN 9781479812844 (ebook other)
Subjects: LCSH: Hispanic American gay people—California—Los Angeles. | Gay culture—California—Los Angeles. | Aesthetics—Political aspects. | Hispanic Americans—California—Los Angeles—Social conditions. | Mexican Americans—California—Los Angeles—Social conditions.
Classification: LCC HQ73.4.H57 G89 2024 (print) | LCC HQ73.4.H57 (ebook) | DDC 306.76/608968073—dc23/eng/20240124
LC record available at https://lccn.loc.gov/2024000919
LC ebook record available at https://lccn.loc.gov/2024000920

This book is printed on acid-free paper, and its binding materials are chosen for strength and durability. We strive to use environmentally responsible suppliers and materials to the greatest extent possible in publishing our books.

Manufactured in the United States of America

10 9 8 7 6 5 4 3 2 1

Also available as an ebook

CONTENTS

Introduction: Brown Power and Its Discontents   1

1. The Style Politics of Nausea: X, Sartre, and Asco   37

2. Stripped Life: Women of Color Punk, Lo-Fi Attitude, and Feminist Print Culture   75

3. Desiring in the Dark: Framing Ambivalence in the Works of Gil Cuadros, Ray Navarro, and "Gay Latino Studies"   111

4. Twilight of the Idlers: Gregg Araki, Felix Gonzalez-Torres, and the Aesthetics of Malaise   151

Conclusion: Dream Damaged, or, A Portrait of Queer Latinidad   195

*Acknowledgments*   201

*Notes*   205

*Index*   233

*About the Author*   247

A change of speed, a change of style
A change of scene, with no regrets
A chance to watch, admire the distance
Still occupied, though you forget

It was me, waiting for me
Hoping for something more
Me, seeing me this time
Hoping for something else
—Joy Division, "New Dawn Fades"

# Introduction

*Brown Power and Its Discontents*

Weeks after their debut show at Josie Roth's studio in Los Angeles, a weird and androgynous-looking punk-synth band of four took the small stage at a corner in Lace Gallery in Hollywood ready to gear up for their set at a benefit for the Los Angeles Women's Video Center (LAWVC). A component of the Los Angeles Women's Building, a feminist arts cultural space that lasted from 1973 to 1991, LAWVC was cofounded in 1976 by the feminists Nancy Angelo, Candace Compton, and Annette Hunt.[1] It was an unusual mix of attendees, especially for a feminist, all-women event. But by far the most memorable moment of the benefit seemed to be the opening act: the genderfucking band Nervous Gender, which both titillated and confused its audience. Nervous Gender was formed in 1978 by two queer East Los Angeles Chicanos who attended junior high school together, Gerardo Velazquez and Michael Ochoa; an Irish expatriate via London, Edward Stapleton, who had met Velazquez at a Screamers punk show; and Phranc, a lesbian separatist folk musician who knew Stapleton from a previous punk show and who characterized the band as not feminist but queer. According to a review of the show in the legendary Los Angeles punk magazine *Slash*, the benefit was a feminist-meets-punk-meets-queer religious experience and raised something like an antiseparatist consciousness:

> Nervous Gender was supposed to play on Good Friday and they sort of did, passing up an offer to open for the Plugz in order to play this benefit. I liked the idea of them playing for the women's building. There was a time when lesbians got together for heavy swaying concert where feminist folk singers sang songs that make the Modern Lovers sound

pessimistic, but these women are wild and crazy guys and Lace Gallery's Punk Meets Art show a year ago inspired this full moon Easter ritual.

Then Nervous Gender's Phranc announced "We're not nervous" and the band performed "Suburbia Diptheria" and "Berlin Redhead" for a half-pleased half-offended audience. A member of the Tracers [the other punk band billed that evening] had his fingers in his ears while a girl was dancing and yawning at the same time. Punks and separatists cheered when "Do the Gestalt" was dedicated to Dr. Toni Grant, and Phranc swatted [her] head with an L.A. Weekly. . . . Then producer Annette Hunt announced that the 40 minutes were up and she didn't want to stay all night. "Pussies!" screamed Phranc to the audience before doing their last song, "Mommie's Chest." She left the stage snarling about the "goddamn dykes" while Gerardo [Velazquez], Michael [Ochoa] and Edward [Stapleton] seemed to take it more philosophically. Nervous Gender toys with being the first "out" punk band, "but people think we're weird 'cause we're queer." Their brand of electronic chamber music and their sense of humor makes them one of my favorite bands.[2]

In the history of punk, Nervous Gender occupies an inspirational position to what critics have deemed the "queercore movement," a subgenre of punk culture that centers on sexual deviancy, gender-bending performances, lyrics about gender and sexuality, and a general do-it-yourself (DIY) aesthetic in opposition to mainstream culture and the emerging hardcore punk scene of the 1980s, the latter of which fashioned itself around a white male masculinity displaced from often-affluent regions such as Orange County. Already in the band's second performance, one detects its abrasive, confrontational, and discordant attitude. This was partly due to their physical performance, screaming, insulting, and baiting the audiences with comments about gender, sex, and religion, all of which only exacerbated the frenzied noise of the band's analog synthesizers. But at the same time, the band was able to organize the variegated audience members around a shared disdain for the antifeminist talk-radio host Dr. Toni Grant, who propagated psychological advice draped in heterosexual and sexist presumptions about the need for women to help men become better selves. Phranc, in "swatting her head" during a song whose title names a school of thought in psychology about perception and order, mimics and ridicules the repetition function of gender.

Figure I.1. Founding members of Nervous Gender (*left to right*): Gerardo Velazquez, Phranc, Edward Stapleton, Michael Ochoa.

At once performing her disbelief in such a sexist ideology, she also questions the coherence of a feminism tethered to strict notions of gender and sexuality. Similarly, Nervous Gender's deliberately offensive lyrics about deviant sexuality, drug usage, rage, violence, sadomasochism, and sacrilegious imagery were generally delivered in insincere though bitingly humorous anger.

The name Nervous Gender came to Stapleton in a bricolage manner. He conjoined the first word of a Patti Smith poem he had encountered ("nervous") while listening to an Ultravox song, "My Sex," when suddenly John Foxx's bourgeoning new-wave voice earnestly arrived at another decisive word: "My sex / Is savage, tender / It wears no future faces / Owns just random *gender*." Stapleton would receive cassette tapes of the glam-rock-*cum*-new-wave band from his friends who were attending art school in East Ham, which helped Stapleton enjoy the electronic side of punk rock music. In fact, "My Sex" was one of the first songs to feature heavy use of synthesizers in the new-wave genre. Like Stapleton, Ochoa was drawn to the synth's electronic sound and had bought a modular stereo prior to meeting Stapleton. Disturbing his fellow Chicano neighbors in East Los Angeles, Ochoa would loudly play with the input/output sockets, producing exciting feedback noise for the young queer Chicano, noise that became central to Nervous Gender's performances and sound.

It was Velazquez who took the lead in determining the band's aesthetic interest, however, often designing by hand their fliers and performance outfits and writing their lyrics and even poetry that accompanied their performances and song releases. Colin Gunckel explains their aesthetic as "at once visual music, and performance based. Its flyers departed from the handwritten or crudely collaged efforts of many early punk bands, and instead were provocative visual orchestrations of gay sexuality, violent nihilism, caustic humor, religious reference, and sci-fi futurity."[3] Nervous Gender's minoritarian aesthetic becomes clearer when we see Velazquez as a conceptual thinker, because despite the reviewer in *Slash* characterizing all three of the men in the band as more philosophical, it was really Velazquez who incorporated a conceptual aesthetic to Nervous Gender's repertoire. He attended California State University, Los Angeles, where he studied classics, creative writing, and physics, subjects that influenced his aesthetic interests in science, sci-fi, poetry, and Greco-Roman sexuality. In many ways, Nervous Gender was as thoughtful as it was abrasive, if not more so. They were stylizing a critique into one of playful confrontation, a performance of dissatisfaction that *feels* before its time.

Nervous Gender and Velazquez's creative output were conditioned by what Mark Fisher calls "popular modernism": a queer tendency toward forms of collectivity forged within the very ruins of modernism, where a focus on circulating and provoking alternative desires through experimental music, underground presses, public radio and television

Figure I.2. Nervous Gender performing at a benefit for the Los Angeles Women Video Center, April 13, 1979. (Photo by Steve Sharp)

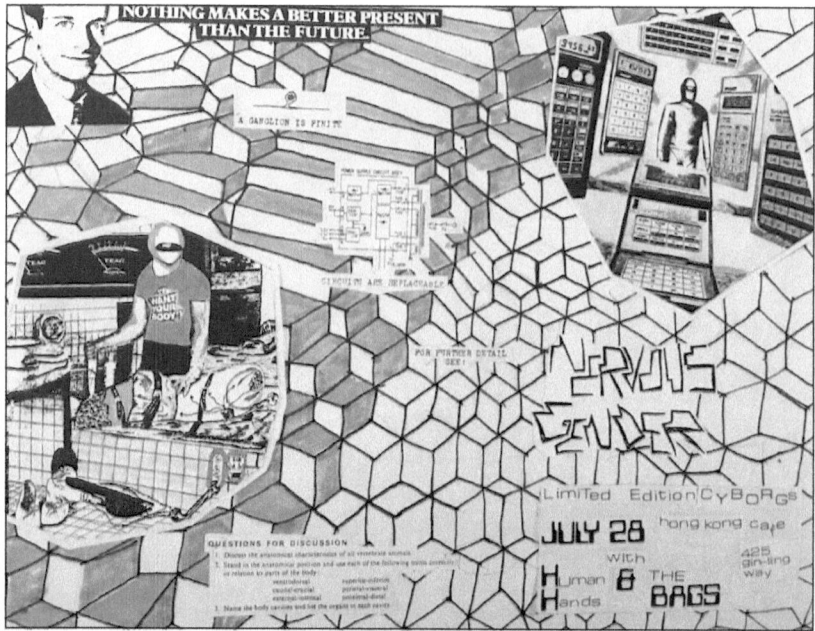

Figure 1.3. Nervous Gender flier designed by Velazquez for a show at Hong Kong Café in Los Angeles featuring The Bags, July 28, 1979.

broadcasting, loitering in public spaces, and a whole other host of networks where communal creativity abounds.[4] In fact, Ultravox's "My Sex" serves as a good example of a song that both lyrically and sonically registers Fisher's popular modernism. For example, its early use of synthesizers to describe a landscape of desire "geared for synchromesh," sputtering up images of "suburban photographs" and "skyscraper shadows on a car crash overpass," all come to echo a similar historical condition unfolding across the Atlantic. These sounds and images also speak to Los Angeles's popular modernist setting, where despite the rapid privatization of the public sphere under Reaganite policies, queer creatives anxiously made do with the at-hand while yielding excitingly new cultural production. One such example is Velazquez's own incorporation of synthesizers, which made Nervous Gender one of the first electropunk bands in the United States, a new configuration of punk sounds that evoked the future within a very syncopated, which is to say off-beat, and disappointing here and now. Here, the very affective structure of minoritarian aesthetics gleaned through Velazquez and Nervous Gender mirrors the dialectics of play and labor central to the argument of *Dissatisfactions*, whereby the popular modernist conditions of Nervous Gender's run from 1978 up until Velazquez's death from AIDS complications in 1992 at the age of thirty-three come to figure within the band's experimental work as a self-awareness of its own demise: anticipating a loss of resources, ideas, energies, and attention to the modern impulse to create something new yielded a yearning, at the very least, to try. Such self-reflexivity inherent within minoritarian experiences, I argue, comes to figure as stylized discontents and not unlike Velazquez's own proclivity for journaling and doodling on early-1980s computational grid paper, notes that would turn into his signature "provocative visual orchestrations" and where we find one line in a flier reading, "Nothing makes a better present than the future." In this statement, one can read "nothing" as a composition of the present, a preferred moment than the future. And nothing *but* the future better serves as the present. In both cases, we have a syncopated temporality, one where the future is experienced as loss in the present *and* something less than nothing. The anachronism announced here grounds the argument of *Dissatisfactions*, which aims to periodize post-1968 Los Angeles through a series of stylized discontents. In turn, these stylized discontents formalize the loss in the here and now while attending to the unrealized desires of the historical subjects of this book.

*Dissatisfactions* begins in California just after the height of the Vietnam War. In fact, a critical dissatisfaction permeated much of Los Angeles in 1968, the year when many Chicanos mobilized and walked out of their high schools in East LA in protest of the inequity of the Los Angeles public school system and the way this inequity disproportionately affected Chicano and Black youth. And it was also at this time when modernist expressions of art in New York City and Paris were being challenged (if not displaced as the art capitals of the world) with the growing interest and production of feminist, pop, conceptual, and performance art. The burst of aesthetic expression and the various style politics that came with it worked in tandem with many of the social movements emerging around the historical flashpoint of 1968, namely, gay liberation, feminist, and Black and Brown Power movements.

Importantly, however, *Dissatisfactions* stages a theoretical and historical shift away from the origins of the Chicano movement to foreground the underground, the minor, and the understudied cultural influence of the intersection of Chicano politics, the early LA punk scene, and AIDS activism and art. This book concentrates around a cluster of historical events such as the Chicano Walk-Outs in East LA (1968) and then-Governor Ronald Reagan's mobilization of the National Guard to the campus of the University of California, Berkeley, in 1969, the first time a US governor ordered troops to a college campus to suppress political dissent. Important here is how Reagan borrowed this tactic after having witnessed a similar move executed in Mexico City some months earlier, resulting in the Tlatelolco Massacre in October 1968. At Berkeley, student activists were organizing in response to the war in Vietnam, which serves as a backdrop for much of the discontent felt within Chicano communities in California during this period. This desperation culminated in the Chicano Moratorium March of 1970, which saw the police assassination of a prominent Chicano journalist, Rubén Salazar, who covered the 1968 Olympics a year prior for the *Los Angeles Times*. In a posthumously published article, Salazar offers an important definition of "Chicano," when he writes, "a Chicano is a Mexican-American with a non-Anglo image of himself."[5] Key for Salazar's definition is the way "Chicano" marks an awareness of historical knowledge outside the fantasy of acculturation. But this definition further comes into crisis when we hold the tension between representation and embodiment in conflict and when misrecognition becomes the ground for a shared politics.

"Chicano" was first used as a pejorative against poor Mexican Americans by wealthier Anglo-Americans in the US Southwest and subsequently reclaimed during the political activism and the rise of political consciousness initiated in the farmworker movement of the 1960s. Marrying Marxist anticapitalist critique with Chicano nationalism and cultural pride, "El Movimiento" posited "Chicano" as a form of political and class consciousness. In the 1970s, the Chicano scholar and theorist José Limón set out to document the contradictory usages of the term, understanding first how "*Chicano* . . . is both an intra-ethnic class-based slur and a nickname."[6] Limón is interested in the ambivalence inherent in the term, since on the one hand, working-class poor Mexican Americans seemingly rejected the use because of its origin as a "caustic slur," while on the other, "the word's very association with the lower socioeconomic classes may be responsible for its potentially positive meaning in other contexts." However, Limón rejects the idea that the working-class, poor Mexican Americans were inherently conservative and posits the idea that perhaps what was being rejected was "a 1960s counter-cultural political *style* which involved exaggerated rhetoric, dress, and other personal habits: adventurist confrontation tactics; etc." What becomes clear for Limón is how "the source of disharmony" in the term's use lies "not in differing political attitudes, but rather in the disparate ways of performing '*chicano*' in the activist and non-university sectors of the total community."[7] In 1979, an important year in this book, Limón was already foregrounding the significance of performance, attitudes, and styles when one takes seriously the cultural limits of a political ideology.

Yet it also must be said that as a field of study, Chicano Studies often centers on male-identified sensibilities when the Chicano's "non-Anglo image of himself" fails to fully subsume into "intra-ethnic class-based" discourses. Sandra K. Soto reminds us that "feminist critiques of foundations and origins" (leveled by scholars like Sonia Saldivar-Hall, Norma Cantú, Norma Alarcón, Emma Pérez, Gloria Anzaldúa, and Cherríe Moraga in the 1980s and 1990s, along with Soto and Maylei Blackwell and others in the twenty-first century) afford queer and nonmasculinist analytics of *chicanidad*.[8]

Meanwhile, the increase in state violence against the Chicano community fueled the social justice sentiment of "Brown Power" in the hope of organizing Chicanos to combat the violent disenfranchisement felt by the minoritarian population. It was also at the time serving as a predicate to the beginnings of the Los Angeles punk scene, which often included many young Chicanos and other queers of color gathering in venues like The Masque in Hollywood and The Vex in East Los Angeles a decade later. This book argues that the Los Angeles punk scene and the queer Chicanos who participated, whether directly or marginally, in this scene present, on the one hand, a disjuncture between Chicano nationalism and gay liberation while, on the other, a possible juncture between the Reagan era and the unwarranted deaths of many Chicanos/Latinos under the AIDS epidemic.

As a form of civil resistance, gay liberation, also emerging in the late 1960s and intensifying throughout the 1970s, was a response to the caustic societal shame imposed on gay, lesbian, and trans communities. Important here is how AIDS activism in the 1980s challenged and changed the composition of gay liberation to include questions of health, medical access, and housing. Also noteworthy are the ways that the AIDS epidemic countered much of the pride and some of the successes gained in gay liberation in the years prior. The AIDS crisis made clear the palpable tension arising from cultural gains won, to then be challenged in the backlash spurred by intensifying homophobia during the AIDS crisis, often articulated in the anxieties around "returning to the closet." It was not until September 17, 1985, in response to a reporter's question, that then-President Reagan mentioned the disease, four years after the first cases were announced in Los Angeles. At that point, approximately five thousand people, mostly gay men, had died of the disease. This served as a chilling reminder of the slowness of social change.

The rise of the Reagan era and the subsequent disenchantment following the historical events around the image-event of 1968 and the social movements that lingered thereafter conditioned much art production in Los Angeles. What I see as the "social comedown" of post-1968 Los Angeles reveals how style remains an essential concept in the study of the social and the political, which have increasingly become untethered from each other under neoliberalism. Style, as Limón attests earlier, tells us something about the ambivalence structuring politics within what Theodor Adorno described as the fully "administered world" of late modernity, a world in which *freedom* "cannot even be conceived as an isolated thing, that is, in the absence of social freedom," which is to say the freedom of all from the administration of social differences into rational equivalencies.[9] The ambivalent function of style is due in part to how style, as the art historian James Ackerman has argued, marks the "tension between stability and change," that is, between the reproduction of the same and the promise of something new.[10] In this way, style becomes actively political, since to speak of style is to acknowledge the dialectical tension between identity and difference. Dick Hebdige's *Subculture: The Meaning of Style* (1979) stands as the first study of its kind to approach style in relation to subcultural politics. Building on social Marxist theories of culture, hegemony, and ideology, this influential work emerged from British cultural studies at a moment when many

Chicanos were engaging with a punk style as a mode of political dissent against Chicano nationalism. (These debates are further explored in chapter 2.) *Dissatisfactions* is indebted to Hebdige's thinking of style as a form of bricolage, a creation of work through the assemblages of variegated objects and things, by translating bricolage into a method of interinanimation, discussed at the end of this introduction. With regard to periodization and the importance of studying "Reagan's America" for queer studies, Latino studies, and performance studies, *Dissatisfactions* not only is concerned with how Chicanos/Latinos created modes of survival in the face of these policies but also offers three significant interventions: (1) an expanded frame of what to consider "performance art" that includes the "body" of the audio/visual medium as historically contingent yet capable of *doing* things in the world (like Asco's misleading photo-performances or Ray Navarro's television-guerrilla-activism, both discussed in this book); (2) an investigation into the equivocal nature of negative feelings and their potential to enact social change by acknowledging how noncathartic emotions structure the everyday lives of workers moving from the Fordist production line into a post-Fordist economy, one requiring more communicative labor; (3) a different theoretical language and framework that hold both the political significance of collective action and the psychic life of those Chicano subjects potentially ousted from that collective's sexual/gender mainstream.

In addition, this historical period marks notable increases in cultural production conditioned by major changes in economic production, the redistribution of wealth and public space, and the consumption of new commodities on an emerging credit system. These major economic forces conjoined with social movements, reconfiguring the relationship between politics and aesthetics, where a shift in politics came to mirror a shift in aesthetics. One aspect of this shift included the supplementation of politics with expressive political culture. *Dissatisfactions* argues that it is exactly this shift that registers the significance of style as a political tool for social change. As the sociologist Edward J. McCaughan argues, "The projection of a social movement's identity and agenda through art clearly involves formal and other aesthetic considerations as well as subject matter. . . . The stylistic and formal choices made by [Chicano] artists were loaded politically."[11] As a result, McCaughan discovers that many artists during this historical hot moment of politically infused art (especially in Los Angeles and Mexico City) indeed created a set of new "visual discourses" demanding "fuller democratic rights and social justice for working people, women, ethnic communities, immigrants, and sexual minorities throughout Mexico and the United States."[12] One clear aspect to the advent of expressive culture from political subjects often responding to experiences of marginalization centers on the marrying of representation with identity in aesthetic production.

Much of Chicano art within this period initially revolved around the paradigm of representation and usually indexed traditional forms of family, national belonging, and uplift ideologies in efforts to cohere an identity around the sign of "Chicanismo." This dominant trend in Chicano art actively disavowed its queer subjects, along with other ways of doing art such as conceptual, minimal, and performance, by insisting that Chicanismo was a *knowable* identity and capable of being represented and unproblematically assimilated within the confines of the nation. Most of this was accomplished through the affective current of cultural pride, where one must happily wear the burden of representation as a minor cost for solidarity for "la causa," or "the cause." However, by foregrounding the queer styles of many Chicano punk artists assembled in this book, we see how style enables convergent and diverse forms of recognition not predicated on the force field of identity but rather something like what the philosopher of language Ludwig Wittgenstein called "aspects," that is, an object's capacity to be seen in multiple ways, an illusory fact perception.[13] The aspects of queer Chicano punk art are symptomatic of an aesthetic embedded within shifting temporal and spatial registers, mainly the paradigmatic shift from modernity to postmodernity, Fordist production to post-Fordism, when the "centuries-long dialectic" between state and capital "came to an end" and when "corporations now ruled the earth."[14] Therefore, style brings us to a study of a brooding intensity within the Los Angeles punk scene, a discontent mediated through a queer Chicano politics unaligned with the dominant way that movement politics *appeared*. I should note here that "discontent" and "dissatisfaction" are used interchangeably throughout this book to describe a structure of feeling while maintaining etymological ties to other terms that share in such a structure of feeling, such as malaise, dis-ease, ambivalence, melancholia, nausea, and a generalized unsettledness.

One aim of this book is to critically engage with ongoing conversations between performance studies, Latino studies, and queer theory, to analyze how these fields are crucial in thinking through the aesthetics and politics of ethnic-racial and sexual difference in late modernity, otherwise mobilized here as minoritarian aesthetics. The theoretical and methodological approaches to the archive assembled in this book represent a commitment to interdisciplinarity as a necessary and productive form of *doing* critique. Like the field of performance studies itself, this book is informed by multiple disciplines and fields of study, such as media studies, film studies, psychoanalysis, critical theory, punk studies, and women of color feminism.

*Dissatisfactions* moves away from *and* with scholars who work at the intersection of queer studies, Latino studies, and performance studies. First and foremost, the book is indebted to the oeuvre of José Esteban Muñoz, who insisted not only on future-dawning queer world-making practices predicated on the "educated desire" he named as hope but also on a "critical dissatisfaction" that puts pressure on the here and now. At the end of his *Cruising Utopia*, the theorist asserts, "From shared critical dissatisfaction we arrive at collective potentiality."[15] *Dissatisfactions* lingers at the point of departure from shared critical dissatisfactions and stops short of arriving at collective potentiality, to ask, What might the absence of the future in the here and now *do* to the Chicano/Latino cultural imaginary? Indeed, this question is animated by a negativity that Muñoz ushered into the field of Latino studies via questions of enactments, doings, critiques, and situations *within* the social world: internal contradictions are gleaned as opportunities for greater understanding of what politics looks like and what aesthetics can do for minoritized populations. He writes at the end of *Disidentifications*, "I've opted against an epistemological approach to disidentification and have instead attempted to offer descriptions of what disidentification *does within the social*."[16] Key to the argument of *Dissatisfactions* is that one of the things disidentification does within the social is open the gap between having to assimilate and having to resist. This gap constitutes a loss that in turn becomes productive for the subjects of this book because much of their creative output was imagined under its sign.

Similarly, Antonio Viego's watershed monograph *Dead Subjects* opens with the confession that his book too was written under the sign of loss.

*Dissatisfactions* earnestly heeds Viego's call for Latino studies to think seriously through a politics of loss, one that both highlights the social elements that constitute losses in resources, language, land, and rights and maintains a keen eye on the constitutive loss at the center of the Latino subject of desire. But most importantly, both Muñoz's and Viego's work affords an incredibly productive overlap between Marxist and psychoanalytic theories and methodologies. For to combat the contemporary rise in anti-intellectualism in US popular culture, one must be nonallergic to concrete, historically grounded theory and its potential usages and limitations for studies of ethnic-racial, gender, and sexual differences. Whether insisting on utopianism from a German Idealist positionality or reminding readers of the inadequacies of subjectivity best articulated through a Lacanian-inflected psychoanalysis, together they gesture to both the incompleteness of Latino subjecthood and the world it finds itself in.

Circumventing narratives of completion, wholeness, and a general affirmative vibe, *Dissatisfactions* aligns with Sandra Ruiz's theoretical treatise on Puerto Rican and brown existentialism by agreeing with the argument that "negation may lead us to the spaces where the unwanted are essentially desirable on their own terms, and outside of pellucidity."[17] As in Ruiz's work, the reader will encounter existentialist thoughts-in-action that come to form much of the aesthetic work in this book. But this is not imposed as top-down theorizing; instead the book takes its cues from the cultural producers themselves, since "the philosophical and political quests of these artists produce an aesthetic event whereby existential concerns meet performative ways of being-different-in-the-world."[18]

Indeed, belonging-in-difference is but another way of saying unbelonging. In line with Ruiz, Muñoz, and Viego, Iván Ramos foregrounds the "aesthetic gestures of refusal in Mexican and Latina/o contemporary art, gestures expressed primarily through an incongruence between sound and identity."[19] Similarly, I hope *Dissatisfactions* makes good on the incongruencies *within* identity and social movements to further explicate the style politics of unbelonging. Like Deborah Vargas, who has also shifted the field's ears to the discordant and dissonant, to the "chaos, cacophony, disharmony, commotion [and] static" disruptions *within* the status quo, Ruiz and Ramos chart aesthetic forms of inauthenticity, which, when taken all together, yield a remarkable insistence against equivalency, adequation, and coherence. From within the very parameters that desire connection, it would seem like the norm makes all the wrong connections.

These bad connections that the norm facilitates present opportunities for otherwise-unlikely resonances between disparate social differences, geographies, and temporalities. Richard T. Rodríguez investigates the transatlantic intimacies between US latinidad and British post-punk by attending to what he calls the "touch" registering the imaginative potential of "unbounded haptic intimacy" across "temporal and spatial divergences."[20] Rodríguez's creative interpretations of cultural production unmoored of identarian constraints refuse to take the social for granted, which is to say the author understands the social as not static but active. And not all activity ought to be surmised as having to do emancipatory work. Pleasure too can be multidirectional in the way Rodríguez conceives of touch, and sometimes it can amount to nothing more than just that—pleasure. Juana Maria Rodríguez insistently reminds us of the centrality of sexual politics to utopian longings, where gestures in general, from touch to kiss to brushes of acknowledgment and parting glances, image futurity from *within* the confines of remote proximities.[21]

Like Juana Maria Rodríguez, Amber Musser has thoughtfully advanced an analytic by which to grapple with sensuality's excessive doings, in particular to ethnic-racialization and sexist histories of sexual objectification of Black and brown bodies. Not taking for granted the opacity inherent in ethnic-racialization and the subjugation of bodies by an unknowable externality (the big Other) renders what Musser calls "brown jouissance," the nexus of body as both object and abject.[22] Abjection as a negative framework affords Musser a retooling of the pleasures and displeasures of belonging. This negative insistence stretches to another key scholar of negativity and Latino studies. Leticia Alvarado's generative work on abjection challenges the disciplinary protocols in Latino studies to think critically about "the relationship between politics and aesthetics by challenging the limited conventions upon which political art rests within the field of Latino studies, namely community building and ego reinforcement through recuperative identity formation."[23] Both Musser and Alvarado foreground the epistemological limits of identity formation and restage them as a site of performance, opacity, and illegibility within perverse pleasures. And lastly, Robb Hernandez and C. Ondine Chavoya have led the way in the field of queer Chicano/Latino studies to show the importance of the archive and the ethical acts of collecting and protecting otherwise-ephemeral evidence of queer Latino life lived through art and aesthetics.[24]

What this cohort of scholars represents is a sustained engagement with the tension between material culture and the aesthetic dimension. Crucial to this strand of scholarship is the affective and relational comportments to unbelonging, memory, and imagination, which I find to be productive sites for an ambivalent, equivocal style politics. What could be termed a "new wave" of queer Latino scholarship ought to be viewed, I contend, as *negative* extensions of previous debates about loss and oppression, that is, the politics of the *lack* of unity and coherence effected by the sign of latinidad, for, as Ruiz reminds us, "a lack of wholeness, and racial and sexual transparency, does not delimit the prospects of being in the world."[25] Yet, what also marks the "new wave" as different is its unflinching critique of representation and identity politics. This book shares a skepticism over a normative compulsion within the fields of Latino and ethnic studies to scrub clean representational and identity politics of their determinate contradictions, which *Dissatisfactions* finds very productive to questions of political action.

Though much great scholarly, artistic, and activist work has been done under the banners of identity and representation, the significant problem with these patterns concerns the often-uncritical engagement with the internal contradictions of these paradigms. To best explicate this point, it is important to define some crucial terms operative for the study. "Politics" is taken to mean the grating tension between the individual and community (imagined or otherwise). Any claim to structure, systems of oppressions, or forms of violence, discrimination, and the like invariably plays out within the theater of (un)belonging. When accounting for this conflict, politics not only interrogates a norm imposed by a dominant culture but also, and sometimes more importantly, exposes the ways norms calcify within minoritarian spheres. This is why aesthetics must follow any claim to or about politics, for the aesthetic articulates the thin line between memory and imagination. If norms are naturalized through processes of forgetting and, in particular, the forgetting of their emergence, then desire becomes governed by a pragmatism that hides its own purpose. Significant here is that queerness has been key to disclosing this truth.

The operative definition of "queer" for *Dissatisfactions* follows Eve Sedgwick's astute argument in her 1993 book *Tendencies*: "Queer is a continuing moment, movement motive—recurrent, eddying, *troublant*."[26] "It seems true to say that queer politics are both antiseparatist and anti-assimilationist," Sedgwick contended some years later: "antiseparatist in the sense that we don't take it for granted that the world is neatly and naturally divided between homosexuals and heterosexuals, and anti-assimilationist in the sense that we are not eager to share in the privileges and presumptions of normality."[27] At once negating strict borders while negating the promise of uncritical institutional inclusion, queer's "movement motive" strikes two forms of negation *at the same time*, in turn, *making* queer political. Important for our discussion of stylized discontents within a queer Chicano cultural moment is the way queer politics for Chicanos showcases how any claim to identity requires taking for granted categorical divisions premised on their own "presumptions of normality." Perhaps no one more than Sandra K. Soto has advanced such a productive heuristic within Chicano and Chicana studies, in her wonderful *Reading Chican@ like a Queer: The De-mastery of Desire*. There, the Chicana theorist argues for a racialized sexuality that operates "as an aperture (not an endpoint) onto the sometimes queer, at other times normative (most often, both) representation of race, desire, and intercultural and intracultural social relations."[28] Soto raises racialized sexuality as a queer heuristic that troubles a prevalent positivism in Chicano studies, in favor of an "unpredictable terrain and de-masterful uncertainty."[29] *Dissatisfactions* is greatly indebted to thinkers like Soto, whose cue I take when she says, "We [ought to] be more *wordy* and contingent, that we not look for a shorthand for naming or understanding or footnoting the confounding manifold ways that our bodies, our work, our desires are relentlessly interpellated by unequivalent social process."[30] Indeed, *Dissatisfactions* attunes to the inconsistencies between social relations, while raising delinkages as connections themselves.

When we hold Soto's and Sedgwick's important contributions together, a queer, racialized sexual heuristic brings into relief the (dis)juncture between gay liberation and the Chicano movement by calling into question the banners under which they gather: gay and Chicano.

For any identity like gay or Chicano cannot capture the "recurrent, eddying, *troublant*" movement between experience and knowledge, between the idea and the object. But more importantly, such difficulty in remaining coherent as identity knowledges relies on the denial of a clear migrancy between identity positions and more specifically the minoritarian survival strategy of having to occupy multiple spaces at once.[31]

Meanwhile, this (dis)juncture between gay liberation and the Chicano movement provides an excellent theoretical entry into the ways that queer Chicanos navigated feelings of disenchantment with both liberal complacency and social activism. Much of the style politics utilized at that historical juncture, this book contends, were politically ambiguous forms of aesthetic expression. In ways that will hopefully become more evident to the reader, the following negative aesthetic expressions present equivocated politics. Such efforts at categorizing stylized discontents inexorably self-efface and are experienced as a crisis of categorization.

Therefore, this book is indebted to the study of *negative aesthetics*, in which the aesthetics of discontent are linked to, though not exhausted by, "sentiments of disenchantment" with, on the one hand, the promise of social change engulfing the global 1960s and the subversive 1970s and, on the other, a larger disenchantment with national belonging, US imperialism, and the nation-state's subsequent disenfranchisement of ethnic-racialized and queer populations.[32] Accounting for the disconnect between ideation and materiality conjoins queer politics with aesthetic experience.

Read as an extension of Shoshana Felman's notion of "radical negativity," negative aesthetics cannot be subsumed under negation, opposition, contradiction, or correction.[33] Rather, they operate "outside of the alternative" as a "scandal" of nonopposition.[34] In this way, negativity works as a transgressive shift in form, resembling what David Carroll calls "paraesthetics," "a faulty, irregular, disordered, improper aesthetics."[35] Attributing a politics to an aesthetic that refuses catharsis, definition, and determination uncovers a critical approach to theory for which the noncathartic, unverifiable, and *in*formative are at once a mode of *making* theory political while leaving open the question of politics itself. Negative aesthetics foregrounds the politically ambiguous work of cultural production, particularly subcultural artifacts situated within an ambivalent and oftentimes exhausting/exhaustive relationship to the dominant culture and systems of disenfranchisement. This is to say, the cultural objects assembled in this book perform the very gaps and pauses within the now-canonical fantasy of the agential, autonomous subject of resistance.

Building on Tavia Nyong'o's work on "brown punk," negativity shares an affinity with "the topology of the punk," in that it makes present an absence despite its failure and passivity at containing any knowable matter that might give it definition. The form of punk resembles an "inner tube shape whose center of gravity lies outside its volume, whose inner exterior is topologically continuous with its outer, whose shape is for both of these reasons ex-centric to itself, . . . a veiled, unavailable body that makes an available space."[36] Negative aesthetics is an investigation into the archival apertures that *suggest* a history left behind, forgotten, or suppressed. Negative aesthetics, like punk, is passive not so much in resigning to systems of disenfranchisement but as a style of "withdrawal from the constraints of an affirmative culture."[37] This withdrawal from the affirmative is not necessarily reducible to its opposite (pure negation) but rather acts as a *suspension* of history, "a pause between past and future," a temporal puncture that discharges or performs an aesthetics of negativity—this is what I mean by a loss in the present.[38]

But if this interval in time is performative, it counterintuitively suggests that we rethink the sovereign, agential subject that is often conditioned by normative time and space. In other words, the suspension of history allows us to think of the performative force behind the suspension of agency as well, or what Lauren Berlant terms the "non-sovereign social and subjective formations."[39] As a result, this book is organized around four styles of suspended agency articulated as feelings of discontent: nausea, lo-fi, ambivalence, and malaise. Operating also as heuristics, together these stylized dissatisfactions provide a genealogy of queer Chicano punk, moving through different moments of gendered formations that are often formalized as a structural delay, a sort of suspended agency conditioned by late modernity. Deploying performance theory in line with minoritarian aesthetic objects never assembled as such, I emphasize how performance may also be a way of analyzing the *effects* of recording technologies and how recorded content always deals with audio/visual performance. In this way, an emphasis on mediation introduces the idea that audio/visual performance (looking at photographs or videos or listening to sound recordings as ways of evidencing) carries its own performative force because it is always already situated within shifting temporal and spatial registers; specifically, these objects are situated within the pause, very much like the temporal topology of punk discussed earlier.

Meanwhile, style, as defined in this book, allows for a meditation on the intersections and possible disjunctions between performance and media. While some scholars have argued that performance's ontology (being) is rooted in media—think here of experiencing a live performance via a recording of it—in this book the experience of a live or mediated performance inexorably leaves an ephemeral trace. This means that any claim about performance's ontology must account for what this ontology does in the social world, which is to say that one must account for its relationality, a central thematic in this book. The disconnect between live and mediated performance tells us more about performance's possibility of existing outside of mere materiality and instead as an *audiovisual archive*. *Dissatisfactions* approaches the audiovisual archive (live, mediated, and ephemeral performance) as thought-in-action.

In other words, style marks the (un)timeliness that the return of "the Same" poses to the promise of historical change. We can think of "the self-Same" here as another way of talking about identity and the way performance of identities inevitably change with time. Style registers the excess to history as not just conditionally determined, such as "postmodernism's" response to the austere formality of modernist style, as was the case in architecture. Instead, style appears timely when one thinks conditionally about history. But also, style is constitutive to relationality since ethnic-racialized sexuality, I argue, renders inchoate political desire and remainders in the process a nonequivalence between a cause and its effect. In other words, ethnic-racial formations modulate one's or a thing's capacity to do, whereby negative aesthetics articulates this agential displacement in time and space. An attunement to a suspended agency allows a study into how stylized discontents manifest themselves in the intimate spheres of the social and how negative aesthetics tells us something about the politically ambiguous work of cultural production.

## Toward a Theory of Stylized Discontent

Ideology arises from the very structure of experience: it expresses the opacity that binds us together as human. Consciousness is nothing but its own noncoincidence with itself—a repetitive struggle to define and position itself in a world to which it will not conform. Anachronism is its signature: experience is continually outbidding itself, perpetually making demands that it (i.e., the world) is unequipped to realize and unprepared to recognize, and comprehension inevitably comes too late to make a difference, if only because the stakes have already changed. Absolute knowing is the exposition of this delay. Its mandate is to make explicit the structural dissonance of experience. If philosophy makes any claim to universality, this is not because it synchronizes the calendars or provides intellectual compensation for its own tardiness. Its contribution is rather to formalize the necessity of the delay, together with the inventive strategies with which such a delay itself is invariably disguised, ignored, glamorized, or rationalized.
—Rebecca Comay, *Mourning Sickness*

The history of style spans multiple fields of study, such as literary history, art history, philosophy, linguistics, philology, cultural studies, musicology, and aesthetics.[40] Many systems of thought have waxed on or explicated the significance or insignificance of style, on its ubiquity or discrete nature, on whether one is born with an innate style or how to possibly cultivate one, on its gendered meaning or its fascistic quality, on its temporality or capacity for extension, on its politics or lack of politics. Style as a topic both feels abstractly gratuitous and simultaneously registers the prick of its singularity.

Indeed, first and foremost, style articulates the tension between conflicting forces, certain entities in dialectical relation frozen at the moment when something entirely new emerged through the rubble of dominant structures, discourses, and cultures, only to supplant the residual leftovers of a previous style. The tensions at the core of style are perhaps best examined first from its etymology. Stemming from the

Latin *stilus*, a writing instrument such as a pen but also a "piece of written discourse, a narrative, treaties," style's roots bring us to the same source as "stick": a tool, rod, staff (all of which derive from a plant's stalk) used to prick, point, or engrave (think here of the phrase "point of view").[41] One cannot ignore the phallic dimension of style, yet it is a dimension that registers an open vulnerability if we are to take seriously how the mark always *emerges* exposed to erasure. Something pedagogical operates in thinking about style because, as Joseph Joubert aphoristically noted, "style is the thought itself."[42] The sharpest of thoughts might be the proposition that ideas have material effects, just like the idea that an entity who turns something natural into a tool, in its cultivation, in effect, cuts itself off from the very materiality of its extension. The French naturalist Georges-Louis Buffon said, "Style is the man himself," in a 1753 acceptance speech after being inducted into Académie Française, and not without anxieties about his own style, a style for which he was ostensibly being recognized. The French psychoanalyst Judith Miller, daughter to the prominent French psychoanalyst Jacques Lacan, remarked on Buffon's self-reflection on style, "In saying, 'Style is the man himself,' Buffon is 'saying' himself, his fantasy of being a great man—a 'saying' that is irreducible to the knowledge he communicates."[43] Style is a form of anticipatory mourning evidenced in its announced anxieties. Rebecca Comay beautifully reminds us about anxiety's pedagogical abilities when she says, "Transforming past into future, anxiety teaches us how to mourn in advance."[44] Style's signature mark highlights this practice of anticipated mourning. Nonetheless, Miller's definition is helpful in getting us closer to the "irreducible" aspect of style that this book is about.

As is known, Lacan reformulated Buffon's definition of style by adding, "Style is the man to whom one speaks," which appears to bring the question of style under the rule of language. Miller explains Lacan's reformulation as such: "Man is no longer the author of his difference; he is the subject of the law of language; it is in the discourse of the Other with a capital O that he finds that by which he exists. He is situated and designated by his relation to the Other, with a structure divided between knowledge and truth."[45] It would appear that style, then, circumscribes "Man's" own cause for himself, materialized as an object of his desire. However, this concretized causation in the form of style is also residue from the discourse of the Other, or "a writing which does not stop not being written," as Miller proclaims.[46] The prick of style, in other words, registers the incompleteness of the subject of language, a project that takes seriously the implications of desire. The question becomes for Miller and us, "How not to drop this object by virtue of which man is structurally incomplete and from which he is suspended as desiring?"[47] *Dissatisfactions* represents a humble attempt at keeping *that* question fundamentally unsatisfied.

*Dissatisfactions* moves to the side of dominant discourses such as art or literary histories while also not offering a corrective to the archive by refusing to embark on a recovery project. I find productive the desire to recover a correction to the historical record, at the moment when such desire inevitably runs into an antimony fundamental to its search: the aesthetic dimension. Though such corrective-recovery works have proven valuable for larger studies of oppression and dispossession, this book instead unfolds a theory of style in relation to the constitutive and constituted dissatisfaction at the core of the subject of desire and capital, respectively.

Reagan's America involved cultural processes aimed at altering the way society consumed and produced, where the financialization of consumption and lean production generated, at the level of desire, a nostalgic, however ironic, yearning for the past while also making it more difficult for cultural producers to create anything entirely new in the present due to the constriction of public resources. When the neoliberal Margaret Thatcher proclaimed in a 1987 interview with the UK lifestyle magazine *Woman's Own* that "there is no such thing as society," the Randian performative statement did more than prohibit the public's self-perception as an imaginable collective. In saying there was no such thing as society, the conservative prime minister in effect spoke through the Other's discourse, a particular discourse that became quickly aligned with the totalizing effect of capitalism's inexhaustibility, its penchant for reproducing itself ad nauseam, because one started to *buy* the notion that the society they belonged to did not in fact exist. This vampiric quality of capitalism in the form of "dead labor" feasting on living labor, as described by Marx a handful of times in *Capital*, slowly drained the reservoir of futurity sourced from the spirit of 1968. And like a vampire, capitalism turned the future into the very monster that feeds on it, leaving in its wake a horrifying reality.⁴⁸ This is to say that Thatcher's performative utterance made capitalism all the more real, that is, necessary and inevitable, through a negation of a society thought to be its source and thus ultimate limit.

For scholars trained in queer theory, Thatcher's dictum will ring as an attempt at normalizing what *appears* to be given in any period. I agree that Thatcher essentially was attempting to normalize capitalism in taking away the only thing capable of proving its untenability: the social realm. I would add, having driven briefly earlier through some Lacanian formulations concerning style, that the reality that capitalism represents is one that actively represses a constitutive factor, what Lacan termed "the Real," and that, if unrepressed, might reveal the contingency at the heart of the system. Mark Fisher, perhaps better than others, has translated this socio-psychic dynamic as follows: "For Lacan, the Real is what any 'reality' must suppress; indeed reality constitutes itself through just this repression. The Real is an unrepresentable X, a traumatic void that can only be glimpsed in the fractures and inconsistencies in the field of apparent reality. So one strategy against capitalist realism could involve invoking the Real(s) underlying reality that capitalism presents to us."⁴⁹ My contention respectfully trails behind the late Mark Fisher's concept of "capitalist realism," loosely defined as the incessant censorship of any alternatives to capitalism and its twin cause of the decline of popular modernism. Underlined in Fisher's contention is the way capitalism presents itself as whole and totalizing. Yet, significant for our discussion of style is the way style formalizes the "unrepresentable X," that irreducible kernel left over from the inexplicable split between knowledge and truth. In other words, style announces the falseness of given reality—the normative world conditioned by capitalist reproduction—because style often resembles the superfluous production of the copy. If style is innate, it can *also* be cultivated like the stalk of a plant into a stylus. Since the unrepresentable X keeps returning as the Same, we can assume that the given system that seeks to naturalize itself through forgetting this repetition cannot be taken for granted. A necessary dissatisfaction permeates the surface of this so-called reality.

If style calls our attention to the surface, then style attunes one to the production of dissatisfaction, a process that is opaque, though crucial to capitalist realism. For capitalist ideology to function, a certain type of dissatisfaction must lubricate the mechanisms of desire. "The alternative to capitalism inheres within capitalism, and the revolutionary act is one of recognizing capitalism's internal and present future," argues Todd McGowan in his book *Capitalism and Desire*. He goes on to argue that the problem with capitalism is not that it cannot satisfy us but rather that capitalism "doesn't enable its subjects to recognize where their own satisfaction lies."[50]

Capitalism functions through a structural "promise" offered in the form of commodities, commodities that are themselves endowed with more than what they can give. In the eyes of the capitalist, commodities shimmer with an excess, something more than just the mere material commodity, and in turn an image of the consumer's dissatisfaction lurks behind it. This image of dissatisfaction (with the commodity) enables the consumer to continue searching for the perfect commodity, and so on. "The fundamental gesture of capitalism is the promise," McGowan writes, "and the promise functions as the basis for capitalist ideology."[51] Satisfactions are produced under capitalism, to be sure; the trick comes in the form of hiding and obscuring the satisfactions from the consumer. As a result, the consumer invests money for a (promised) future or acquires commodities in search of fulfilling the promised future in the present. In this dynamic, the imagined future that capitalism provokes is the fulfillment of the promise. However, because foreclosed in the present, this satisfaction cannot structurally be attained. Accumulation is the name of the game, a game predicated on repetitively acquiring an object to be dissatisfied with, if only because it stopped shimmering with its excess.

The problem with accumulation (which is important to underscore is but one pillar of the function of capital) is that it obscures, covers over, its own means of producing satisfaction. In restaging the subject's encounter with loss, accumulation exploits the future through a promise that cannot fundamentally be fulfilled. It would seem then that according to the morality of capitalism, too much is *never* enough.

Whereas the fundamental idea of psychoanalysis, and specifically a Lacanian inflection, lies in the opposite direction: too much is *not* enough. The difference here shows how the subject of capital's excessive accumulation results in their unavoidable confrontation with lack, that is, the constitutive loss that in turn moves this subject into the realm of desire.

*Dissatisfactions* meets the subject of capital in their accumulative habits in order to reflect back the loss endemic to the structure of desire where it inevitably emerges. In one blow, this loss announces itself as singular while remaining tethered to something opaquely universal. The tension between singularity and the threat of its subsumption into the universal tells us something about style. On not-so-abstract terms, we can sketch this out as the tension between the majoritarian culture and the minoritarian styles historically grounded in a complex relation that we might call the social realm. In this way, style reassembles a structure of feeling thought as a newly emergent social phenomenon. When viewed from the vantage of minoritarian strife, dissatisfaction appears as the structure to feeling par excellence.

Raymond Williams notably coined the paradoxical term "structure of feeling" in his important *Marxism and Literature*—paradoxical since how might one outline a structure to something fundamentally unstructured like a feeling?[52] Influenced by Italian *Operaismo* and its theories of inheritance—that is, the historical processes whereby ideologies and social forms are passed down and over time some go away, others dominate, and a few continue to remain—Williams developed his famous tripartite scheme to account for this dynamic theory of social history: the residual, the dominant, and the emergent. For Williams, the residual (different from "archaic") and the emergent reveal the effectiveness of the dominant, which hegemonically defines what *is* the social realm. The residual, Williams writes, "has been effectively formed in the past, but it is still active in the cultural process, not only and often not at all as an element of the past, but as an effective element of the present."[53] Williams's definition of the residual as "an effective element" in the present has a profound meaning for minoritarian culture, since "certain experiences, meanings, and values which cannot be expressed or substantially verified in terms of the dominant culture, *are nevertheless lived and practiced on the basis of the residue—cultural as well as social.*"[54] Should something escape or resist what Williams calls "incorporation" into the dominant culture, "residual meaning and values are sustained."[55]

Meanwhile, the emergent marks those "new meanings and values, new practices, new relationships and kinds of relationship . . . continually being created."[56] Both the residual and the emergent can only be understood *in relation* to the dominant, where the dominant figures as totalizing but, because of the dynamic between the residual and emergent, cannot fully incorporate all elements of society: "Therefore no dominant social order and therefore no dominant culture ever, in reality, includes or exhausts all human practice, human energy, and human intention."[57] This is key to Williams's theory of society since the trick actually lies in distinguishing between what the dominant recognizes as oppositional to it and what it deems instead as an alternative social activity, where the latter usually turns into the former once it becomes culturally recognizable. In other words, what can be regarded as emergent social forms (often viewed as oppositional to dominant forms) means that it is already articulable within the hegemonic cultural milieu. Social forms and activities that are not fully articulated on the dominant culture's terms are considered "pre-emergent," a phenomenon that corresponds to Williams's influential concept "structure of feeling." The task for the cultural materialist such as Williams involves articulating "specific feelings [and] specific rhythms" while not ignoring the constitutive sociality of their singularities.[58] Williams writes, "We are then not only concerned with the restoration of social content in its full sense, that of a generative immediacy. The idea of a structure of feeling can be specifically related to the evidence of forms and conventions—semantic figures—which, in art and literature, are often among the very first indications that such a new structure is forming. . . . For structures of feeling can be defined as social experiences in solution, as distinct from other social semantic formations [which are] more immediately available."[59]

Thus, central to a structure of feeling is its lack of "generative immediacy," since the singularity of the pre-emergent is in the process of forming, whereby the singular thus appears in-formational. When constituted socially, that is relationally, experience breaks down and dissolves into something more than itself. The structure to feeling stages a "semantic figure" unrecognizable to itself, if only because its specific coordinate has been distributed elsewhere, leaving in its trace "evidence" of its existence in the form of "forms and conventions." Elsewhere, Williams explains this phenomenon: "When I hear people talk about literature, describing what so-and-so did with that form—how did he handle the short novel?—I often think we should reverse the question and ask, how did the short novel handle him. Because anyone who has carefully observed his own practice of writing eventually finds that there is a point where, although he is holding the pen or tapping the typewriter, what is being written, while not separate from him, is not only him either."[60] Here we may ask, What is this force that tears one from oneself and implants something in between, where unity once was thought to be? Williams thought it was literary force, a force immanent to culture, which means a historically grounded force. However, without forgetting our exploration of style earlier, where one might see a writer's particular style appear, they are really registering the Other's voice, the Other here understood in Williams's inflection as the force of history itself: history is the thing that holds us. However, psychoanalysis also teaches us that where it seems like history, it might structurally be language and specifically the language of the Other. When framed this way, the struggle with the dominant culture does not necessarily become any more apparent but rather more personal. And as the feminist axiom goes, the personal *is* political, a critical dissatisfaction registered at the impressing moment when a totality articulates itself in the inadequate subject it produces.

The other significant point here is how Williams's triad makes the social realm constitutively relational to the materiality of culture, where questions of style are already posited within the interplay between the dominant and something pre-emergent, a social form or sensibility *not yet* articulable, though wholly immanent to culture. In other words, dissatisfaction drives the tension between pre-emergent forms and the dominant milieu. Structures of feelings, therefore, carry within the very concept a dissatisfaction that is subsequently played out in the social realm, a certain struggle against the dominant culture's power of incorporation, a particular striving that in turn reveals something in formation—something appearing as a dissolving singularity.

For now, when we talk about a "politics of style," we mean the particular way style is constituted in culture and how the latest style, in whatever the market, marks a surplus in production. Meanwhile, "style politics," the way politics appear or seem, is about the formalization of an elusive cause of a struggle. Despite seeming tautological, one would err in positing that the politics of style is the same as a style politics. The latter formation gets to the ways the subject's constitutive lack is fashioned; the former tells us about the various cultivated styles within a shifting historical terrain. The style to politics perfumes from the ground where power is negotiated (the politics of style) and where experience belatedly appears as missing the mark. Within the gap between structure and the happening of experience (with particular emphasis on the *hap-* and its reminder of contingency) unfolds the subject of our study: the subject of desire, which it is important not to forget is also the subject of loss.

In cultural studies, one framework dominates questions of style, namely, the way styles emerge in material culture, how style is cultivated into personalities, and how it circulates with other styles. In short, this very productive position investigates how style is *constituted* by capital, language, power, and history. Here, subjectivity is about the choices available to it in the form of style, where desire, if it figures at all, comes second. Consequently, *discourses neglecting desire effectively equate alienation with structure.* That we are without because of some larger structural cause occludes any genuine attempt at critical reflection, if we are to define critical practice in psychoanalytic terms as the desire for desire itself, that is, a general refusal of the object of satisfaction whether it be complacency with the status quo or resistance to the norm. On closer examination, such dominating discourses negatively and, though unaware, correctly posit desire at a structural impasse, where consciousness (*re*-cognition) repeatedly fails to find itself at the immediate coordinate of its conditional awakening—a sense of having lost an object that was never in one's possession. This is to say, a subject is overdetermined by its (structural) causes, which leaves in its trace the very *matter* of contradiction: the variable social forces, conditions of possibility, historical reasonings, and stories about the incompleteness of social totality, which all compose the narrative to "the politics of style." But these causes only *appear* retroactively as determining the subject's position and in effect mask the constitutive delay at the heart of the subject of desire. Indeed, neglecting desire, and its elusive cause, figured as the constitutive lack at the center of subjectivity that leaves subjectivity fundamentally dissatisfied, only highlights how, as Samo Tomšič elegantly puts it, the "flip side of the production of surplus is the reproduction of lack—the true 'matter' by which the subject is constituted."[61] The "matter" of style politics is a product of lack. The historical actors chronicled in this book make tangible this lack from the conditions of possibility allotted to them in post-1968 Los Angeles. But allow me to restate this complex interplay between constituted and constitutive alienation and their relation to surplus and lack in a different way.

In the 1980s US, the consumer market intensified with new commodities like the cordless phone, the personal computer, and a purchasing power enabled by a credit system resulting from the economic collapse in the previous decade. Coupled with circulating images of the good life replicated in beauty magazines, endless commercials, TV shows, and films about wealth that no one *really* had seen or thought about having *until then*, mass consumer culture posited a false demand. Generated by a fantasy of having, the "more and more" logic of Reagan's America revealed that more was never enough, and so back to the store we went. The production of surplus is founded on a fantasy of a demand, which is to say an exploited demand, entailing the extraction of pleasure from precisely *not* having. The worker was replaced with the figure of the consumer, and with the supplanting came a perverse rearticulation of freedom whereby an atomized, individuated freedom replaced the collective struggle for liberation just a decade prior. The freedom articulated in 1968 was an entirely different configuration than Reagan's; '68's freedom was a freedom *from* oppression (capitalism, empire, patriarchy, homophobia, and racism), which aggressively insisted on an Outside to a totality like discourse, power, language, or capitalism. Reagan's "different" idea of freedom, though not entirely a new form, which replaced the "spirit" of 1968, was one projected *within* social logics, at the level of dispersed singularities communicating with one another in a similar vein, to what Jodi Dean calls "communicative capital," or the freedom to endlessly create/circulate content, which in turn obscures the formerly practiced freedom.[62] As a result, *consuming* in excess outed its twin phenomenon, the production of surplus enjoyment—of lack. A new mode of production was needed, a need expressed as a wager on the endless supply of the singular, keeping in mind that the goal was to capture surplus enjoyment's remarkable capacity to reproduce itself... ex nihilo. The lack of an outside came to reflect in the autonomous subject of resistance an "opacity that binds [them] together as human," as Comay claims in the epigraph to this section. The consumer saw their freedom in the objects they accumulated *because* of their perpetual dissatisfaction: the consumer consumes consciously in order to sustain the unconscious pleasure they receive from forgetting about their primal loss (of freedom).

Said differently, the consumer consumes to remember an event that could not and cannot occur.[63] This is one reason why the consumer and the activist appear as foils to each other in this book: since one insists on a constituted Outside (the activist), while the consumer repeatedly disavows the constitutive without (or lack) within (their possessions). I say "foil" since they are not opposites or mutually exclusive operations. In fact, neoliberalism may be thought of as the lamination of these two functions into an image, a process Freud called "condensation," or if you prefer, a metonymic image of a larger whole. However, one significant capitalist goal is to collapse their distinction with time, since the short distance between the activist and the consumer contains what Elizabeth Freeman beautifully named the "undetonated energy" leftover from the spirit of 1968.[64] In disentangling the two functions from each other, a diffused multiscalar study of formal strategies responding to two conflicting and complementary demands came as a result. The performativity of the investigation is best exemplified by the way *Dissatisfactions* suspends the lamination process, almost in a style of a freeze-framing, to mind the layering involved when getting to the structural conditions behind the coarticulation of the consumer and the activist. In short, the following stylized discontents formalize the middle range—the gap—between the demand to consume and the demand to resist; for style underscores the anachronistic attribute inherent in the historian's mantra—"change over time"—and how a necessary gap renders time noncoincidental to itself as history.

## Lingering with Questions on Method

Ideas are to objects as constellations are to stars.
—Walter Benjamin, *The Origin of German Tragic Drama*

Questions regarding the cultural history of aesthetic objects within queer Latino studies and performance studies inform this book's research method. A question that links all three fields concerns the ontology of performance as that which disappears (Phelan), as always already mediated (Auslander), as productively ephemeral (Muñoz), or as transmission, either understood psychoanalytically (Pellegrini) or through a "nonarchival system of transfer" known as the repertoire (Taylor).[65] These diverging theories not only posit different methodologies in approaching the archive but also show how performance is always a contested site of analysis. The archival material explored in this book range from video recordings and photography, punk ephemera and audio recordings, to literature and performance art. These materials make up what I understand as the audiovisual archive, an "archive of feelings" that discloses recorded content and ephemera as possessing their own performative force as they come into contact with their observer.[66] In this way, the audiovisual archive is *both* about what is collected in the archive *and* what the researcher "brings" to the archive.

For example, Fred Moten posits a heuristic that takes seriously the fugitive and moving elements of material texts, whereby an aesthetic expression of one medium is displaced and located in relation to another medial expression, simultaneously *yet* in motion. This practice foregrounds the performativity of materiality rather than looking for the "meaning" of any specific medium anterior to what the text might enable. I understand this method as coterminous with what Moten names "interinanimation"; *Dissatisfactions* ought to be read as an extension of this form of critical engagement with archival objects.[67] These cultural objects are at once situated within a historical moment while also exhibiting their own conditions of possibility to account for what is systemically unaccounted for, forgotten, or lost within the historical record. I accomplish this through close readings of song lyrics and musical performance, while also deploying literary and film analysis to show how the artists and cultural objects assembled resonate with one another in a way like what Walter Benjamin calls a "constellation," that is, the *relation* between ideas and concrete objects.

This book employs a few existing archives. Los Angeles was the site for two major exhibitions featuring avant-garde Chicano art: the Los Angeles County Museum of Art's retrospective on the Chicano performance art group Asco and Pacific Standard Time's *Mapping Another L.A.: The Chicano Art Movement*. Though both shows were exhaustive in presenting never-before-seen material, queer Chicanos fall out of the art-historical texts available, obscuring the cultural memory of post-1968 Los Angeles in relation to the discourse of AIDS. While there is a small amount of cultural analysis that looks at this period and these groups, punk rarely ever is understood in relation to these movements and in particular how the queer punk scene as a site of analysis troubles Chicano nationalism by setting the foundation for the aesthetic responses to the AIDS crisis. I was then inspired to wonder how one methodologically accounts for a group of cultural producers that are systematically forgotten, lost, and obscured within the confines of the archive, while refusing categorization as either "gay/lesbian" or "Chicano" cultural production.[68]

With performance studies as my primary field of interest, I see this book as contributing a performance analysis of aesthetics to the emerging field of queer Latino studies. Interinanimation as a method requires me to place these fields in conversation so that they may call and respond to each other in ways that are productive in thinking with, through, and against the blind spots and limits of the archive. Queer Latino studies can potentially challenge the exclusion of queer subjects within Latino scholarship and foreground how any queer scholarship is always already about ethnic-racialized desire. Therefore, if queer Latino studies is primarily a study of lost objects, performance theory allows one to show how this loss is made visible and material through the audiovisual archive.

Each remaining chapter of the book is framed by a specific stylized discontent: nausea, lo-fi, ambivalence, and malaise. Though the study is situated within a period (post-1968 up to the early 1990s) and a place (Los Angeles), the arc of the archive assembled necessitates a cross-analysis with other artists not necessarily read as Chicano or Chicana. This is in part due to the bricolage nature of the argument, since one of the major goals of the book is to insist on the creative mapping that theories of aesthetics and politics afford scholarship invested in unearthing material that often gets occluded. This fragmentary and pastiche nature does not have to reflect only a symptomatic result of "postmodern" style of writing and thinking. It is also an effort to reassemble and realign thinking in order to make present the opaque mediation *between* objects and ideas. In addition, *Dissatisfactions* also performs its own punk ethos by adhering to certain aesthetic traits such as the style politics of the auteur and the bricoleur we see in the new-wave movements in French and German cinema, the commingling of revolutionary aspirations with Mexican countercultural aesthetics, and the possibilities of non- or antirepresentational strategies best articulated in conceptual and feminist performance art of the 1970s, all aspects that carry through the subjects of this book.

The book begins with an analysis of the way punk and queer Chicano subcultures responded to the immediate period after 1968 in Los Angeles. Chapter 1 focuses on the Chicano performance group Asco (Spanish for "nausea") and traces a genealogy of "nausea" from Jean-Paul Sartre's novel of the same name and the staple song by the notorious LA punk band X, which shares the same title, "Nausea" (1980). The chapter argues that nausea resembled a style endemic to Los Angeles and articulates the emotional situation of the city post-1968. Chapter 2 then posits an individuated attitude within the nauseating emotional habitus of the city articulated as a style of lo-fi performance, which mirrors the Chicana punk feminist ethos best exemplified in Alice Bag's and Teresa Covarrubias's attitudes. I argue that lo-fi performance also informs the way early feminist makeshift presses circulated their ideas through lo-fi means and not unlike the way early LA punk shared its subculture, best articulated in the 1977–1980 punk magazine *Slash*, in which Bag and others were prominently featured.

The following half of the book shifts in tone because of the arrival of the AIDS crisis in 1981 and Reagan's assuming the presidency. This shift reflects a split in Latino identity that is the focus of the remainder of the book. Chapter 3 begins with a critique of a strand of thought in Latino studies called "post-positivist realism" (PPR) and its influence on gay Latino studies to foreground the importance of ambivalence as a stylized way of articulating one's discontent with the status quo, identity, and the authority of experience. Ambivalence as a Chicano style politics, I argue, results from the splitting in Latino gay identity at the pinnacle of the AIDS crisis. By close reading Ray Navarro's writing and his AIDS activism in ACT UP with the experimental prose of Gil Cuadros's *City of God*, this chapter posits ambivalence as a stylized discontent that is really about a passionate and sensuous relation with death in the world, best captured by Cuadros's best friend, the late queer Chicana artist Laura Aguilar, and her altar to him after his death from AIDS complications.

Chapter 4 moves into the early 1990s after the fall of the Berlin Wall ("the long 1989") and compares two non-Chicano artists while arguing that they should be considered in line with a tradition of stylized discontent ranging from Asco, the queer LA punk filmmaker Gregg Araki, and the late queer Cuban-born minimalist artist Felix Gonzalez-Torres. First, the chapter begins with the last artist discussed in chapter 3, Laura

Aguilar, except this time in relation to Aguilar's 1995 video art pieces *Talking about depression*, *Talking about depression 2*, and *The Knife*. Aguilar opens the chapter's discussion about "talking" about depression and Freud's pessimistic prediction of civilization's inherent *Unbehagen*, translated to English as "discontent" or "malaise," the final stylized discontent. The chapter argues that the aesthetics of malaise yields a spatial relation structurally akin to besideness, echoing *Dissatisfactions'* interinanimating methodology. The chapter offers a cluster of aesthetic objects produced by Felix Gonzalez-Torres during his time in Los Angeles and in response to the death of his lover from AIDS. Juxtaposed with an early video art piece by a twenty-one-year-old Gonzalez-Torres, of which little scholarly analysis exists, I explicate a theory of temporality offered by the queer artist. Gonzalez-Torres's theory of time mirrors a spatial theory that Araki unfolds in his oeuvre and especially in his 1993 film *Totally F\*\*\*ed Up*, in which he uses a queer Chicano character to stand in for his authorial voice. Through his use of intertextuality, Araki creates a blasé tone that when coupled with the beauty of Gonzalez-Torres's minimalism yields a general malaise right at the height of the AIDS pandemic. I argue how this malaise offers a spatial agnosticism that helps illustrate the contours of queer latinidad, namely, by diffusing the weight of Chicano identity in favor of analogically disclosing its sensibility across social difference. The conclusion then attends to the cultural imagining of what queer latinidad looks like if we take seriously the stylized discontents it affords politics and the "labor and suffering" of the negative.

Finally, this book's argument is best disclosed to the reader in chronological order, such that, in moving through each stylized discontent—nausea, lo-fi, ambivalence, and malaise—the reader is in fact periodizing post-1968 Los Angeles by way of aestheticized affects. The conceit of the book recognizes the affect of dissatisfaction and its subsequent stylization in Los Angeles, as a product of the shift from modernity to postmodernity—late capitalism's general mood—and a site for playful manipulation for minoritarian subjects. In the end, the demand to either resist oppressive logics or assimilate to them short-circuits into a failure that necessitates further play, further care, and further concern for those who do not coherently, fully, and transparently figure in the political imaginary.

# 1

## The Style Politics of Nausea

### *X, Sartre, and Asco*

The instability of levels produces not only the intellectual experience of disorder, but the vital experience of giddiness and nausea, which is the awareness of our contingency, and the horror with which it fills us.
—Maurice Merleau-Ponty, *The Phenomenology of Perception*

Today, you're gonna be sick, so sick.
You'll prop your forehead on the sink,
Say, "Oh Christ, oh Jesus Christ,
My head's gonna crack like a bank."

Nausea, bloody red eyes, go to sleep.
—X, "Nausea," from the 1980 album *Los Angeles*

Penelope Spheeris's 1981 documentary about Los Angeles's late-1970s punk scene, *The Decline of Western Civilization*, opens with a blue-tinted close-up of Eugene, a young punk musician whose tired visage complements his mumbly, Southern California accent. Eugene argues that the label "punk rock" is "stupid" since it is really just a new form of rock and roll without the "bullshit" of rock stars taking center stage—an assertion complicated by Spheeris's use of confessional camera techniques. As Eugene ruminates on the punk phenomenon, the character's face takes up most of the screen, suggesting an overall intimacy with the viewer that is nonetheless muddled by the young punk's performance of disaffection.[1] The point here is that while Spheeris introduces this emergent scene by way of a consumer of punk music, an attention to the audience as opposed to the bullshit rock stars becomes aesthetically structured by an ironic coolness.

Eugene's mediated intimacy with the viewer mirrors the sprawling soundscape of punk Los Angeles, and his disaffection is further clarified by the failure of Los Angeles to materialize its glamorous promise. For instance, later in the documentary, one of Los Angeles's well-known punk bands at the time, X, performs the song "Nausea," appropriately lifted from its 1980 album titled *Los Angeles*. As the opening credits run over shots of sweaty punks dancing or standing idly, characters extemporize about how the new phenomenon of "punk rock" fares differently than other musical genres. The most striking account comes from Brendan Mullen, the late owner of the well-known punk venue The Masque, which operated from 1977 to 1979 at 1655 North Cherokee Avenue in Hollywood. Mullen attributes punk rock's distinctive style to its speed: 250 to 300 beats per minute "is well above the speed of a dance," creating an "abnormal level of adrenalin" and peculiar forms of movement such as pogo-dancing, which can be seen throughout the documentary. Mullen believes that the speed of punk music might correspond to the occasional eruption of violence at punk shows, perhaps because of the "kids [being] more desperate or more bored" than the previous flower-power generation of the 1960s and early 1970s, who advocated an ethos of passive resistance and nonviolence. Mullen astutely argues that an allegorical connection exists between the acoustic guitars of the 1960s protest songs and the raised speed of punk music. What both have in common, in keeping with Eugene's dialectical assessment of the continuity of punk music from rock, is a desire to bring attention to the same issues that plagued youth culture just a decade prior—that is, a general grievance "about how their air is poisoned out there; the air in utopia is poisoned, . . . the final joke."

I find this moment one of the most telling in the documentary for various reasons, none of which ignores Mullen's background and the lingering smog hovering over the Los Angeles cityscape, almost making indistinguishable the horizon's splitting of the city from the sky. Both Eugene's and Mullen's arguments about punk's continuity from 1960s protest music and the rise of rock and roll underscore how the utopia promised during the social movements of the 1960s and 1970s in the United States might well have arrived, albeit polluted by government malfeasance and the stark realization that utopia still carries with it desperation and boredom. Thus, just as the image of bustling highway

Figure 1.1. Screenshot of Eugene's confessional mode describing the feel of punk, from *The Decline of Western Civilization*, 1981.

Figure 1.2. Screenshot of Brenden Mullen with a view of Los Angeles and its smog, from *The Decline of Western Civilization*, 1981.

traffic under a stagnant cloud of smog displays two dynamically involved speeds, the unusual quick speed of punk music too comes in direct contrast with the slow progress of social change.

There is no better way to inaugurate a stylized, documented investigation into what was then perceived as a fairly new subculture outside the ordained capitals of countercultural production at the time (New York City and London) than with the negative feelings of desperation, hunger, boredom, and nausea. However, in Los Angeles, these decisively punk feelings are *spatially* situated; to see Los Angeles through the eyes of its contemporary punks requires an attunement to the amorphous cloud of smog ominously hanging over the sprawling city and its populated highways. In Spheeris's documentary, smog manifests itself as a pervasive force and feeling, a structured-unstructuredness that forms a striking picture of post-1968 Los Angeles as a polluted utopia. If this is in fact utopia, then its image of futurity carries an *autopia* of malfeasance, to use a word that the architectural historian Reyner Banham applied to the four ecologies of Los Angeles in 1971. For Banham, who reveled in the majesty of the Los Angeles freeway system, it was "a comprehensible place, a coherent state of mind, a complete way of life," and thus an ecology onto itself.[2] For others, such as Brock Yates, the longtime executive of *Car and Driver* magazine, the freeway system represented "an existential limbo where man sets out each day in search of western-style individualism."[3] Yates's sentiment is perhaps best captured in the 1993 crime thriller *Falling Down*, whose protagonist abandons his car in a traffic jam, triggering an existential break with reality that begins his crime-filled journey throughout Los Angeles in search of his estranged ex-wife and daughter. The utopian allure that Los Angeles occupies in the collective imagination was always a trap, an "existential limbo" initiated by an ever-increasingly atomized culture: in reality, utopia can only become manifest as a failure in trying.

This chapter requires attending to this historical impasse on the levels both of social change, in a moment suspended between the promises of 1968 and the onset of Reaganite neoliberalism, and of the agential subject's account of itself. This latter impasse is what Banham calls the "limbo of existential angst," spurred by the moment when the status quo comes under duress, or at least *feels* as such.[4] The phenomenal crisis initiated by the tension between the monotony of the status quo and the promise for social change requires attuning to the way, as in *Falling Down*, social change comes with the fall from reality. This "fall" registers the disorienting experience of being projected/ejected from the given world, which might feel exhilarating, if not equally terrifying. Meanwhile, if the "instability of levels" between one world and another, according to Maurice Merleau-Ponty in the epigraph to this chapter, produces "vital experience[s] of giddiness and nausea," it is because the *multiple scales* (or the range) by which to account for the phenomenological experience of a body in fact cultivate an attunement to the contingency of historical events (their uneven givenness) and the subject's position within them: this is what "fills us" with horror. However, Sara Ahmed cautions against ascribing disorientation to queer politics even if queer politics might involve the experience of disorientation.[5] The gap between the world perceived and its outside figures as the necessity of historical change; this is because the ground by which the world is perceived has now shifted with the realization of its insufficiency. And as we shall see, nausea stylizes this queer political experience of history.

Meanwhile, the horror of utopia saturates many punk images of Los Angeles after the promises of liberation articulated by previous social movements fade. Punk stories of disenfranchisement and desperation, even if told with an ironic tone, were modes of tarrying with the unintended consequences of the previous generation's desire to "dream big," as it were. Los Angeles's punks and the Chicano avant-garde inherited a world damaged by Governor Ronald Reagan's incipient deregulatory policies, disillusioning them from psychedelic dreaming and the belief in flower power's image of peace. Yet, one notable affect served less as an individuated experience in polluted utopia than others. Though nausea more popularly connotes a physical response to disgust, even to the brink of vomiting, nausea also carries an often-unacknowledged genealogy stemming from the philosophical tradition of existential thought. This particular strand, I argue, provides an apt heuristic to approach Reagan's America in general and Los Angeles specifically, because those who were involved in a nauseous youth subculture created an existential condition felt, understood, studied, lived, and reproduced out of a dissolving modernist project. Thus, the ways in which nausea ricochets through the queer networks in post-1968 Los Angeles are best gleaned through the songs, writings, and performances amplifying—in concert—this emotional habitus into a generalized style characteristic of Los Angeles at this historical juncture. This ironically diffused emotional habitus can be thought of as the excess to *autopia*'s polluted reality: a hazy consequence hanging between this world and another.

José Esteban Muñoz has argued that X's first four albums (including *Los Angeles*) were "attuned to the ways in which populism was becoming savagely privatized and unmoored from society or publics and instead substituted with flattened individuals, self-absorbed couples and the ravenous and all-encompassing family."[6] No doubt X's stringent cultural critique cemented the band as the voice of Los Angeles punk at the turn of the decade to the 1980s. And yet these malcontents did not come without their own controversies, even for a shock-ridden punk scene like Los Angeles's. Recorded in January 1980 and quickly released some months later, *Los Angeles* provided a different interpretation of what the affective field of punk sounded like. For example, unlike the more hardcore and DIY punk bands of the scene, like The Germs or The Circle Jerks, X displayed musical virtuosity that only augmented its tongue-in-cheek lyrics. X's description of Los Angeles became the unspoken backdrop to the punk scene of the early 1980s. Taken as a whole, *Los Angeles* painted the "terrible beauty" of an emerging postmodern Los Angeles, itself a pastiche of the materially driven, sexually shallow denizens of "Sex and Dying in High Society," the desperately disenfranchised youths rummaging from apartment to apartment in "We're Desperate," and even the naïve white transplants turned homophobic and racist because of the city's growing multiculturalism in "Los Angeles."[7] Taken together with the other songs, "Nausea" offers a decisively existential take on the experience of living in Los Angeles as a poor, young malcontent, where the promise offered by 1960s social movements is consumed and spat out by systemic poverty, social disorientation, and a larger sense of feeling tired and expired. The future tense of the song's lyrics, standing in contrast to its declarative opening word, "Today," performs a mode of anticipation, where the future (in the present) is marked not as bright but as grim and dark.

By 1980, we begin to see a deterioration of public space, a slowing economy, and hyper-commodification against a backdrop of crumbling infrastructure. By July 1979, the United States experienced its second oil crisis of the decade, causing then-President Jimmy Carter to deliver what was aptly dubbed his "malaise speech," in which he lamented that the country had failed to come together to solve its dependency on oil. The autonomist Marxist economist Christian Marazzi pinpoints the watershed shift from a Fordist economy to post-Fordism just a few months after Carter's lament, on October 6, 1979, the day that the US Federal Reserve increased interest rates to nearly 20 percent, which in effect ushered in supply-side economics, leaving some heads, in X's words, "crack[ed] like a bank." Notably, X's lyrics emphasize an odd dissolve between the romantic desire for a collective agenda and one's own syncopated separation from the group: "Talking out of harmony, you can't remember what you said. Cut it out, you feel retarded. Take the scissors; saw the head." These irreconcilable realities lull the dissonant subject to sleep, a subject described by Marazzi as "psychologically damaged" by capitalism: "Nausea, bloody red eyes, go to sleep."[8]

If in fact the United States after October 6, 1979, entered a new phase of capitalism, then the denizens of Los Angeles's punk subculture were well situated to register some existential ramifications because of this change. The affective field of Los Angeles punk responds directly to a suspension of satisfaction initiated by a cluster of socioeconomic shifts that in turn obstructed the subjective experience of actually attaining the very thing one desires. This is the reason why utopia seems polluted to Mullen and his punks; for the very thing desired (utopia) can never really actualize the promised end to its search. Instead, the emotional habitus of the city materializes through a suspended smog bank that is in effect *holding* the city together. And just as smog positively relates to the traffic beneath it—more traffic means more smog—nausea too is susceptible to amplification due to its positive relation to social circulation. Movement amplifies nausea and makes it more contagious and more shared. A reader might be struck by some new questions here: How does a subject's feeling of nausea amplify into a shared, almost preconscious, structure of feeling? Are we talking about the ontological compartments of *a* feeling or *the* feeling of existing in shifting modes of production and consumption?

Many scholars of affect have argued that its ontology is equivocated, or obscured, by the subjective experience of how it is felt. This in turn makes affect synonymous with emotion, where the subject can consciously account for its phenomenological effects. In this way, affects are determinate and subjected to a self-reflective process and thus imbued with intentionality and meaning. Other theorists, particularly those influenced by Deleuzian thought, argue that affect, unlike emotion, is preconscious, existing outside of subjective thought as *virtual*, as the potential to be affected and to affect, forming an indeterminate plane that connects all bodies together as emergent.[9] Though there are other camps within the "affective turn," I focus on these two, seemingly irreconcilable positions to theorize how the question of *style* might emerge from this productive epistemological impasse. Investigating the potential of affect's intersubjectivity—its social, rather than individuated, quality—leads to this chapter's core polemic. Is the nausea in X's song the same nausea for all folks in the punk scene, let alone for all denizens of Los Angeles? Can existential nausea feel the same across the multiple particularities of subjectivity, such as race, gender, and sexuality? Is nausea in this form mostly a class-determined ontological state? If nausea is to be understood as a style and is thus singular, how can we account for nausea as an emotional habitus signaling some collective composition without romanticizing the signifier "community"? With these questions, something might strike the reader in the chapter's tracing of a loose genealogy of nausea and its implications for Chicano politics, namely, the string of racially unmarked cultural objects used to make this argument. X and many of the other bands featured in Spheeris's documentary are mostly white and mostly heterosexual participants. And as the chapter foregrounds, the French existentialist philosopher Jean-Paul Sartre and his novel *Nausea* also do not represent any obvious ethnic-racial politics that might help our understanding of a Chicano performance art group's politics in post-1968 Los Angeles. However, and as mentioned in the introduction to this book, it is in the *relations* between these cultural artifacts across time that any meaning might be said to reveal the material, aesthetic, and theoretical resonances between their respective immediate historical situations.

I argue that subjects cast out of the mainstream yet caught at the margin of their own *marginal* "communities"—ironically due to the same particularities of class, race, sexuality, gender, and so on—find themselves lodged between two seemingly conflicting ideologies. The subjective position of being caught between two opposing forces, compounded with the failure even to belong to any "third space" they effectively carved out, represents a threshold to the negative feelings constitutive of such a drama. The aesthetic and literary theorist Sianne Ngai's *Ugly Feelings* is a study of the aesthetics of negative emotions constituting the administrative apparatuses of late modernity. Following Paolo Virno, Ngai warns that we must be careful not to romanticize negative emotions as only "sentiments of disenchantment that once marked positions of radical alienation from the system of wage labor—anxiety, distraction, and cynicism—[which] are now perversely integrated, from the factory to the office, into contemporary capitalist production itself."[10] Ngai's project opens up new ways to think about minoritarian emotional situations, highlighting emotions that are explicitly amoral and noncathartic. Ugly feelings such as irritation, envy, paranoia, and anxiety (and I would include here nausea) are constitutively weak. Because of their minor status as affects, they manage to endure in ways that other feelings of virtuosity and passion, such as anger, fear, and hate, cannot. Noncathartic feelings offer "no satisfactions of virtue, however oblique, nor any therapeutic or purifying release."[11] The failure of release and catharsis foregrounds an aesthetic of "suspended agency" that I find to be an appropriate description of X's song "Nausea" and the larger sentiment surrounding the Chicano performance group Asco, which is a focus later in the chapter.[12] Following Ngai, I argue that it is precisely the ambivalence of sentiments like nausea that makes them open to politics. On a larger level, this book argues that four stylized dissatisfactions—nausea, lo-fi, ambivalence, and malaise—are constitutive of a Chicano politics that refuses catharsis.

For Ngai, the noncathartic feeling of disgust acts as the negative limit to negative affects themselves (and thus cannot be subsumed by that category) since, unlike other ugly feelings that confuse subject and object, the structure of disgust involves directionality, aim, and a clear distinction between subject and object. Think of a child caught in a heated argument between their parents, with each proclaiming over the child, "*I* am disgusted by *you*. No, *you* disgust *me*." And yet, this confusion itself often emerges affectively as disorientation, or a queer sense of being lost within the flows of social change. Ngai ascribes this phenomenon to "tone" or "mood," which are certainly akin to the way we have been discussing nausea's structure. The diffusion attributed to nausea differs from disgust in that nausea has no object; it pulls the subject outside of itself into a process of differentiation, which is to say nausea self-externalizes the subject. The subject's uncanny experience of suspension (to have its agency obstructed) means it acts as both subject and object of this meta-feeling of nausea. We may say that one does not *have* nausea (*tengo asco*, a common Spanish phrase) but rather nausea has you, just like the smog holds its city. In short, nausea is more amorphous than the way Ngai theorizes disgust, which is "never ambivalent about its object" and in fact "policies" the boundary between subject and object.[13] Nausea, then, figures as *in-formation* (in the process of forming), whereas disgust seems always to be performative (creates the thing in its act). Or, said differently, disgust registers a politics whereas nausea resembles a style. However, these two attributes are not necessarily in opposition to each other, since their dynamic relationship relies on their mutual imbrication with the social realm.

The affective field of Los Angeles punk reverberates through the stylized discontent we have been describing as nausea and touches another contemporaneous Los Angeles performance group by the same name: Asco, the Chicano performance art group that sought to laminate a politics of disgust with a style of nausea. Asco's oeuvre can be read as positioned simultaneously at the limits of its Chicano community and at the limit of Reagan's America. What allows a reader to access Asco's singular position is precisely its style, understood as an unsubsumable cultural sensibility, which the group utilized as a tool to interrogate the limits of Chicano nationalism and particularly its insistence on culturally affirming representations in a very contentious post-1968 Los Angeles. Asco not only created an alternative visual discourse to a culture of affirmation propagated by movement politics but also illuminated a queer driving force within its aesthetic production, infused with a low hum of discontent, that reached outside the dominant Chicano aesthetic imprints of the time, such as *mestizaje*, tropes of *la familia*, or what the Chicano scholar Raúl Homero Villa calls the "culturally affirming [barrio-logical] spatial practices."[14] One way Asco articulated this queer drive was through redefining and *refining* disgust into a style, much in the same way its philosophical precedents did with signifiers, like "indifference" for Albert Camus, "ambiguity" for Simone de Beauvoir, or "nausea" in the case of Jean-Paul Sartre.[15] Therefore, in tracing a loose genealogy of the cultural production of nausea, especially through attention to one of Asco's main influences, Sartre's 1938 novel *La Nausée*, we can begin to see how Asco's "attachment genealogy" to nausea/asco, to borrow Kadji Amin's term, underscores an often-neglected intellectual strain of Chicano activism and art that, as Amin argues, "excavates earlier and more transnational modes of queer attachment to both historicize and expand queer's current affective orientations" beyond the dominant set of early twenty-first-century American assumptions and priorities.[16] By foregrounding Sartre's novel, written while Sartre himself was attempting to reconcile his existential phenomenology (and psychoanalysis) with Marx's historical materialism, I argue that Asco's performance work materializes important modern philosophical questions regarding class struggle and the subject's role in revolutionary politics.

To follow this argument, one must account for resonances between cultural artifacts and historical periods. This queer orientation toward history and objects brings our attention to the aesthetic realm since it is here where cultural objects both register a particular world and index other possible worlds by virtue of their anachronistic status. Again, take Sartre's existential novel *Nausea* as an example, one posited *alongside* Asco's work and X's song. Sara Ahmed describes *Nausea* as "a rather queer novel" in its phenomenological description of disorientation.[17] The way the novel presents objects as triggering a strange break with reality, where the givenness of the world suddenly appears absurd or out of tune because a "cold object" comes into perception and is touched, evidences for Ahmed the novel's queer capacity.[18] *Nausea*'s queerness also lends itself to questions of "nausea" as a name and its attachment genealogy to global processes of ethnic-racialization, especially when juxtaposed with Asco's historical situation in Chicano Los Angeles.

The postcolonial thinker Franz Fanon was greatly influenced by Sartrean existential thought and psychoanalysis and translated Sartrean phenomenology into his own form of anticolonial critique. The sentiment of nausea significantly figures in Fanon's work, usually as a visceral reaction to racism and colonial ideology. Neetu Khanna's study of the "visceral logics of decolonization" encourages a shift in decolonial inquiry away from the psychoanalytic unconscious to "the somatic unconscious."[19] In so doing, "the physiological reflex" of the colonized body reveals the "colonized psyche as constitutive rather than merely expressive of thought and feeling."[20] Fanon's nausea is an apt point of entry for

Khanna's study, in which she describes Fanon's nausea as a "failed laughter."[21] The "trope" of nausea in Fanon and throughout Khanna's own study figures the visceral as an articulation between a "semantic refusal" of colonial reality and a "diagnostic promise" from it.[22] For Khanna, this dialectical dynamic racializes nausea and thus replaces, for the critic, the "more abstracted Sartrean figure of existential nausea with a deeply embodied and often biomedical representation of the colonial subject's struggle with automatized reflexes of the body."[23] In turn, the colonial automatization of bodily reflexes constitutes aesthetic taste and desire.

For our purposes here, Khanna via Fanon offers a vital contribution to the existential renderings of nausea, as a literary trope but also a visceral, embodied feeling imbued with colonial, racial, and gendered dynamics. Indeed, viewed in tandem with Ahmed's queer phenomenology, the structure of nausea sutures the body, perception, and consciousness through the act of *delinking* the phenomenal from normative, colonial reality. And to the extent that nausea indexes a deep dissatisfaction with the normative racial and gender mainstream, it can also be refined, reworked, and deployed as a style.

Therefore, I read *Nausea* as a proto-Chicano text to the same extent as it is a proto-punk one. The addressee in X's existential song mirrors Ahmed's description of the novel's narrator's general "loss of grip" with the objects gathered around him.[24] As opposed to the immediacy of the body forwarded in Khanna's study, it is precisely this *mediating disconnection* between the world and the subject's body, perception, and consciousness that gets stylized in Asco's oeuvre. As we shall see, one of the major questions embodied in Asco's work concerns the irreconcilability between the individual and society, between what Sartre once called "the milieu of scarcity" (a milieu later exacerbated under Reagan's policies) and the internal structure of the subject of resistance. Or, better yet, Asco's work formalizes the tension between (Chicano) identity and its (romance of) community.[25] But first, let us revisit the story behind the title of Sartre's rather queer novel.

## Sartre's *La Nausée*

*Nausea*, Fredric Jameson claims, is "unquestionably Sartre's most perfect novel."[26] If this is the case, this perfection did not come without some misgivings over the novel's reception. Jean-Paul Sartre's title for his 1938 novel, *La Nausée*, published by Gallimard Press, is well known not to have been Sartre's initial choice for the book at all. In fact, Sartre submitted the original manuscript to Gallimard under the title "La Mélancolie," which was rejected since this title seemed too steeped in the Romantic overtones of nineteenth-century literature, which, by the interwar period, had become antiquated. Sartre's second suggestion, "The Extraordinary Adventures of Antoine Roquentin," bypassed some of the major (post)-Romantic tropes of the novel, such as themes of malaise and ennui, in favor of an ironic ploy to cast the beginnings of Sartre's literary work (and perhaps even his philosophy) as a frolicsome entry into his "factum on contingency," Sartre's thesis that chance determines Being.[27] After all, if a theory of everything as contingent and random does not mean that life is an adventure, then what does it mean that something is extra-ordinary, that is, superfluous to the quotidian fact that "there are no adventures" to be had?[28] For this and other reasons, Sartre's second title amused Richard Howard, the English translator of the New Directions edition of *Nausea*. In his foreword, Howard meditates on an uncanny scenario in which a contemporary reader encounters Sartre's original lost title, "Melancholia": "How *deceived* we should be, as the French say when they mean *disappointed*, if confronted today by a novel with that original, all-too-human, sentimental or psychiatric appellation."[29] That is, as readers encounter the original title in retrospect, they would quickly understand the melancholic subject as an "all-too-human, sentimental" deception and disappointment to itself, an inadequate subject that does not quite grasp the heavy anguish permeating Being. As the Sartre scholars Alistair Rolls and Elizabeth Rechniewski explain in their volume *Sartre's "Nausea": Text, Context, Intertext*, melancholia fails to produce a deep shame over living; *mélancolie* fails to capture the young Sartre's "boredom and frustration of long days spent in front of a blank sheet of paper; the contempt for the bourgeois, their respectability, their rituals, their smugness and philistinism; the condemnation of art that flatters and gives them a good conscience, that hides their faults, . . . the final project of writing a novel which will be as bright and hard as steel and will make people ashamed of their existence and bring salvation."[30]

These tropes, evident throughout the novel and the context in which it was written, echo themes of disenchanted Romanticism that run throughout *Dissatisfactions*. But for the purposes of this chapter and our exploration of nausea as a stylized discontent emerging in post-1968 Los Angeles, *Nausea* reminds us that the distinction between melancholia and nausea begins to dissolve at the level of style. When Antoine Roquentin, the sullen, white, male protagonist of Sartre's novel, realizes the capaciousness of his moment in the famous chestnut tree scene of the narrative, he writes in his journal,

> This moment was extraordinary. I was there, motionless and icy, plunged in a horrible ecstasy. But something fresh had just appeared in the very heart of this ecstasy; I understood the Nausea, I possessed it. . . . The essential thing is contingency. I mean that one cannot define existence as necessity. . . . I believe there are people who have understood this. Only they tried to overcome this contingency by inventing a necessary, causal being. But no necessary being can explain existence: contingency is not a delusion, a probability which can be dissipated; it is the absolute, consequently, the perfect free gift. All is free, this park, this city, and myself. When you realize that, it turns your heart upside down and everything begins to float.[31]

*Dissatisfactions* in general and this chapter in particular take as their starting point the moment when everything begins to float, at the very instant when the Chicano agential, political subject is in suspension and "all is free" from any politics of redemption, completion, or recognition. As a result, the subject's suspended agency resists any catharsis promised by an affirmative culture, whereby the subject's stylized discontent eludes valorization and even value in resembling the melancholic's recessive activity. Contingency figures as determinate where the loss of meaning or value results from the loss of one's grip on the world, as in the case for Roquentin in the scene just quoted. But what does this have to do with style?

In our study, style serves as a heuristic for investigating the gratuitous and superfluous aspects of politics, giving us a window into the contingency of the world and value's uncertain status within any style whatsoever. For, if style marks a singular voice or touch, its value only accrues relationally, that is, in conjunction with other various styles. In a sense, style both originates from an identity, signaling its possession to some identifiable thing or person (like how Roquentin possesses his nausea), and yet must also escape its identitarian confines in order to matter, as it were—style appears self-caused but yet floats among other styles. In this sense, style contains an "effeminizing shame," as D. A. Miller argues, "a shame that Style at once incurs and inflicts" on itself and others.[32] And here is the contradiction, whereas style, like shame, "points and projects," in Eve Sedgwick's words, style's effeminizing shame for Miller is a "very *narrowly* distributed abjection."[33] Precisely because of its absurd subjective status, that style questions any coherent identity, pulling identity into a definitional crisis. An effeminizing style's pointed abjection can also become, as Leticia Alvarado argues, "an aesthetic strategy that reverberates in the social realm."[34] An effeminizing style might cause a narrowly distributed abjection per Miller's point, but it in effect racializes its object as well, as explored in scholarly debates about abjection and the effeminizing effect of ethnic-racial difference.[35] The point here is that abjection's "attraction and repulsion" dynamic, the way it stages a productive impasse for desire, oddly mirrors the function of nausea as style.

In the end, Sartre's publisher, Gaston Gallimard, named the novel *Nausea*, a decision that had much more of an impact (amplified through some thirty translations across the world since) than the text itself. At first, both Sartre and his partner, Simone de Beauvoir, worried that the nomenclature "nausea" would make the text seem too "naturalistic," thus forgoing the experimental and philosophical impulses behind the writing. Instead, as Howard points out, "What actually happened is that the word ['nausea'] somehow changed its meaning because of the novel's title: capitalized and clearly in reference to the novel, 'Nausea' no longer evokes physical *malaise* to the point of vomiting, but is a nickname for existential anguish."[36] Gallimard's renaming of the novel *did* something to the epistemological scaffolding of the generic term. *Nausea*'s popularity and circulation altered the word's definition through a particular performance of amplification that I also find operative in the works of Asco. Perhaps recognizing that Sartre's text performed the very definitional distortion to language that we witness in Roquentin's "extraordinary adventures" in Bouville (translated to English as "Mud-Town," a name that evokes the sordid living conditions that many punks in Los Angeles endured and best exemplified in Spheeris's documentary), Gallimard skillfully tapped into the political workings of writerly and philosophical style—the same experimental attributes that Beauvoir and Sartre were anxiously defending during debates over the titling of the manuscript.[37] Gallimard's title repackages the novel's tropes of ennui, malaise, melancholia, and boredom—which extend from the early nineteenth-century Romantic novel, a form that favors an inward, self-reflective gaze on a particular and irreducible subjectivity—to suggest the dissipation of individuated melancholia. In *Nausea*, Sartre's original appellation "Melancholia" becomes both personally felt and social, tethered to the experience of collective existential angst. In other words, readers anticipated in *Nausea* to find the effects of a physical malaise only to encounter the novel's Romantic tropes, albeit distorted by the modern impulse to translate the malaise of a body into a social phenomenon.

## *La Nausée* of Asco

Much as the renaming of Sartre's novel successfully manipulated the cultural definition of nausea, Asco also sought to manipulate and amplify a sentiment that hovered above the city of Los Angeles in the early 1970s. Harry Gamboa Jr., Gronk (Glugio Nicandro), Patssi Valdez, and Willie Herrón III formed the core and original members of the Chicano experimental art group Asco (Spanish for "nausea"). By most accounts, the four began collaborating in 1972, and after 1975, the group fluctuated in size as original members diverged to pursue individual projects and second-generation Asco members came and went, until the fluctuating group officially disbanded in 1987. Participants in the East Los Angeles "blow-outs" protesting inequalities in the city's public school system, Asco members drew many of their artistic tactics from Chicano activist impulses of the 1960s and 1970s. Recently, the field of Latino/Chicano studies has seen a significant increase in scholarship on Asco, which has contributed to a robust conversation over the importance of art and style in social movements. For the sociologist Edward J. McCaughan, Asco demonstrated how style and aesthetics were central to critiques of social movements in the 1960s and 1970s, in their incorporation of a global sensibility drawing from German expressionism

Figure 1.3. "Asco, 1982," from the Asco era. ©Harry Gamboa Jr., 1982. Performers (*left to right*): Harry Gamboa, Glugio Gronk Nicandro, Patssi Valdez, and Willie Herrón.

and dadaism, while combining these styles with more local and readily available references such as Hollywood glamour.[38] In addition, the feminist performance studies scholar Leticia Alvarado has theorized Asco's work as articulating an "abject structure of feeling" that created a queer "counterculture community" in contradistinction to the respectability politics characteristic of the more family-oriented ethos of Chicano culture at the time.[39] Richard T. Rodríguez leans on Asco in his work on nonnormative kinship relations in Chicano cultural politics to describe how Asco's art actively challenged heteronormative and sexist representations of family values through its experimental methods and queer aesthetics.[40]

Meanwhile, a groundbreaking retrospective of Asco's work, which I had the privilege of attending at the Los Angeles County Museum of Art (LACMA) in the fall of 2011, was organized by Rita Gonzalez and C. Ondine Chavoya and reintroduced Asco to the art community from an institution that rejected its artistic contributions some three decades prior—more on this point later in this chapter. To accompany the retrospective, Chavoya and Gonzalez edited the incredibly generative exhibition catalog *Asco: Elite of the Obscure, 1972–1987*, in which, in collated images, writings, and ephemera, one can see how distinctive Asco's experimental, DIY, and generally "cool" style appeared before its time. What most scholars land on with regard to the art group's stylistic and representational politics is its name: Asco. The moniker was meant to articulate an attitude to the dominant Chicano sensibility, one that deviated from the norm in style, politics, organization, and dissemination to distinguish the group as a self-generated community of misfits within a larger disenfranchised community. Indeed, scholarly conversations on Asco continue to attend to concerns about the way we think about and represent those who are doubly excluded from social belonging. It is this attribute that churns much debate on Asco's style politics and its asynchronous alignment with the Chicano cultural sensibility of its time.

The origin of Asco's name is of particular interest for performance studies scholars since Asco articulates the very effect that the group intends. Many of the original members of Asco, like their comrades, expressed a shared sense of nausea and disgust with the war in Vietnam, state-sanctioned violence in the form of police brutality in the barrios of East Los Angeles, and the general political, economic, and social disenfranchisement of minoritized populations in the United States during the 1970s and '80s. For those subjects outside the racial and sexual mainstream, the status quo meant the sedimentation of norms caustic to what the scholar Grace Hong elaborates as "the impossible politics of difference." Following Audre Lorde's (at times vexing) utilization of the term "difference" throughout her oeuvre, Hong deploys the notion to reference "a cultural and epistemological practice that holds *in suspension* (without requiring resolution) contradictory, mutually exclusive and negating impulses." "'Difference,'" Hong continues, "names an epistemological position, ontological condition, and political strategy that reckon with the shift in technologies of power that we might as well call 'neoliberal.'"[41] Hong's astute reading of Lorde's use of "difference" uncannily mirrors Merleau-Ponty's phenomenological argument highlighted in this chapter's epigraph, where the "instability of levels" produces an experience not only of disorientation but of giddiness, nausea, and horror, which responds to the neoliberal "technologies of power."

Asco, too, understood these economic and cultural destabilizing forces amid an "impossible politics of difference." The status quo nauseated the members into recalibrating the social, sifting out an aesthetic way of being from the debilitating effects of hostile government policies. This is to say, what we have is a historical notion, the word "difference," which corresponds to the multiscalar social realms that a subject may inhabit. The historical force behind the politics of social difference thus suspends— "without requiring resolution"—positionalities (Chicano, gay, woman, poor) that are falsely pitted against one another and productively makes visible what Hong describes as "the exacerbated dispersal of minoritized death" culturally and systemically disavowed in Reagan's America.[42]

But in accounting for social difference, the difference between identities, one must also account for the unbridgeable difference within oneself. This is central to the argument of *Dissatisfactions*. Los Angeles and its Tinseltown reputation as a land of make-believe allow one to *feel* different from their own reality, almost as a joke or an ironic ploy. This is what Harry Gamboa Jr. captures in his description of LA's smog: "If the smog is not too severe when you stand atop nearly any rooftop in Los Angeles, you can see the Hollywood sign as it beckons to the world with its multibillion-dollar myth. When you climb back down into your own backyard and walk along the streets, everything can be considered a façade, everyone can be acknowledged as an 'extra,' and you can be the brightest burning star."[43] Once again, we have the smog acting as a protagonist in Los Angeles's existential landscape. According to Gamboa, Hollywood's hazy myth lulls the denizen down to a reality draped in dreamy aspirations. One forgets if they are the actual star of their own show or just an extra in someone else's. Everything is a façade, a decoy, a surface to project fantasies of belonging, financed by a "multibillion-dollar myth" hardly discernable through an atmosphere of failed hope. This is the unbridgeable difference externalized into a false sense of totality, into an aura of misperception, where one cannot discern whether the given world is real or staged.

Take, for instance, a photograph that captures much of the driving argument of this chapter. The photograph, titled *Decoy Gang War Victim*, was taken by Asco in 1974 on the streets of East Los Angeles (figure 1.4). *Decoy* depicts one of Asco's members lying in the middle of an empty street, seemingly dead and surrounded by magenta

Figure 1.4. "Decoy Gang War Victim, 1974," from the Asco era. ©Harry Gamboa Jr., 1974. Performer: Glugio Gronk Nicandro.

traffic flares, suggesting that a scene of criminal proportions has just occurred. In fact, Los Angeles witnessed a rise in Mexican American gang-related violence in the early to mid-1970s, which scholars have attributed to three political developments: the Chicano movement, the war on poverty, and the Vietnam War.[44] With the election of Richard Nixon as president of the United States in 1968, many of the previous Johnson administration's economic initiatives aimed at reducing the poverty rate in the United States were significantly curtailed, thus eliminating jobs in the already economically marginalized populations of Los Angeles. Johnson's war-on-poverty policies now under duress included the expansion of many government welfare programs, such as food stamps, Social Security, and access to primary and secondary education. Meanwhile, as the Chicano scholar James Vigil contends, the Vietnam War displaced a generation of Chicanos from the barrios and into war zones.[45] As a result of the systemic breakup of the Chicano family over the course of two decades and the staggering death toll of Chicanos in the Vietnam War, many Chicano youths who were left behind cultivated alternative forms of kinship and belonging, spurred by a decrease in access to social welfare programs and an increase in cultural pride and awareness articulated in the intensifying Chicano movement. Asco created aesthetic responses to these cultural events in efforts to suspend (and thus display) the fantasy of the Chicano gang victim, a victim that altogether registered structural and historical modes of dispossession on the body and on the ground.

Asco mischievously sent the photograph, produced on a thirty-five-millimeter color slide, to local news stations with the caption "last gang member," as if to facetiously claim that gang violence had come to an end in the Los Angeles barrios. One strategy deployed by newspapers in their increased coverage of gang violence in Los Angeles in the 1970s was to publish the names of victims, their family members, and gang affiliations to facilitate the reciprocation of violence and thus increase newspaper sales. In the words of one Asco member, "the desired effect of *Decoy Gang War Victim* was to generate a *pause* in the violence in order to rob the newspapers of their daily list of victims."[46]

KHJ-TV, however, reported the image as evidence of growing gang wars within the unruly Chicano barrios of East Los Angeles. Of course, the evidence behind this news report was not necessarily "true," but the photograph did *do* something: Asco's photograph performatively substantiated the very problem that Asco sought to pause. One Asco member, Harry Gamboa Jr., explains that works like *Decoy* aimed "to alter sentiment or to provide false information or to augment existing information in a way that might guide the viewer's attention, which again has been . . . a very important thing in working with Asco—to create this *aura* of [the event being photographed] . . . being much bigger than what it might have actually been." To an extent, Gamboa's diagnostic confirms the newly emerging economic reality unfolding in Los Angeles, one where, in the words of Christian Marazzi, "communication and production overlap."[47]

Upon reflecting on the relationship between photographic performance, mass media, and the circulation of information and "sentiments," here we see how Asco questions the artistic capacity to represent an event. In its photographic staging, Asco cultivated a style or an aura "being much bigger than what it might have actually been." In this way, Gamboa's use of "aura" resembles less Walter Benjamin's description of the lost (because of modernity's drive toward art's mechanical reproduction) distance between the artist and their artwork. Rather, the aura created in *Decoy* falls more in line with the way Theodor Adorno describes the art object's *Schein*, its semblance or illusion of formal unity. Such semblance of total identity produces what Rei Terada calls *Schein*'s "illusory fact perception" and ought to be considered as a function of style's tendency toward refinement—more on this point in the final section of this chapter.[48] Most importantly, Asco's aesthetic choices and intents register larger socioeconomic factors unfolding in Los Angeles by the mid-1970s. *Decoy* sets the stage for the 1979 watershed moment that Christian Marazzi attributes to the shift in capitalist economic production, where, in 1979 and increasingly by 1980, the world witnessed a shift to "lean production"—that is, a change from instrumental forms of production indicative of Fordism to "communicative action," otherwise known as "immaterial labor" in the then-emerging post-Fordist economy.[49] Consequently, what is produced are "information workers" caught in an ever-increasing speed of information "transmitted through complex technical systems that go faster than the human brain."[50] Think here of the symptomatic and oddly fast, syncopated punk beat responding to the slowness of social change; think here also of how the feeling of nausea marked for X the ongoingness of the present. In producing false information meant to circulate in local news outlets, Asco's "communicative action" amplified nausea into a style. What we are left with is a commodity of the information worker's work.

*Decoy* images an event that has not occurred, despite displaying credible signs of barrio gang violence, in order to shift our critical optic back to the importance of its stylistic and photographic form for a Chicano cultural politics. In crafting a highly stylized and formally refined image with a deceiving caption of misinformation, Asco lodged a node of what Anne-Lise François calls "recessive action" into the broadcasting of information, whereby a performance of "self-canceling revelation permits a release from the ethical imperative to *act* upon knowledge."[51] The photograph's mixture of cyan and magenta colors filters the image, dispensing with the harsh realities of what Raúl Homero Villa calls "barrioization" and transforming what would normally be an ugly image of violence into something formally astute: a photographic composition laying bare the consequences of gratuitous violence.[52] Asco calls into question the proliferation of violence perpetuated by the media, framed by the state, and intensified in the barrios. Yet, in its photo-performance, the violence is contained, staged, reframed, and controlled. The decoy lies alone on an empty street with the silhouette of distant witnesses in the background, reminding the viewer of the impersonality of everyday violence and punctuating, like the white mercury gas lamps in the photograph that conjure Los Angeles's neighborhood-specific street lamps, the frame of any *given* reality. In other words, what Asco enacts in its misinformation campaign is a turning away from the *givenness* of an event, evincing a general dissatisfaction with the normative pretense to accept the conditions in which one finds oneself and one's community. We can perceive in Asco's artistic intention the same coincidental implications of Gallimard's renaming Sartre's novel: a stylized mode of disappointment (or deception, in the French vernacular) taking shape as an aura (*Schein*) that makes an event seem bigger than what it might have actually been, thereby calling into suspicion the dominant culture's complacency with acceptable appearances. Finally, *Decoy Gang War Victim* perversely literalizes, in its aesthetic qualities, both the "burden of representation" and "the burden of liveness" placed on bodies outside the racial and sexual mainstream.[53]

## The Burden of Live Representation

How might one represent the demand for culturally affirming politics? In what ways do minoritized subjects live within the confines of liveness—that is, the cultural demand for minoritized subjects to exist *in the moment* for elite consumers of spectacular difference? These questions structure Asco's interventions. Much of Chicano art surrounding Asco's initial collaboration revolved around the paradigm of affirmative cultural representations and usually indexed traditional forms of family and national belonging in efforts to cohere an identity around the sign of "Chicanismo." For instance, Chicano mural art, a widely theorized and recorded art practice that particularly sharpened under movement politics, risked representing traditional signs of heteronormativity and nationalism in order to evoke cultural pride in the face of damaging ideologies that sought to negatively cast marginal groups as criminal, illegal, and unassimilable into the larger (unmarked) culture. For this reason, movement representations of Chicanos have been accused of reproducing the same paradigms of cultural whitewashing that fueled and justified the erasure of difference through the homogenizing effect of that force field we know as identity.[54] Consequently, Asco always fell outside conventional meanings and appearances ascribed to Chicanismo. This could not be more evident than in its perversely comical and at times form-breaking performances of mural-making.

In *Walking Mural*, considered one of Asco's first performance pieces, performed on Christmas Eve 1972 in East Los Angeles, we see a gothic *Virgin de Guadalupe* (Patssi Valdez), stripped of her notable Mexican-national color palette of green and red, walking in a morbidly discontented posture. Yet, next to her, the missing green and red elements explode in the ridiculous costume of her fellow performer (Gronk). This ensemble is supposed to represent a Christmas tree, almost in an effort to bridge Mexican and American cultural and religious symbols, while Valdez's getup remakes "our" *Virgen de Guadalupe* into an angsty teenage girl, horrifying pedestrians strolling down Whittier Boulevard. Following closely behind is fellow Asco member Willie Herrón, whose head protrudes from a large painted cardboard canvas exhibiting three other grotesque-looking heads, each paired with aluminum arms reaching outward in a zombie-like gesture. Here, however, it is not so much the disgusting backdrop of a multifaced mural come to life—Herrón is the actual walking mural—nor the many confused Chicano pedestrians afflicted by what they may have dismissed as simply a lofty performance art piece that makes this moment of a live performance remarkable. Instead, what strikes the viewer in this photograph, taken by fellow Asco member Harry Gamboa Jr., is the singular punctum of an illuminated green neon crosswalk sign captured at the decisive moment reading, "WALK," thus reminding the viewer from the confines of the seemingly static photograph—a mediated documentation of a live performance—of the value-forming effect of circulation. Asco situates its aesthetic critique of the representational politics emerging from *within its own* marginalized Chicano community at the level of the body, linking it to a self-reflexive construction of a perverse performative framework in which to reinterpret anew that marginalization (at the scale both of the minoritized subject and of its marginalized community). The second component builds on the first by emphasizing that the embodied question of critique—which I have been describing here as part and parcel of the structure of nausea—must circulate and move if it is to free the minoritized subject from the demand to *act* on a situation in which the prevailing ideology is inadequately interpellated. If at this emerging-postmodern juncture, it becomes more difficult to parse critique from art by virtue of the latter's increasing awareness of its discursive circulation, that is, the ability to incorporate a critique of the artwork into the art itself, then Asco formalizes its own double exclusion from both criticism and the art world. This move redirects attention back onto the audience and institutions, confirming Ngai's astute observation when she says, "A culture in which the making of art is institutionally mediated thus encourages art's internalization of history and thereby theory."[55] Mediation becomes Asco's target and vehicle for critique, and this is what makes the group both alluring and objectionable.

First, we will examine Asco's relation to the function of the audience in live performance, followed by its awareness of its exclusion from art institutions. The performance studies scholar José Muñoz has argued that the framework of the live event in performance studies scholarship serves as a "precritical aura that shrouds some performance research."[56] In effect, "the burden of liveness," a term Muñoz reworks from Kobena Mercer's important 1990 essay "Black Art and the Burden of Representation," names the ways some minoritarian subjects are forced into live performance for "an audience of elites" as "the only imaginable mode of survival."[57] In disentangling liveness from performance, the temporal logic of liveness becomes more apparent: "'The burden of liveness' affords the minoritarian subject an extremely circumscribed temporality. To be only in 'the live' means that one is denied history and futurity. If the minoritarian subject can only exist in *the moment*, she or he does not have the privilege or the pleasure of being a historical subject. If that subject needs to focus solely on the present, it can never afford the luxury of thinking about the future."[58] What I would like to suggest is that Asco enacts a productive addendum to Muñoz's staunch critique. *Walking Mural* demonstrates how the "burden of liveness" does not always necessitate "elite audiences" for it to be a burden on the minoritarian subject. And although Muñoz recognizes that, for example, the Latina lesbian is "triply susceptible" to the burden of liveness, the dominant culture cannot or refuses to register the many particularities in which the subject is hailed to perform for it. This is one limitation of Muñoz's theorization since Asco challenges the unidirectionality of which the burden is placed. Asco disidentifies with the burden of performing its cultural affirmation of Chicano identity (underscored in its work's reference to mural-making) and instead throws back the interpretive responsibilities of its performance onto its community and the quotidian Chicano passersby in East Los Angeles. What Asco's performance affords to its makeshift audience in the barrio is the very possibility of thinking not necessarily about futurity (since its audience was already living in the foggy promise of social change) but of the rudely proximal desire to police its own culture and thus of the audience's own superegoic status in *that* moment. This displacement of interpretive responsibility comes as the effect of Asco's embodying the question of critique. By *giving* people *asco*, the art group interpellated its audience into a larger social milieu that confused the distinction between the burden of liveness and the burden of affirming one's lived, however marginal, experience.[59]

In "Black Art and the Burden of Representation," Kobena Mercer argues for types of art and cultural criticism that do not adopt a dominating posture over their object of critique. He states, "Instead of assuming an authoritative position, in which criticism takes on a judgmental stance, it is more helpful to conceive it as an on-going conversation or dialogue that seeks to deepen our knowledge of the way texts 'work' as they circulate in the public sphere."[60] Mercer warns of a form of criticism that seeks to foreclose dialogue. He sees this exemplified by a style called "populist modernism," which foregrounds the ethnic-racial identity of the artist in an effort to explicate the "accountability to the community" that the artist must acknowledge. Dismissing it as "cultural insider-ism," Mercer says proponents of populist modernism undertake what he calls "ideological policing of 'correct' or 'right-on' *attitudes*." According to Mercer, demanding that an artwork unequivocally correspond to the ethnic-racial identity of its creator means that critiques of the artwork become predetermined and fully knowable. This move obscures the material conditions that enabled the artist to create the artwork in the first place, while reinforcing insidious binaries of high/low culture, white/Black art, and even structure/agency. In a sense, Mercer challenges the cathartic mood of this criticism, cathartic in the sense that it satisfies the politics demanded of the artwork's aesthetics, a catharsis that obscures audience consumption. What becomes important for Mercer regarding cultural criticism lies in the critic's (or performance artist's) own capacity to "recogniz[e] the contingent and contextual character of the relations between authors, texts, and readers as they encounter each other in the worldly space of the public sphere."[61] This semantic contingency, Mercer reminds the reader, does not allow us to claim that "no one 'definition' has more truth-value than the others, [but] simply [that] what matters is whose definitions are more powerful, more hegemonic, more taken for granted, than others."[62] As mentioned, the governing political distinction in Mercer's argument is class since questions of access to art markets and what kind of audience the art is for (specifically, Mercer's discussion of Black art turns on the question of the white audience's consumption and thus the reification of the white/Black binary) are structured by class relations: "It seems to me that the 'burden of representation' is constructed as an effect of the hierarchy of access to institutional spaces of cultural production in the visual arts, . . . [where] hierarchical distinctions between vernacular and literate culture, or popular culture and elite culture, . . . is a hierarchy structured by relations of class."[63] In short, the burden of representation eschews the material reality of the artist by circumscribing and projecting an image that the artist can never fully fulfill unless they are willing to forfeit the sovereignty of their aesthetic incalculability. In turn, Asco repurposes its aesthetic incalculability into the impossibility of Chicano art *tout court*.

Asco's work provides those who are interested in the relations between aesthetics and politics with a different way into Mercer's argument, one that does not stop at merely illuminating the materialist conditions by which works of art are recognized in institutional spaces, though this significant point remains salient for the argument of this chapter. But rather, how do these material conditions govern culturally affirming spaces—that is, within the *barrio* itself? One of Asco's early and most notable pieces, *Spray Paint LACMA* (at times later referred to as *Project Pie in De/Face*) encapsulates the very problem that Mercer outlines. In 1972, young Asco members orchestrated a response to a LACMA curator's statement dismissing the absence of Chicano art in the museum, since in the curator's view, Chicanos made graffiti, not art. From LACMA's position, Chon Noriega explains, "'Chicano art' was a categorical impossibility."[64] This impossibility became an opportunity for Asco to reframe given distinctions between high and low aesthetic production into class distinctions, and so one evening, its members graffitied their names on the pristine, unmarked entrance to the museum.

LACMA, located in the largely white, mainly affluent mid-Wilshire area of Los Angeles just south of the gay enclave of West Hollywood, was "defaced" by the graffiti of brown folks. Perhaps understood as a sign of the continuous browning of America, *Spray Paint LACMA* revealed an unsettling anxiety produced by white America's proximity to ethnic-racialized others.[65] This is to say, Asco performed the very thing LACMA expected of Chicanos: the impossibility of Chicano art. By situating Chicano art *tout court* as impossible through Asco's documented happenings, *Spray Paint LACMA* and *Walking Mural* underscored this impossibility in two different contexts: both outside LACMA's walls and within the barrios. One might be reminded of Grace Hong's evocation of the "impossible politics of difference" while also considering how *Spray Paint LACMA was* and *is* Chicano art. The nauseating reality imprinted on LACMA's blinding walls makes difference visible and reflects the burden that Chicanos are forced to carry not only for elite audiences but also through the streets of East Los Angeles.

Asco, in inciting *asco* in its fellow Chicanos through performative means, in effect *created* its audience, despite that audience's subjective refusals. All the while, Asco registered the existential dread of belonging in a nation-state that cultivated its own experience of *asco*, an experience perpetuated by the exclusionary, value-ridden tactics of institutions like LACMA—even if LACMA now, thanks to Asco, broadcast information concerning the impending encounter with ethnic-racialized others (pie meets face).

Two years later, this collective action of walking and gathering an audience, however disgusted, confused, or shocked it may be, vanishes in an instant in Asco's 1974 performance piece *Instant Mural*. In the performance, Gronk taped his colleague Patssi Valdez to a bright yellow wall, amplifying the colors of her red jacket and white-powdered face. At one point, another Asco member joins them, and Gronk begins to tape him to the wall as well. One photograph shows the taped-down bodies exploding out of their bandages with laughter. On the one hand, a literal

Figure 1.5. "Spray Paint LACMA, 1972," from the Asco era. ©Harry Gamboa Jr., 1972. Performer: Patssi Valdez.

interpretation of the work's title satirizes the act of creating a mural by making it ephemeral through liveness. On the other hand, it calls into question the politics of representation in the performance of shoddily taping a Chicana body onto a wall, evincing an almost confining need to represent a body that just will not stick at all. Both performances and conceptual pieces, like much of Asco's oeuvre, utilized a punk DIY ethos that often read as a political and stylistic refusal of the stale Chicano "art objects" propagated by Chicano nationalism during this period. These tropes also populated much of the dominant Chicano literary canon of the late 1970s and '80s, when Chicano political consciousness was tethered to the often-guilt-ridden genre of the coming-of-age novel, such as Rudolfo Anaya's *Bless Me Ultima* and, to a lesser extent, Sandra Cisneros's *The House on Mango Street*. Asco's style, on the other hand, diverged from the Chicano mainstream and participated in an understudied intellectual culture of Chicano activism.

The Chicano scholar Randy Ontiveros reminds us in his book *In the Spirit of a New People: The Cultural Politics of the Chicano Movement*,

Figure 1.6. "Walking Mural, 1972," from the Asco era. ©Harry Gamboa Jr., 1972. Performers (*left to right*): Patssi Valdez, Willie Herrón, and Glugio Gronk Nicandro.

"Chicano/a activists avidly read C. Wright Mills in the classroom and informal reading groups. They also read work by feminists Simone de Beauvoir, Betty Friedan, and Robin Morgan; by Brazilian radical Paulo Freire and Algerian anti-colonialist Frantz Fanon; by Mexican and Mexican-American intellectuals Jose Vasconcelos, Miguel León-Portillo; by Martin Luther King Jr. and Malcom X. . . . The diversity and rigor of Chicano intellectual life during the 1960's and 1970's is one of the movement's most underappreciated *aspects*, and also one of its most important legacies."[66] It should be no surprise to the reader, then, that Asco's members were also readers of Jean-Paul Sartre and specifically of his 1938 novel *Nausea*. Thus, these minor forms of cultural scaffolding require an attunement to how style endures and intensifies with time as partly a performance of minding or lingering with time's capacity to enact change. There is no better example than what Ontiveros shows us. The vast literary and theoretical bibliography of the Chicano movement reveals its *internal* queer drive to expand the production of Chicano culture, literature, and thought *outside* the dominant Chicano literary canon, much like Asco members playfully exploding off the wall.

## Asco's Style as Refinement and Whateverness

Asco's work extends a literary and cultural genealogy of nausea that allows us to think both with and against Sartre's early development of his existential philosophy. First, Asco gets us away from a solipsistic construction of an individual's embodied experience of nausea as existential angst and toward something more collective—something like a social form or a social body—at the precise moment when the Chicano agential subject comes into tension with a promise for collective action against a dominant ideology, all unfolding during the Chicano movement. Though, in *choosing* neither assimilation nor a ready-made counteridentification with the US nation-state found in movement politics, Asco selects nausea—a structured feeling and nomenclature—as its style politics. Take a 1975 photograph featuring Willie Herrón, Humberto Sandoval, Patssi Valdez, Gronk, and Harry Gamboa Jr. in the middle of an empty downtown Los Angeles street, contorting their bodies to spell the name of the art group: ASCO. On closer examination, the group appears to be spelling A-S-K-O, with Valdez and Gronk together forming the letter *K*. Yet, Valdez is decisively further back behind her male counterparts, with her hands tucked into her timeless denim shorts, shoulders a bit shrugged as if to communicate a slight discomfort in belonging, a sense of being out of place, or both sentiments simultaneously. Valdez's inadequately erected posture suggests some internal conflict within the performance and photograph, a struggle animated by an internalization of nausea. Here, Valdez's subjective "I" embodied in her stance foreshadows our next stylized discontent in signaling a lodged bad attitude at the core of "A-S-C-O" and deepens the seemingly surface play that her male colleagues present for the viewer with a withdrawn uncertainty.

Meanwhile, the cool blue tint of the photograph evokes the photograph discussed earlier, *Decoy Gang War Victim*, yet here Asco displays, in the words of C. Ondine Chavoya, "a convergence of language, body, and city."[67] Downtown Los Angeles (buildings, streetlamps, and streets) figures as a background character in the photograph, suggesting Asco's own fascination with the dissemination and movement of information, bodies, and affects. This point makes sense when considering how the city at the time was undergoing great urban renewal at the cost of the working poor and the displacement of many ethnic-racial communities,

Figure 1.7. "Instant Mural, 1974," from the Asco era. ©Harry Gamboa Jr., 1974. Performers (*left to right*): Glugio Gronk Nicandro and Patssi Valdez.

a great concern for Asco members as denizens of East Los Angeles. But also, Asco intuitively understood that these material changes were conditioned by a shift in economic and cultural relations, where the increased circulation of commodities and information necessitating constructions of new highway infrastructure, power lines, streetlights, and telecommunication systems were increasingly made visible *as* forms of mediation and thus susceptible to the group's playful manipulation. Therefore, it is necessary for us to understand how Asco's engaged experimentation with media was self-understood as their way of refining the social detritus produced in the wake of this shift, a refinement composed of mockery and contempt for societal change.

In a 1983 interview, when Asco was asked how the collaborative group came up with its name, Gronk explained, "That was generally the reaction to a lot of the work that we were doing, when we first started doing work, is people would say, refer to our work as giving them, 'Uuhhll! *Asco*.' . . . So, the reaction by the community, or by different people that would see the work, it was giving them nausea. So, we liked the word." When the interviewer inquired whether the audience's response had since changed, Gronk replied, "No, but the vomit has probably refined itself a little."[68] Asco articulates an affective traffic that runs like a two-way street. On the one hand, the Chicano community's disdain and ill reception of Asco's work exclude the art group from the domain of "Chicano." On the other hand, Asco members too were repulsed by the rampant homophobia and machismo characteristic of Chicano nationalism, which in their view was complicit with the dominant white culture of racism and bourgeois consumerism. It is in this two-way exchange where we must take a closer critical look at what happens to the fetid feeling of nausea. Certainly, this dynamic shows the negative affective registers of Asco's work. Leticia Alvarado argues that Asco forwards a "queer present without place," which in turn provides "alternative grounds for disruption and inclusion through uncivic comportment."[69] I agree with Alvarado's astute reading that Asco's politics of displacement reworks loss into a refined negativity, because we can then say Asco effectively stylized its politics of loss.

In returning to Gronk's statement, what does refined vomit look like? What type of style does this refinement entail? The cathartic element of vomiting requires the need for further catharsis, for further expulsion—a refinement of sorts. But what exactly can be cathartic about vomit if the facsimile is always haunted by its inadequacy, its need for further expulsion? Nausea calls the surface of things into suspicion, questioning what was actually desired in the first place, because quite simply, refined vomit obscures any satisfactory release.

Let us conclude with a telling example of this nauseating dynamic by turning to one of Asco's 1985 short video art pieces, *Baby Kake*. The short is about six minutes long and features Barbara Carrasco (Harry Gamboa's partner) as a fed-up wife and mother who murders her husband, played by Gronk, after her man-baby, played by the queer Chicano artist Humberto Sandoval, chokes and dies due to parental neglect. The short also features another queer Chicano artist, Ruben Zamora, dressed in drag as Marie Antoinette, who functions as a fairy godmother to both men in the film (that is, the ideal mother). In Harry Gamboa's 1998 essay, titled "Past Imperfecto" as a play on his first video production from 1983, *Imperfecto*, he explains the material conditions under which this new phase of Asco had to work to create some of its video pieces: "The few videos which I was able to produce during that year were each shot and edited within a 48-hour period that was often dictated by restrictive scheduling practices of the TV cable company. The conditions which affected the production also included ongoing poverty, poetry, and painful impropriety. . . . All the video works which were produced for public access were each cablecast a minimum of ten times."[70]

One can imagine here Kobena Mercer underscoring Gamboa's insistence on understanding the material conditions surrounding *Baby Kake* as a refusal of the burden of (affirmative) representation, demonstrated in *Baby Kake*'s themes that Gamboa describes as "alienation, dysfunction and hatred which can be found beneath the veneer of romantic/manic relationships."[71] Concerning the representational politics of the video piece, Richard T. Rodríguez, in his excellent book *Next of Kin*, offers an apt description of the familial drama at play in *Baby Kake*. Rodríguez argues that Asco's video production, "throughout the 1980s and 1990s, also represent[s] an important moment in Chicano/a media culture in which shooting the patriarch precisely means taking aim at paternal authority."[72]

At the end of the short, after both men are dead, Zamora's character laments, "Now I have two men to depend on my love and affection," drawing the viewer's attention to their ghostly presence as a queer figure who has to subsume the two patriarchal deaths. Mother responds, "I don't want anyone to depend on me or me to depend on anyone." She then turns to the camera with a smirk of relief: "At last I'm free. At last I'm happy." Rodríguez argues, "While *Baby Kake* is undeniably comedic and campy, it pointedly uproots the social norms ascribed to women in conventional representations of the Chicano family by highlighting Mom's freedom from codependent relationships. Moreover, by killing off Dad (which Baby threatens to do prior to the choking incident), Mom short-circuits the privileges granted to the father who once took for granted his ability to 'come and go' and to elide any responsibility for Baby, therefore delegating it to Mom."[73] I agree with Rodríguez that Asco's nonnormative narrative and stylistic techniques, features common among queer video pieces emerging during the 1980s and 1990s, aimed at killing the "paternal authority" to leave the Mother/Wife happy and free. Moreover, what makes *Baby Kake* radical in its form is precisely its stylized discontent, its production and circulation of nausea, which leaves the closing of the piece indeterminate and the viewer with an almost blasé shrug of "whateverness" to the video's supposed ending. Therefore, I would like to move away from Rodríguez's generative reading of the film as a family romance to underscore the ways in which *Baby Kake* stylizes a dissatisfaction through the given material reality of its production. As Gamboa points out, videos produced around *Baby Kake*'s time showcased a "raw stylistic technique of straight cut edits, poor lighting, and rough camera motion."[74] These stylistic choices reflected the material conditions available to Asco's production. Yet, most importantly, the artist's techniques created nausea-inducing visuals for the viewer. In attending to Gamboa's and Rodríguez's explanations, one cannot ignore the spatial metaphors deployed in highlighting *Baby Kake*'s subversive qualities: *Baby Kake* "uproots" conventions, pointing to a false familial "veneer" beneath which lie hatred, alienation, and dysfunction. These spatial descriptions evidence Asco's awareness of how ideology lurks beneath a refined culture industry and its subsequent uncovering of such ideologies through the manipulation of the medium, coupled with *Baby Kake*'s queer, feminist content.

For instance, viewers cannot ignore *Baby Kake*'s campiness, which harks back to other aesthetic expressions of 1980s queer counterculture, such as the films of John Waters and the Kuchar brothers or the video works of Mark Morrisroe. When not focused on brown bodies, Asco's camera pans over a cluttered room where objects like a painted blue broom taped to a manikin or chewed-on balloons plastered on the walls or the mess of Mr. T cereal and Gerber cranberry juice spilled on the table compose a *constellation* of revolting objects that adds to the very nauseating atmosphere of the small room. This is certainly a scene of disgusting proportions, amplified by the old analog video's color and dystopian soundtrack.

The blue and purple hues of the video's frames suggest a futuristic tone, recalling the ominous inflection of Asco's *Decoy Gang War Victim* and X's song "Nausea." Coupled with the cool synths of Gerardo Velazquez's soundtrack, which evoke something like a Chicano space odyssey, the visuals of *Baby Kake* create a twilight zone of indeterminate affects that are coming into formation. As I have been arguing, Asco is primarily concerned with the circulation of ethnic-racialized "(dis)information," which mirrors the structure of nausea. *Baby Kake*'s color palette of magenta and cyan evokes many of Asco's photo performances, leading viewers to question, What surface or veneer is deceiving us here? Reminiscent of Eugene's blue-tinged confession in *The Decline of Western Civilization*, the general disaffection produced in Asco's video is ironically intensified by Barbara Carrasco's flippant and at times intentionally bad acting, creating a weird and cool distance between her and the camcorder. Furthering this effect, the video's tinted frames dissolve with the indeterminate closure of a fade-out that deprives viewers of a cathartic ending.

Mother's distant flatness or irony is also a characteristic feature of weak affects as Ngai theorizes them, such as envy and irritation, both prevalent affects circulating around Mother's positionality in the video piece. Recall Muñoz's remark that, under Reagan's California, populism was "substituted with flattened individuals, self-absorbed couples and the ravenous and all-encompassing family." Perhaps this was true at the beginning of Asco's tenure in 1972. But by 1985, amid a growing AIDS crisis and media hype around the racist- and sexist-charged figure of Reagan's "welfare queen," women of color and effeminate men became the faces of moral and financial poverty in the United States. It is also no surprise that envy, irritation, and nausea are all culturally marked as effeminate, whether in psychoanalytic narratives of penis envy or the irritable feminist killjoy, leaving such queer subjects, in the eyes of mainstream society, as simultaneously lacking power and excessively affective. Therefore, Mother's shooting the paternal authority cannot be seen as a culminating, cathartic gesture, since she internalizes the scene's nauseating environment and reconstructs it into a "bad" attitude that inadequately expresses fidelity to the event of the murder.

Carrasco's ridiculing performance reworks nausea into a mode of ironic indifference that is really about a being-in-difference with regard to the dominant machismo and heterosexist imprints of late modernity. In effect, nausea is dedramatized, flattened, and embarrassingly ordinary, down to her character's murderous act. Chicano nausea is aestheticized as queer insofar as nausea acts as the ambiguous precondition or subaffect to its more dramatic, object-oriented, politically inflected, and hot counterpart, disgust. Nausea is never quite coincident with disgust but rather surrounds it as a paraconceptual mode of confusion. In *Baby Kake*, this affect plays out in the irrational appearance and disappearance of Marie Antoinette and the panning of the camera over disgusting objects and acts—the video's undisciplined direction.

*Baby Kake* ran on Falcon Cable Television, a public-access channel in a suburb of Los Angeles, allegedly for two years. One can imagine the shock and perhaps enjoyment of young teenagers who tuned in to their local public-access channel and by chance encountered something novel, revealing in turn the, however waning, possibilities of the public domain. As I have discussed, Asco's work was continuously engaged with flows and circuits of information, bodies, and feelings. For example, the group's early conceptual art pieces, in addition to the live murals discussed earlier, included mail art sent to various artists and institutions (some even to Latin America) and guerrilla art acts on Los Angeles's busy highways, in addition to video art like *Baby Kake* that aired over public-access television in Southern California. Asco's constellation of communicative art production demonstrates a commitment to the dissemination of an informational aesthetic that comes to structure the affective map of nausea. *These information artists slowly learn to refine vomit, to clean up and sell back the expelled unwanted (thus unconsciously desired) parts of a social body smashed under Reagan's America.* Just as those viewers who tuned in (by chance or not), Asco attunes to the range of discontent that style affords.

Stylized nausea tells us something about how we remain collected and percolate within a system aiming to pull apart, privatize, and individuate. In this way, Asco's style of politics seems to uphold a particular queer and ethnic-racialized nausea that at the same time points to a "pluralized whateverness ... in a sea of stylistic variety," to borrow Ngai's productive description of style.[75] Whether it is through the group's refusal of the dominant Chicano style of the time (Brown Power, the family, heterosexuality, Chicano nationalism) or of the lack of style in the white walls of the museum, Asco's work underscores what Ngai describes as the very "uncertainty about the significance of any particular style."[76] Asco's *style politics* can be understood as "cool" in its flatness and disinterest toward the Chicano movement and mainstream art circles and even from itself, as articulated in Carrasco's and Valdez's feminist performances. For Asco, nausea equivocally represents the state of remaining cool within the confusing activity of political disorientation.

This chapter ends with *Baby Kake* because Carrasco's feminist act exemplifies what Asco also does best: that is, it (re)injects the human body into representations of networks such as streets, highways, public-access television, and postal services. Carrasco's refusal of routinization suggests an internalization of Los Angeles's circulating nausea, whereby her bad attitude, at once punk and feminist, registers a nonconformist desire to be free of social constraint. This cool Chicana feminist act of shooting the Chicano patriarch and her overgrown son subjectifies nausea, returned back to the body not as existential angst but instead as an attitude of low fidelity to normative culture—another stylized discontent and the subject of chapter 2.

2

# Stripped Life

## Women of Color Punk, Lo-Fi Attitude, and Feminist Print Culture

[Advanced industrial civilization's] productivity and efficacy, its capacity to increase and spread comforts, to turn waste into need, and destruction into construction, the extent to which this civilization transforms the object world into an extension of man's mind and body makes the very notion of alienation questionable. The people recognize themselves in their commodities; they find their soul in their automobiles, hi-fi set, split-level home, kitchen equipment. The very mechanism which ties the individual to his society has changed, and social control is anchored in the new needs which it has produced.
—Herbert Marcuse, *One Dimensional Man*, 1964

When you look in the mirror do you see yourself?
Do you see yourself in the TV screen?
Identity
Is the crisis
Can't you see
—X-Ray Spex, "Identity," 1978

In a recording of a live 1978 punk show at Hong Kong Café in downtown Los Angeles, we hear The Bags perform a cover of the song "That's Life," made popular in the 1960s by Frank Sinatra. But The Bags' version is actually a cover of a cover of a popular TV commercial from the 1970s for Sanyo home electronics, featuring the alluring actress Susan Anton. In the overproduced clip, Anton dances in a slim white dress in front of Broadway-style flashing lights that read, "That's Life," while lightly crooning the tagline, "That's life. That's what people say.... Sanyooooo!"

as if in an ecstatic daze. Anton's soft voice only exaggerates the ethereal glow of her blond hair, as she swirls and prances to the manufactured jingle for Sanyo Electronics. Her wavy tresses and perfectly manicured nails glamorize the TV-buying experience: "The easy life at an easy price," she whispers. The game-show style of the commercial intends to convince the audience that somehow they have won the "good life," while Anton, with an almost *Wheel of Fortune* virtuosity, caresses the gleaming boxes of entertainment. Everything is hi-fi in the commercial: clear, crisp, and at a great price.

In The Bags' version, lead singer Alice Bag disidentifies with the commercial piety of Sanyo Electronics and instead produces an apparently meaningless texture of extreme noise, encapsulated by Bag's punk crackling scream punctuated with an ironic pinching of the *o* vowel in "Sanyo." Shrieking, "That's life. That's OK. Saaanyooo," with a dissonant, throaty timbre, Bag pushes Anton's performance to its rational limit by rendering the commercial and Anton's own excited flailing as absurd, ridiculous, and irrational. Bag's performance may seem over the top but only in relation to the more hi-fi, subdued, and affectively weak Susan Anton. Whereas Bag's lo-fi version of the jingle is excessive in noise and feedback, the hi-fi original tone of the commercial production version approximates a standard normalcy so closely as to be imperceptible. A hi-fi aesthetic seeks authenticity and clarity; it wants to make things transparently knowable through a kind of tacit identification with it (i.e., a desire for TVs) rather than a critical distance. We can hear in Bag's punk grimace, the dark fleshiness of her voice, a hemorrhaging of sense that vibrates out of the here and now and suggests an unknown aspect to the "good life" that the Sanyo commercial promises. Bag's scream serves as a comical response to the market's serious demand to buy, consume, and produce.

This chapter foregrounds another stylized discontent emerging in tandem with the amplification of nausea, one that I identify as lo-fi, or low fidelity to cultural norms. Whereas we might characterize nausea as a diffuse emotional habitus holding Los Angeles in suspended relation, lo-fi shows us how a subjective internalization of this external atmosphere—inhaled by its residents like a fetid smog—can in turn *de-amplify* conceptions of identity to reveal fraught processes of identification.[1] In other words, identification takes the form of a low fidelity to the norm. What is meant by "the norm" is what the status quo presents as the given. Within the context of this chapter, the following historical actors often interpreted the given as the material world that one could utilize for survival. Indeed, do-it-yourself (DIY) culture and aesthetics rely on an established "given" as the material world for what the self can make do. By the late 1970s, the norm in question was represented in quotidian forms of mass culture as a version of the "good life" dependent on the conspicuous consumption of the previous generation's commodities, such as television sets, stereo systems, beauty magazines, cars, and larger houses. What was new by the late 1970s and 1980s is how this consumption was lubricated by an emerging credit system as an effect of the financialization of the economy, which in turn deferred the cost of the good life to the future: "A good life, on credit!"

Another norm central to this chapter's argument concerns the norm of identity, the ways "Chicano" essentializes difference into stereotypes and the way identity norms circulate in minoritarian communities. The punk or the feminist, like Asco in chapter 1, understand the double bind between the mainstream and the norm-within-minoritarianism. The "good life," then, serves a double function. Pictures of the "good life" reveal "the commodification of social relations" in mainstream culture but also fashioned them as the only acceptable avenue for social belonging allotted to subjects outside the racial and sexual mainstream: identity comes to equal cultural representation.[2] These commodified social relations distort into conceptions of identity, like Chicanismo and punk, and create their own forms of alienation.

However, this is not without historical context. The norms in question emerged in response to the depletion of social relations under a deindustrializing US economy. Even more so, social relations became the target of commodification within an economic system shifting to a service-based model in the 1970s. It was also at this time that culture benefited from "the working-class inventiveness," which Mark Fisher claims is central to his notion of "popular modernism."[3] Fisher also points out how "this was also a time when casual racism, sexism, and homophobia were routine features of the mainstream."[4] The dialectic between creativity and oppression provides context to the significance of popular modernism, which will help further define the lo-fi aesthetic circulating in Los Angeles's early queer punk subculture explored in this chapter.

Before we consider specific case studies of lo-fi performances in Los Angeles punk and feminist print culture, it is useful to explicate the aesthetic consequences of assuming low fidelity to the norm. A technical definition of lo-fi invokes sound recordings that are not filtered for accuracy and clearness. Lo-fi audio recordings usually exhibit flaws in the recording process, such as scratching, background noise, feedback, and deliberate distortion of sound. Lo-fi aesthetics underscore the deliberate use of imperfect and damaged sound-recording equipment in order to create a style that is dense, raw, and heavy. Along with its technical definition, lo-fi signifies an aesthetic that is normally associated with a do-it-yourself ethos and shares with Chicano culture an "underdog" resistant sensibility that Tomás Ybarra-Frausto calls *rasquachismo*. Through appropriation, inversion, juxtaposition and reversal, *rasquache* aesthetics also invoke the experiential aspects of lower- and working-class lifestyles. The *rasquache*, Ybarra-Frausto argues, "respond[s] to the direct relationship with the material level of existence or subsistence," which engenders a "*rasquache attitude* of survival and inventiveness."[5] Key in Ybarra-Frausto's definition is how survival and inventive strategies in working-class Chicano situations appear attitudinal. In fact, he plainly states, "*Rasquachismo* is neither an idea or a style but more of an attitude or taste."[6] Though lo-fi as a stylized discontent happily corresponds to Ybarra-Frausto's productive aesthetic concept of *rasquachismo*, it does so at the level of an embodied affective performance, a stylized taste or attitude. As we will see, lo-fi can index working-class lived experience and translate this experience into a way of being, that is, into a stylized affect or attitude. Important to underscore for the reader here is that unlike the other stylized discontents in this study, lo-fi is an *aesthetic* and needs to be translated into an attitude to be considered an embodied affective performance like nausea, ambivalence, and malaise. However, this attitude does not simply express what Joan Scott has aptly critiqued as the "evidence of experience." As Scott claims, lived experience as "uncontestable evidence and as an originary point of explanation" naturalizes difference.[7] Instead, a lo-fi attitude is unequivocally contextual and *transmits* knowledge below the frequency of established codes of communal belonging, rather than claiming any self-evident truths.

Such an attitude was a strategy implemented by many underground punk bands and women of color feminists to demonstrate their own refusal of belonging within a consumerist culture *and* within minoritarian communities that equally practiced prejudicial behaviors. The early Los Angeles queer punk attitude traced in this chapter effectively stages what Simone de Beauvoir philosophized as "the positive aspect of ambiguity," whereby one's "aesthetic attitude" recasts their willful refusal of a given norm into a concrete action: an action intended to free oneself.[8] Yet crucial for Beauvoir is that in the act of freeing oneself, everyone else ought to be free in return. And significant here is the particular freedom from the demand to consume.

This chapter looks at the lo-fi performance of the Chicana punk feminist Alice Bag and other musical performers who too utilized lo-fi production. Their performances tell us something about how a makeshift materiality composed cross-affiliations under the sign of Chicanismo. But first, we detour through a queer Los Angeles performance artist's early desire to transmit minoritarian knowledge through popular modernist means—specifically, the Xerox copy machine.

## Women of Color Makeshift Presses and Lo-Fi Knowledge Sharing

One important cultural producer looms over the intersection of Los Angeles's queer punk scene and women of color print culture that emerged in the latter half of the twentieth century. The moniker Vaginal Davis, concocted in homage to the feminist scholar and activist Angela Davis, belongs to a prominent queer punk performance artist who came of age in post-1968 Los Angeles, where the burgeoning punk scene of the 1970s became a refuge for people seeking community outside the dominant culture. Despite this movement's succumbing to cultural whitewashing by the mid-1980s and its frequent encounters with aggressive homophobia, which characterized punk masculinity in the city, Vaginal Davis left a legacy of Los Angeles punk that is unquestionably queer. She formed the Motown-resembling punk group The Afro Sisters, whose first EP, *Indigo, Sassafras and Molasses*, was released in 1978 and produced by one of the scene's early punk impresarios, Geza X. In addition, Davis became recognizable for her hilarious zine, *Fertile La Toyah Jackson*, and its extension, *Shrimp*—both catalysts for what would later be called the "queercore zine movement." These publications exhibited an experimental, DIY aesthetic that trafficked in celebrity gossip and the personal tales of Dr. Davis (as she sometimes liked to be called). The makeshift zines worked as a piece of fabulation, suggestive of Kenneth Anger's scandalous 1959 exposé *Hollywood Babylon*.[9] In fact, gossip and fabulation have been some of the most generative vehicles for Davis's art, an oeuvre that actively accommodates illicit encounters with Hollywood celebrities, art stars, and alter egos and culminates in an ongoing art practice that at times has elicited descriptions of the performer herself as a "walking installation piece."[10] Davis is often heard recounting her cultural heritage as Chicano and African American, claiming that her parents only met once when she was conceived at a Ray Charles concert at the Hollywood Palladium in the early 1960s.[11] By the late 1980s, she continued to explore her Chicana roots by teaming up with other women and men of color, most famously with the Chicana punk rocker Alice Bag, to form another band, ¡Cholita!, or, as Davis often recites, the female equivalent of Menudo.[12]

Most of Davis's performances, art events, and everyday interactions with people are undeniably difficult to categorize as historical facts, since Davis excels at the art of gossip. This is evident in the performer's many alter egos, such as Fertile La Toyah Jackson (who was often played by a friend and often confused for Bag herself), La Cicciolina (a half-Hungarian, half-Italian porn star), and Graciela Grejalva (the lead teenage Latina bubblegum pop star of ¡Cholita!), to name just a few. In one performance, Davis reads a text called "My Favorite Dead Artist," describing a peculiar encounter with Andy Warhol, who allegedly took a Polaroid of Davis dressed as Frida Kahlo (though Warhol claimed that she looked more like Helen or Harry Morales).[13] In the performance, Davis recounts further encounters with Warhol in Los Angeles at the downtown hangout spot of Bibbe Hansen (a former Warhol Superstar) and Sean Carrillo, Troy Café, and a supposed collaboration of the Afro Sisters in the 1986 "Best Of" issue of *Interview* magazine, which the artist claims is one of the last issues Warhol oversaw. The commerce of gossip surrounding Vaginal Davis's oeuvre is also present in much of her early 1990s video and film work, such as *Designy Living* (1995), an homage to Jean-Luc Godard's *Masculin Féminin* and an obvious play on Noel Coward's title *Design Living*, and *Dot* (1994), a hilarious tribute to the famed alcoholic, witty poet, and muse to many queer modern artists and writers Dorothy Parker.

A 2012 exhibition at New York City's Participant Inc. restaged the punk/DIY exhibition space that Davis founded in her small Los Angeles apartment, Hag Gallery, which the artist ran from 1982 to 1989. Constantly seeking to create spaces for those who do not belong, Davis is often a muse for artists and cultural makers outside the mainstream. The *New Yorker* profiled Davis's work as a "sacred mythology for the outside," while the *New York Times* called the artist "the bedrock of cultural life [in Los Angeles]" before her move to Berlin in 2006.[14] Yet what becomes evident is that the litany of Davis's many queer performances and alter egos cannot be separated from her commitment to knowledge sharing; she is an artist who challenged the modernist divide between high and low art through popular means. Take for example Davis's aforementioned early zine *Fertile La Toyah Jackson*, which according to Davis was produced in a clandestine way while she was working at the University of California, Los Angeles's Placement and Career Planning Center under the pseudonym Kayle Hilliard. As Hilliard, Davis would command the Xerox machine after business hours to print copies of her zine and would then have "stapling parties" with friends to help assemble them. Davis would disseminate the magazine to friends in the queer community, which splintered out of the early Los Angeles punk scene in response to the straightening male bravado induced by the hardcore punk crowds flooding Hollywood from Orange County and surrounding suburban areas.[15] She would also leave copies of the magazine around campus with the back of the cover page explaining to any innocent reader, "Fertile La Toyah Jackson, the living, breathing TV movie, rock video, xwoman and magazine is published whenever Fertile becomes so indignant, so frustrated with the goings on of our critical times in which we live that she feels it's time for her to make comment."[16]

*Fertile La Toyah Jackson* was foundational to the beginning of the "queercore" movement that centered queer aesthetics and sensibilities during Los Angeles's post-punk era. Central to the queercore movement were lo-fi means of expression. Davis's use of her employer's Xerox machine in efforts to create and circulate subcultural content that was otherwise sidelined by popular culture borrowed from a certain modern understanding that what was given had to work for you in some way; function over form was very much *Fertile La Toyah Jackson*'s content. Davis drew on popular culture as a form of critique of the status quo. Though Davis's zine was not necessarily populist in the sense that some of its content was derived from cultures one needed literacy in, it nonetheless represented a popular *use* of working-class inventiveness against mainstream culture.

Davis's art can be classified under Mark Fisher's "popular modernism," a cultural and materially grounded expression prevalent in both the United States and the United Kingdom during the punk and post-punk era, thus coinciding with the rise of Ronald Reagan and Margaret Thatcher, respectively. Fisher describes popular modernism as such: "In popular modernism, the elitist project of modernism was retrospectively vindicated. At the same time, popular culture definitely established that it did not have to be populist. Particular modernist techniques were not only disseminated but collectively reworked and extended, just as the modernist task of producing forms which were adequate to the present moment was taken up and renewed."[17] What Fisher points us to is a cultural ecology—comprising Penguin paperbacks, post-punk music, brutalist architecture, public-service television, and eventually the camcorder, music presses, and affordable art school education, to name just a few examples—that circulated new ideas and experimental forms of expression enabled by the intersection of popular culture and "high theory." The makeshift elements comprising popular modernist expression often resulted in a lo-fi aesthetic. Indeed, the desire to change the world by injecting new and experimental ideas through the very media economies one sought to critique also describes the feminist understanding of consciousness-raising through small press production. At the end of the 1970s and the beginning of the 1980s, many feminist makeshift presses were seeking to publish and circulate their own ideas through lo-fi strategies.

Take for example the Chicana feminist theorist Norma Alarcón and her founding of Third Woman Press in 1979. While a doctoral student at Indiana University, Alarcón acquired funding from three different academic units to help kick-start *Third Woman*, a journal and an early incarnation of Third Woman Press, before her arrival as faculty at University of California, Berkeley, in 1989. Her fear was that funding from only one unit would hinder the academic integrity of the press, forestalling the intellectual promiscuity that drove the original incarnation of the project. Indeed, the press sought to center the lives, theories, and experiences of women of color and Latinas, recognizing the dearth of literature on the subject at the time. In the inaugural issue of the press's eponymous journal, Alarcón explains the project as such: "*Third Woman* is one forum . . . [for] self-definition and . . . self-invention, which is more than reformism, more than revolt. The title *Third Woman* refers to that preordained reality that we have been born to and continue to live and experience and be a witness to, despite efforts toward change."[18] Alarcón's point here underscores the cultural straitjacket that Mexican American women faced during the dizzying transition from modernity to postmodernity. Sara Ramirez and Norma Cantú home in on this problematic when, in outlying the impact of Third Woman Press, they underscore the confining choices presented for contemporary Mexican American women: "1) defend tradition in conjunction with modernization to be in tune with the times; 2) mimic Anglo-American feminism to the extent necessary; 3) practice self-invention, that is, reinvent themselves to create a new self."[19] Alarcón undoubtedly assumed the third option, one tethered to a long tradition of feminist work.

For example, with little funding to hire professional typesetters, Alarcón did it herself for the first issue. In addition, almost as if to borrow a page out of Davis's playbook, Alarcón invented in the first volume a contributor with the pseudonym "Marisa Cantú," under which she published a book review in hopes of making *Third Woman* appear more staffed than it was. Alarcón's work (and Davis's early guerrilla printmaking for that matter) extends from a long tradition of women of color publishers using material means as a practice of self-invention. Ramirez and Cantú go on to detail,

> Publications by Latinas and Chicanas in the United States date back to the previous century. In the early 1900s Jovita Idár published revistas, newspapers, and books in her family's printing press in Laredo, Texas and

later in San Antonio. The Idár family published the newspaper *La Crónica* (circa 1890–1917). While Idár's experience was a family endeavor initiated by her father, . . . it would be over fifty years later that a Chicana would single-handedly establish a literary press. Only July 4th, 1976, during the Chicano Movement, Lorna Dee Cervantes founded Mango Publications in San José California, with the intent of publishing radical and progressive books.[20]

Following Alarcón's desire for self-invention, Third Woman Press utilized lo-fi means to find an alternative to following tradition or mimicking the (white feminist) norm. But what exactly does Alarcón mean when she describes her embryonic makeshift press as *more than* both reformism and revolt? For one, Alarcón's assertion complicates any easy identification with a position that ultimately maintains the status quo (reformism) versus a counteridentification with the norm (revolution). Instead, the search for collective liberation (in this case, Chicana authorial freedom) involves minding the tricky relation between individual and community, whereby self-determination and self-invention spring from the force of an encounter with something entirely new. Indeed, popular modernism laid bare the potential for new forms of music, writing, artistic expression, and communal belonging by injecting popular formats with fragments of other realities, in hopes of refashioning the given norm in a mode that was altogether *queer*.

Another example is salient here in unpacking such a complex dynamic. Surely, makeshift feminist presses of the time, spiraling out from the cultural advantages afforded by the feminist movements of the 1960s and '70s, sought to challenge traditional academic writing. Norma Alarcón's own academic trajectory speaks to the unequal burden on women to produce a monograph-length study, since quite simply, it proved more difficult for women, and especially women of color, to produce full-length books in a patriarchal society seeking to void "women's voices" by denying them the means of production. As a result, anthologies became accessible vehicles to showcase new and emerging feminist experiences and democratize feminist writing by collecting poems, short and long essays, reflections, reviews, and experimental prose. Barbara Smith makes this point in her introduction to the *Home Girls* anthology published in 1983 by Kitchen Table

Press, an early woman of color makeshift press founded by Smith that was the only press at the time to publish women of color who were not established writers or academics. Smith points out how the anthology as a medium accommodates various styles of writing "suited to the multiplicity of issues of concern to women of color."[21] This is to say that makeshift feminist presses multiplied styles of writing with the desire to include various intellectual, artistic, and literary commitments. Jennifer Gilley describes "multi-genre anthologies" as "indispensable tool[s] for the feminist movement in general and for women and color feminism in particular."[22] Maylei Blackwell has forcefully argued for the feminist utility of the "technology of the anthology": "Women of color anthologies . . . made women of color the subjects of knowledge rather than its objects. In many ways anthologizing was also a strategy of collective self-knowledge construction and played a critical pedagogical role for vastly different groups to learn about each other and themselves."[23] Blackwell corroborates Alarcón's commitment to self-invention through the enlivening of collaborative conversations about and for the people central to their enactment.

However, the will to anthologize is not virtuous in and of itself. In tracing the cultural impact of race and empire on the relationship between the page and music, Alexandra Vazquez underscores the performative aspect to the "anthological impulse."[24] Vazquez reveals how performance can be thought of as one iteration of the anthology: "To perform is to anthologize," she writes.[25] Specifically speaking within the context of musicological "studies protocols" (a term she borrows from Hortense Spillers), through which the impulse to anthologize mirrors the critic's (failed) attempt at grasping the performer's intent, Vazquez asks us to think of the anthology as "the idiom of the corrective."[26] In this way, the feminist performance studies scholar envisions the anthological drive in its fundamental equivocality to be a desire for mastery. Meanwhile, Brent Hayes Edwards argues, within the context of diasporic literature, that anthologizing might open a "space of 'new creation' in the performance of reading that takes place in the subjunctive, . . . in which diaspora can be articulated only in forms that are provisional, negotiated, and asymmetrical."[27] In other words, to anthologize might be a corrective action but also might be a creative act for marginalized subjects. This ambivalent function to anthologizing renders it open to manipulation and play, while affording a multitude of styles.

Similarly, independent feminist of color presses like Kitchen Table, Third Woman, and Aunt Lute Press (founded by Barb Wiseser and Joan Pinkvoss in 1982) sought a corrective to the dominant discourse, which excluded the voices and experiences of women of color, by harnessing a space of new creation, a performance widening the cultural consciousness with dreams, desires, and criticisms aimed at ushering in an alternative to the antifeminist environment of Reagan's America.[28] In many ways, early women of color makeshift presses formalized a dissatisfaction at the core of knowledge production. Through popular modernist material that was available though vanishing under Reagan (and Thatcher), lo-fi knowledge sharing proved pivotal in changing readers' attitudes to difference. Even though some of the presses mentioned could not sustain their viability with minimal financial support and labor power, the short-lived tenure of these zines, presses, and other ephemera indeed served, if fleeting, a purpose. These feminist presses, in their lo-fi production and assemblage, showcase a working-class creativity by understanding the transmittable capacity of their (marginal) knowledge. Before the onset of capitalist realism, a quality inherent in the transmission of marginal knowledge through lo-fi means was also an exercise in imagining a secure future by actively creating alternatives to the status quo *within* the present. This was also the case with a notorious magazine that projected a picture of world-making *in process* and transmitted knowledge about the outskirts of society as a place for creativity, destruction, and play.

## "Steal This Mag!": *Slash* (1977–1980)

*Slash* was a short-lived fanzine founded by its publishers and editors, Steve Samiof and Melanie Nissen, in 1977 with the aim of capturing a bourgeoning new scene of misfits then unfolding in Hollywood. Often regarded as the paper of record for the early Los Angeles punk scene, *Slash* featured editorials written by the notorious French punk writer Claude Bessy (aka Kickboy Face), some adventure cartoons of *Jimbo* drawn by Gary Panter, and documentation of punk nightlife taken by a group of photographers including Kerry Colona, coeditor Melanie Nissen, and Philomena Winstanley, an editor and key player in the early success of the magazine. *Slash* showcased high-contrast images of loitering youth captured by a seemingly amateur eye, its overall aesthetic invoked a cinema-verité style of journalism through its collection of lo-fi photographs. Many of the images that populated the makeshift publication feature local scene-makers in their everyday lives, punctuated with documentation of punks' seemingly unusual antics on the streets of Los Angeles. Issues often featured photographs of early punk bands such as The Clash, The Weirdos, and The Screamers performing onstage, pictures of their encouraging audiences, and many images of friends hanging out. Altogether, the slices of life gathered in *Slash* evidence the makings of a new subculture that had traversed the globe and found a singular expression in Hollywood.

According to an interview, Samiof and Nissen cooked up the idea of starting a punk magazine after Samiof read an article in the *Los Angeles Times* describing the evolving punk scene in London. After some research, Samiof and Nissen, who were romantically involved, decided to launch their own publication to document a similar scene in its nascent stage in Los Angeles. Samiof contacted his friend Claude Bessy, who was working at a fish restaurant on Santa Monica Pier and had started his own Xeroxed zine on reggae music titled *Angelino Dread*, to see if he was interested in writing editorials for *Slash*. Bessy, aka Kickboy Face, roped in his girlfriend, Philomena Winstanley, who edited many of Bessy's pieces and described the idea of the magazine as a "street paper." After cruising through some early punk shows, the original founders of the magazine attended a show featuring The Damned, the first British punk band to perform in Los Angeles, at The Starwood, a music venue known for its early punk shows on Santa Monica Boulevard and Crescent Heights in West Hollywood. Samiof managed to arrange an interview with the band, and Nissen snapped some style-setting photographs including a portrait of David Vanian, the lead singer of The Damned. The high-contrast image featuring a vampire-like Vanian adorned the cover of the first issue, along with the magazine's name spelled out in its signature red lettering. Samiof titled the fanzine *Slash* after British slang for "taking a piss," committing to this idea after seeing the word written out with dripping Pelican ink on a paper bag. Within three months' time, the first *Slash* issue was printed in May 1977. It featured Bessy's first editorial, which came to define the ethos of the new punk magazine. Under the heading, "SO THIS IS WAR, EH," Bessy's article opened with,

> This decade's biggest musical fad has been the dreadful dripping sounds of disco music. Up to now. Because lately there've been rumors of strange goings-on on the fringes of the music world. Violence at concerts both on the part of the performers and of the audience, outraged editorials in daily newspapers, foul-mouthed interviews on live TV and frightened record companies dropping contracts faster than a chimp would with a hot potato, oddball fashions of slashed clothing, repulsive make-up and bondage paraphernalia and of course music, dirty primitive music that has little to do with the stuff music stations have been pouring in our ears for what seems to be an eternity.

Bessy's editorial set the philosophical mood of the fanzine, a periodical that "never wrote down to readers," according to Kristine McKenna.[29] *Slash* assumed that the reader had some knowledge of the scene, music, and style being described, while simultaneously eschewing a "snobby" tone. In fact, Bessy's opening paragraph captured the spirit of 1977, as it were, in the languid sounds of a dying musical phenomenon known as disco, whose faddishness relied on narcissistic consumerism undergirded by a hi-fi aesthetic. In fact, in the Sanyo commercial featuring Susan Anton, the hi-fi style of disco structured much of the commercial's visuals, which in turn only synaesthetically makes Alice Bag's rendition sound counterdisco. This point is further ironized when Alice Bag adorns *Slash*'s 1978 cover in what appears as an homage to Studio 54's classic tuxedo attire and bow tie often found on the club's busboys, bourgeois patrons, and famously on Andy Warhol (figure 2.1). There, Bag's mouth agape calls attention to the opening between her white lapels revealing her black bra below her black bow tie and contrasting against her black coat. However, the punctum of the photograph, the small detail that pricks the viewer, is the safety pin and its shadow clipped to the right side of the white shirt just below the bra. Even in Bag's chic rendition of 1970s disco flare, her small safety pin reconfigures the style

Figure 2.1. Alice Bag on the cover of *Slash*.

into something altogether lo-fi and corroborates José Muñoz's claim when he waxes on punk and what clearly are its lo-fi stylings: "Punk is about inelegantly cutting and stitching a sense of the world together; it is about imagining a commons that is held together by nothing more than a safety pin."[30]

## Alice Bag's Lo-Fi Performance

Alice Bag, born Alicia Armendariz in 1958 to a working-class family in East Los Angeles, is a Chicana punk feminist who was the lead singer and cofounder of the notorious Los Angeles punk band The Bags, which Bag formed in 1977 along with her friend Patricia Morrison. She is known as one of the pioneers of and a major feminist influence on the Los Angeles/Hollywood punk scene of the mid-1970s. While she was growing up and attending school in the late 1960s and early 1970s, Bag underwent constant bullying from her peers for being overweight, wearing glasses, and possessing a peculiar interest in glitter rock stars such as Freddie Mercury, David Bowie, and especially Elton John—all of whom would later influence her music career. In her 2011 memoir, *Violence Girl: From East L.A. Rage to the Hollywood Stage—A Chicana Punk Story*, Bag poignantly underscores how her coming of age in East Los Angeles during the height of the Chicano Power movement bore the unforgivable reminder that she was "NOT NORMAL" and consequently did not fit in.[31] As a young adult, Bag moved to Hollywood, where she immersed herself in a community of misfits living in the now-famous Canterbury Apartments. There, scenesters such as Belinda Carlisle of The Go-Gos, Darby Crash of The Germs (a friend of Bag's), and Nicky Beat of The Weirdos (who later dated Bag and would occasionally drum for The Bags) would collaborate, circulate, and influence Bag's personal and creative lives. The Bags performed their first concert at the famous punk venue The Masque on September 10 of that year, opening for the already-notable band The Germs. Gaining notoriety, the queer Chicano performance artists and conceptualists Gronk, a founding member of Asco, and Jerry Dreva, a cofounder of the queer conceptual art group Les Petites Bon-Bons, invited Alice Bag to open their art exhibition *Gronk/Dreva: Ten Years of Art Life* in 1978 at LACE Gallery. The Bags would later disband in 1981, having released one record including the singles "Survive" and "Babylonian Grogon"; however, The Bags remain one of the original and most influential punk bands of the early Los Angeles punk scene.

While singing for The Bags, Bag became known for her distinctive and often aggressive performances, landing her a cameo in Penelope Spheeris's 1981 documentary on the Los Angeles punk scene, *The Decline of Western Civilization*, and in Marc Spitz's important oral history of Los Angeles's booming subculture, *We Got the Neutron Bomb* (2001). She collaborated with Phranc, a member of the queercore punk band Nervous Gender, and Dinah Cancer in forming an all-female punk band, Castration Squad, and by the early 1990s, she joined the famed zinester and punk drag queen Vaginal Davis's concept band, ¡Cholita! In 2015, Bag released a book, *Pipe Bomb for the Soul*, about a trip she took to Nicaragua as a young aspiring teacher that confirmed her dedication to social justice issues as well as feminist politics and pedagogy.[32]

In her memoir, Bag meditates on some key moments in her childhood that fostered a burning punk ethos and a deep fascination with DIY culture. For Bag, punk was about low fidelity to identities and norms. Her identifications were always slightly *off*. As Bag grew up, her queer identifications led her to an obsession with glam rock, embodied in the repertoire of Elton John. When she was young, Bag saw herself as a "groupie," overenthusiastically following Elton John to every concert premiere, endlessly waiting outside to catch a glimpse of her all-time hero. At one point in the book, Bag begins to take an increasing interest in Chicano politics after witnessing the Chicano Moratorium march on August 29, 1970. At the march, a deputy sheriff infamously shot and killed Rubén Salazar, a Chicano journalist and outspoken critic of police brutality. This event quickly prompted Bag to sign up and join MEChA, a Chicano student organization, at Garfield High School. However, the students made her feel rejected and unwelcome, asking her why she was sporting an excessively glammed-out outfit. "I guess I looked a little too freaky for them," Bag writes, "and they thought I couldn't seriously care about Chicano politics. . . . They were wrong."[33]

Bag's style (of) politics was never easy to pin down, since it was both "too freaky" and excessive, that is, a low-fidelity approximation of how Chicanos were expected to self-present. Sometime after the MEChA rejection based on style, her aesthetic interests in music and fashion continued to change, and Bag understood what it meant to be a Chicana, and "now [after her rejection, she] was looking beyond that."[34] Bag's identity makeovers, from a barrio-infused Chola aesthetic to a glitter-freak style and eventually fusing the two under a darker punk flair, allowed her to gesture beyond the normative codes of acceptable styles and identities. When Bag proclaims that she is now looking "beyond"

Chicano, we must not infer a teleological pull toward closure. Instead, Bag challenges identitarian claims through her understanding that what is *different* comes from the equivocal spatiality of the beside: How do we come to *know* what is beside "Chicano"? Bag was beginning to put pressure on the blind spots of minoritarian identity categories. A vortex was opening, pulsating with the same fervor of Bag's own identificatory ambivalences.

Identities were never fixed for Alice Bag. Instead, they were performative and experimental, and more often than not, they reflected a style of low fidelity to the parent culture and her own Chicano culture. For her, identity categories already pointed to what lay outside, beneath, and beside the confines of the identitarian. Instead, Bag played with *identifications*, sometimes exposing them to contradictions, which offered pleasures that normative identitarianism could not. These contradictory identifications were messy. Lo-fi performances, not only in music but also in other forms of cultural production, render visible the flaws and mistakes contained within the process of identification with a prototype—the affective cracks, messes, and excesses of belonging. In this way, lo-fi also invokes turbulence through an ethos of syncopated sensibilities, where freedom is found within the ideas, experiences, and aesthetics effectively rendered offbeat by the parental culture. Lo-fi then becomes the aesthetic expression of the cracks and crackles within the spinning vinyl of identity. Indeed, lo-fi is identity's feedback noise operating like an echo outside the claustrophobic, self-enforcing chamber of identitarianism.

At the same time, lo-fi indexes a "stripped-down" version of reality, giving us a grainier and seedier aesthetic production. Punk archives are usually a collection of lo-fi ephemera, scratchy and imperfect recordings of anything-but-perfect songs, places, and things. Lo-fi production enacts a refusal by stylizing discontent with the majoritarian culture and, in turn, centers the minor affective chords within quotidian life. For example, the notable title of Penelope Spheeris's trilogy *The Decline of Western Civilization*, along with the raw, cinema-verité style in which she captures a bourgeoning Los Angeles punk scene, represents lo-fi production par excellence. Yet more interesting is the contested origin of the title. In Marc Spitz's *We've Got the Neutron Bomb*, Claude Bessy of *Slash* claims to have authored the now-canonical punk title.[35] Others speculate that the title was derivative of the German neo-Hegelian social theorist Oswald Spengler's controversial *The Decline of the West*, of which Darby Crash carried a copy around, quoted from, and immersed himself. Crash would later have to separate himself from the Nazi history surrounding Spengler's philosophy (though Spengler himself criticized Hitler's adoption of his work, which led to the censorship of his work in Nazi Germany), telling *No Mag*, "Fascist is extreme right. We're not extreme right. Maybe there's a better word for it that I haven't found yet, but I'm still going to have complete control. . . . One day you'll pray to me."[36] However, it was the music journalist Lester Bangs who wrote in 1979 a piece titled "The White Noise Supremacist" for the *Village Voice* about the racism in the punk scene, criticizing the use of Nazi symbolism and fascist ideology for pure shock value. Predating his astute criticism, though, was a 1970 review of the band The Stooges for *Creem* magazine, where he proffered a larger diagnosis regarding "Amerika" and the West:

> I mean, nowhere else but in Amerika would you find a phenomenon like Iggy Stooge, right? I was at one time going to write a letter to Malcolm Muggeridge over in England telling him all about Iggy and the Stooges, but I didn't because I finally decided that he'd just mark it up as one more symptom of the decline of Western Civilization. Which it's not. Not finally, that is—it may be now, in some of its grosser, semipathological trappings, but then look what it came out of. There's always hope for a brighter tomorrow because today's mess spawned stalwart crusaders for something better like Iggy. And presumably, the rest of the Stooges.[37]

I find Bangs's description generative for our discussion of lo-fi and popular modernism, generally. The critic claims that what slows the decline of the West is creativity, because out of "today's mess" rises Phoenix-like "stalwart crusaders for something better," since there is "always hope for a brighter tomorrow." For Bangs, a declining Western civilization marks not an end but a turbulent process of imagining something new from within. This is precisely what Spheeris captures and what lo-fi indexes, namely, a decline refashioned into a declination, a refusal, of the given norm.

## "My Mind Is Like a Plastic Bag": On Declination and X-Ray Spex

In his own way, the ancient Roman thinker Titus Lucretius Carus was a punk philosopher and poet. Complicating origin narratives and teleological concerns, Lucretius effectively created a form of do-it-yourself philosophy based on the primacy of contingency. His epic poem *On the Nature of Things* usually falls out of the canon of the philosophy of science, mostly because classical rationalism has dominated our way of thinking since Plato. In this section, I stage a brief encounter between the ethnic-racialized punk performance of Alice Bag and the philosophy of Lucretius, particularly his emphasis on the notion of the *clinamen*. This section performs a comparative analysis insofar as I approach both objects in and through each other. That is to say, I read Lucretius through the strong punk ethos demonstrated in the work of Alice Bag; and conversely, I approach Alice Bag with Lucretius's fervor for structuring ancient atomist themes such as turbulence, affect, and declination. I foreground two punk aesthetic techniques: the lo-fi and turbulence. The noisy aesthetic of lo-fi gestures to an undifferentiated flow of energy or potentiality. Meanwhile, turbulence emerges as a process of differentiation that relies on the productive capacity of moments of contingency. This unexpected kinship contributes to my larger argument that an immemorable indeterminacy sets the stage for a queer punk relationality. Declination, another Lucretian notion, illuminates a specific refusal of transparency that unfolded within the material and turbulent sensorium of early Los Angeles punk.

Declination not only is the fall of a single atom but also is manifest as a form of refusal. The Bags deploy a form of declination in their performance of "Sanyo" in order to insist that we may not *know* the good life properly. In fact, their satiric appropriation of the tech company's jingle "That's life. That's what people say!" suggests that the commercial forecloses on the potentiality of the good life by shackling it to the status quo. In this way, "Sanyo" activates a double declination: a decline or fall out of life, on the one hand, and a refusal of a whitewashed, straightened good life, on the other. The Bags' double declination resembles the way the French philosopher Jean-Luc Nancy describes the Lucretian *clinamen*: "Still, one cannot make a world with single atoms. There has to be a *clinamen*. There has to be an inclination or an inclining from one toward the other, of one by the other, or from one to the other. Community is at least the *clinamen* of the 'individual.' Yet there is no theory, ethics, politics, or metaphysics of the individual that is able to envisage this *clinamen*, this declination or decline of the individual within community."[38] Nancy engages atomic theory by pointing to a process in which things are created through chance meetings between two singularities. The *clinamen* marks an inclination of one singularity toward another singularity, producing an encounter, or what Nancy terms "touch." This incline differs from identification insofar as the incline is not always structured as a linear current. To incline means to tend or sway toward something altogether different at any moment. In this way, the individual within a community, as Nancy argues, acts as the *decline* within and away from the sameness guaranteed by what he calls an "operative community," that is, a community produced through conscious work. An operative community works to keep things the same by displacing dissent and difference outside its walls. One example of this was when Bag was rejected from her high school Chicano student organization when she failed to perform in accordance with the expectations of what a Chicano community should look and act like.

Bag's performances are not easily folded into the representational economies of "social justice communities." Instead, Bag performs the very decline that Nancy sees as the ontological ground to what is "common." For both Nancy and Bag, the common articulates a displacement of the viability of a community. The ways in which communities do *not* work and become *in*operative expose the very forms of affective coagulation constituting those communities. Communities come about through the constant sustainment of mutual identification, while the commons gestures to the yet-differentiated flows of belonging that resist the confines of identity.[39]

Turbulence defines a mechanism of disequilibrium, a staging of disruption or disagreement with the given status quo. The turbulence circulating through the "Sanyo" lo-fi recording in particular and The Bags' oeuvre in general renders any easily identifiable cultural signature void and inoperative. The Bags cannot be labeled as a Chicano or a feminist punk band, though it has affinities with each identity group. In chasing resonances versus identities, The Bags intimately resonates with one of its contemporaries that emerged across the Atlantic in a similar bourgeoning consumer culture prior to the election of the conservative prime minister Margaret Thatcher in 1979, Ronald Reagan's "political and philosophical soul mate."[40] In fact, when focusing on punk resonances and their afterlives (in what will be later classified as "post-punk"), *intimacy*, if even remote, maps ways that connect illegible cultural outsiders and unrecognizable forms of sociality across time and space. Karen Tongson argues, after Jennifer Terry's use of the term "remote intimacies," that "suburban queer kids of color" often trafficked in distant forms of belonging enabled by technologies such as television, radio, and the internet.[41] These "networks of desire" inform Richard T. Rodríguez's study of the "touch" between "US Latinidad and British post-punk artist to underscore the interplay of reciprocal intimacy" between these two differing geographies, cultures, and histories.[42] Much of the resonances, affiliations, and inclinations of these two cultural phenomena (British post-punk and US latinidad) are fashioned through similar political events and economic changes that are discussed throughout *Dissatisfactions* as well. For Rodríguez, such a method attunes to the migrancy of sound's and music's "unbounded haptic capability of animating networks of cultural, collaborative, amorous, and political affiliation."[43] And though much resonance characterizes the consuming audiences of these sounds, music, and sensibilities, I also insist that the creators, musicians, and artists themselves were working within networks of desires particularly heightened at the very dissolve between modernist inventiveness and the advent of postmodern reprocesses predicated by the very technologies that afford remote intimacies, such as the television, radio, and the commercial advertisements that followed them. Therefore, through the trope of the shopping bag, a symbol of consumerism, we may glean a similar touch across the ocean between The Bags and the English punk rock band X-Ray Spex.

The same year that The Bags performed "Sanyo" at Hong Kong Café, another female-led punk band released its first album, *Germfree Adolescence* (1978). Though X-Ray Spex's first album received grander reviews and more critical acclaim than anything The Bags ever produced, there are striking inclinations between X-Ray Spex's song "Plastic Bag" and The Bags' performance of "Sanyo." "Plastic Bag" tells a story set in the same year that The Bags formed in Los Angeles: "My mind is like a plastic bag! / 1977 and we are going mad / It's 1977 and we've seen too many ads / 1977 and we're gonna show them all / That apathy's a drag."

X-Ray Spex's brown female vocalist, Poly Styrene, reminds us of the maddening atmosphere of 1977, a year environed with "rubbish that is fed in through [her] ear." Both X-Ray Spex's "Plastic Bag" and The Bags' performance of "Sanyo" respond to their moment's heightened demand to consume. A swarm of ads produces a mind "like a plastic bag"; this suffocating false consciousness cultivates the deadened affect of a hypercommodified culture—apathy. Yet, in Styrene's song, the speaker explains how such apathy weighs on her: "apathy's a drag." Apathy's own structure of noncompassion is doubled as a drag, where indifference folds into an intense feeling of compassionate heaviness. Elizabeth Freeman has argued that sometimes a certain gendered and sexual form of "temporal drag" is experienced by queer subjects as an embodied anachronism.[44] Similarly, the speaker in Styrene's song *feels the historical*, as Freeman would say, insofar as she is aware of her historical indexicality—1977—and how a collective interest, articulated in the pronoun "we," cannot keep up with the temporal progress assumed with the year. In short, the speaker laments the technological progress gained by 1977 while highlighting how consciousness has begun to mirror the ads and commodities circulating around her.

For Styrene, not only mainstream society but also the United Kingdom's punk subculture presented opportunities for critique. As Jayna Brown has argued, "Poly Styrene called out patriarchy from within a counterculture that was supposedly subversive yet was indeed heavily invested in masculinist performances of power."[45] Indeed, Styrene's feminist and queer punk sensibility was an embodied form of anachronism best exemplified in the statement, "Apathy's a drag." Styrene shows how becoming aware of one's disinterest might spark surprise in what one was disinterested in, a sort of boredom with one's boredom. In light of Freeman's argument, Styrene is proposing a way of doing history. Brown continues, "Poly Styrene's politically awake compositions disrupt in some very interesting ways the smooth patrilineal narrative constructing what gets remembered as rebel music, and also challenges the calcifying racial orthodoxy of white riot memory."[46] Styrene and X-Ray Spex's song "Plastic Bag" both variegate the historical context in which

The Bags are performing in Los Angeles and provide productive correspondences between the two bands and lead female vocalists, namely, a staunch critique of mass culture and commodification of social relations, especially with regard to patriarchal by-products. But above all, both feminist singers historicize their indexical moment via affect.

In a particularly telling moment in Bag's memoir, she tells us that she had always hoped to form an all-woman band, but only men would respond to her ads. In this way, Bag's gendered punk voice constantly battled the aggressive drumming and riffs of her male band members. This produced a syncopated call and response, a sort of disagreement between the female lead vocals and the male-heavy instrumentals. Perhaps it is no surprise, then, that one of Bag's early male bandmates suggested that they wear paper bags over their heads to remain anonymous. Bag recounts the first and only performance where The Bags appeared with paper bags over their heads. The performance had barely begun when the rambunctious Darby Crash of The Germs, who then went by the name Bobby Pyn, stormed the stage and tore the bag off Alice Bag's head at the beginning of the set. Darby's action reads not only as an obstreperous repudiation of The Bags' attempt to remain anonymous, though it was very much infused with such spirit. His gesture also springs from a desire to reveal and expose the rarity of a woman of color onstage as a lead singer. Maybe unexpectedly, this queer tear began a lasting and tumultuous friendship between Crash and Bag. And though I do not wish to romanticize a potentially aggressive moment between the two punk rockers, something about Crash's gesture gets to the ways in which turbulence as a mode of relating necessarily involves a structure of differentiation. Especially considered through the lens of X-Ray Spex's song, Crash and Bag's interaction allows us to see how performing with a bag over one's head might promise anonymity but also might produce claustrophobic anxiety in another by displaying a lack of difference. Consequently, Crash's turbulent presence produced something new, a differential outcome, *within* Bag's lo-fi performance, much like the experience of being slammed in a mosh pit.

Crash and Bag's friendship served as an occasion for the two vocalists to work out their own misgivings about identity in different gendered ways. For instance, it was rumored that Crash was gay, an open secret that his fellow scenesters were pressured to conceal, especially during the filming of Spheeris's documentary. In fact, one scene in *The Decline of Western Civilization* depicts Crash and a woman who appears to be his girlfriend standing languidly in the kitchen in an awkward domestic scene. It is rumored that before filming, Crash had his then-boyfriend, Tony the Hustler, a younger male sex worker, move out of their apartment so as to feign a straight romantic relationship with a female friend, because "he didn't want to be seen so unambiguously homo," according to Brendan Mullen.[47] Many women punks in the scene attest to Crash's narcissism in surrounding himself with women who would bring him food or water when he was high on heroin and care for him whenever he walked the razor's edge of overdosing on the lethal drug.

In Bag's memoir, an ambivalence permeates her remembrance of Crash. Revisiting the scene of The Bags' first performance, we can speculate about how Crash's violent and childish disclosure of Alice Bag's persona was driven by an unconscious desire to be discovered or outed himself as much as it was about uncovering a woman of color on a punk stage. Within the framework of the Lucretian *clinamen*, Bag's and Crash's singular rejection of a hypercommodified society, a shared declining away from the advanced industrial civilization that Marcuse describes in the epigraph to this chapter, leaves these two queer punks so radically inclined toward each other that such chaotic antics were both means and ends to a makeshift friendship.

What I have been attempting to demonstrate in this section are the ways in which Lucretian philosophy helps us understand, through the concept of the *clinamen*, that the emergence of an event is always multiple and indeterminate. This fundamental indeterminacy occludes any easy understanding of history as universal, time as linear, or space as finite.[48] Lucretius's philosophy can be called DIY insofar as we are released from origins and final causes. The *clinamen* acts as a radical differential, gesturing to pure potentiality along with the indefinite and infinite ways things may emerge. Alice Bag's punk performance and The Bags' own rendition of "Sanyo" brush on this potential to the extent that they materialize the immateriality of sensing differently. This difference is not always pretty, like Susan Anton's promising voice in the Sanyo commercial. In fact, potentiality is mostly hidden though present within the opaque confines of lo-fi performance. Caught on a stage waiting for someone to rip off the suffocating pleasures of our own anonymizing identity bags, what is potential, then, realizes the actual as always feeling like a drag.

## The Brat and Lo-Fi Style as Attitude

X-Ray Spex claims that in 1977 those who were inundated with images of ever-increasing mass consumerism, represented in the plethora of ads like Sanyo's commercial, understood apathy as the prevailing affect of the time. Yet, one response to the stifling apathy initiated by distracting images of commodities and the "good life" was simply rediscovering interest in the everyday, where the quotidian world, in all its unrefined presentations, became a source of creativity. In this case, the given world was unveiled not as just a static reality but as brimming with potential for change. This was the case for a young Chicana in Boyle Heights in late 1978, Teresa Covarrubias, who was the lead singer of the East Los Angeles punk band The Brat. The Brat formed in 1978 and consisted of three core members: Covarrubias as lead singer and lyricist and Rudy Medina and Sidney Medina on lead and rhythm guitar, respectively. The Medinas were related and also from Boyle Heights. Rudy Medina had previously formed a band with his older brother, who was influenced by David Bowie and DIY culture, but by the time he met Covarrubias, his band was falling apart. Meanwhile, at the behest of Covarrubias's friend Sean Carrillo, a young Chicano artist who would eventually join the performance art group Asco in the 1980s, she went to see the English mod-revival punk band The Jam perform at the Starwood in West Hollywood. There she met Medina, and after talking about their respective musical interests and failing bands, Medina asked if Covarrubias could sing. Covarrubias not only could sing but was also a creative lyricist. Soon after, they formed The Brat.

Covarrubias wrote all the lyrics for the band and drew most of her inspiration from personal experience and the pleasure of watching others within the everyday. She described her writing process, her dissatisfaction with normative Chicano culture, and the explicitly feminist lyrics of The Brat in a 1983 interview with the Chicano automobile periodical *Lowrider*. In the interview, Covarrubias explained that she would often sit for hours at a Yum-Yum Donuts, a chain of donut shops peppered throughout Los Angeles, looking to make something new with what was available to her at that time and place: "I got a lot of influence just from the neighborhood, just watching different characters in the neighborhood. [What] I was writing about were experiences that were happening to me. Sitting at Yum Yum [Donuts] all night and just watching people coming in and out, watching the cops come in and out, just things that would happen. And just on that one little corner. If you sit at Yum Yum long enough for enough evenings, you see the same people coming in. You can start creating ideas about what's going on with them or what they're experiencing."[49] Here, Covarrubias attests to how watching mundane acts resembles a way of reading experiences. The lyricist found inspiration in the transformation of something appearing random and contingent, "watching people coming in and out," to, in turn, becoming scripted, calculated, and recognizable: "If you sit at Yum Yum long enough for enough evenings, you see the same people coming in." For the young Chicana punk, it is within the experience of observing the passersby for hours on end where speculation morphs into narrative and experience inclines to the lyrical.

To "create ideas" about the object of one's gaze shows that some sublimation, some unconscious work, took place. Here, Covarrubias rerouted her pleasure in looking at the anonymous lives and acts around her into an aesthetic experience. Yet, her scopophilic act appears contrapuntal to the dominant psychoanalytic narratives of the male gaze and a general culture of men objectifying women. Such objectification was accomplished through the patriarchal pleasure in looking at them. This point becomes clearer when one critically accounts for the history of the print magazine *Lowrider*. Founded in 1977 by a group of San Jose State University students to give voice to the Bay Area Chicano community during the height of the Brown Power movement, the magazine at first failed to garner a viable readership. Two years after the magazine's initial release, the remedy to the low number of sales was to feature bikini-clad women provocatively posed next to lowrider automobiles. After *Lowrider* originally folded in 1985, with a subsequent revival of the magazine in the late 1980s, some versions of it ran until 2020. One thing proved salient through its tenure: that sexualizing the cover of the magazine aided its consumption while lubricating the circulation of Chicano culture and its subsequent, albeit masculinist, pride.

Meanwhile, lowrider cars have a long history in Chicano popular culture stemming from a 1940s zoot-suit youth sensibility emerging within the rapid change of the Los Angeles urban landscape. By the 1980s, lowrider automobiles often came adorned with customized prints and insignias of Chicano cultural symbols such as Aztec imagery or the Virgin of Guadalupe. However, other adornments featured on lowrider cars were sexualized images of women, often in a pinup-model composition much like the covers of their namesake magazine, *Lowrider*. Both sexist and heterosexist representations of women as equivalent to insignias of cultural pride reveal how women were often subsumed (if not scapegoated) within the dialectic of cultural subordination and cultural pride. This very dynamic can be gleaned in *Lowrider*'s aesthetics, which usually presented a masculinist version of Chicano cultural pride. A key aspect of its aesthetics, according to Brenda Jo Bright, stems from "experiences of alienation based upon metropolitan decline."[50] And while George Lipsitz argues that bands like The Brat "blended the urgency and emotionalism of 1950s rock and roll... with lyrics speaking to the alienations and frustrations of contemporary youth," these related forms of alienations converged with Chicano punk as distinct gendered experiences.[51]

Covarrubias understood these twin-gendered experiences of alienation as two different forms of politics. In the interview in *Lowrider*, the questioner points to how many reviews of the band had been overwhelmingly positive except for a few, including one that claimed that The Brat had no "feelings" for the Chicano community, and asks Covarrubias to respond. Covarrubias explains, "Yes it upset me because it was a cheap and inaccurate shot at us. I see politics in personal relationships. Sure, I have written lyrics about things such as police abuse, but most are more subtle. Most of my lyrics deal with the most camouflaged injustices. The ones we commit between two people or between families."[52] Politics registers in situations "between two people or between two families" for Covarrubias and often appears as "camouflaged injustices." Covarrubias *sees* the immediate experience of a historical situation as a problem within the social field and not just in obviated instances such as overt forms of repression by the police, for instance. To make Chicano politics legible, to "feel" the Chicano community as The Brat's critics would prefer, means one ought not to sacrifice loyalty for

Figure 2.2. The Brat on the cover of *Lowrider*, 1982.

subtly. Once again, this is a problem with the politics of Covarrubias's lyrical style and the style politics of The Brat's "feelings" about being a Chicano punk band from East Los Angeles. Namely, Covarrubias and The Brat's sociocultural significance to the Chicano community hinged on their unambiguous fidelity to a (patriarchal) representation of pride at the expense of nuanced, if often contradictory, political sensibilities.

Covarrubias's lyrics mostly focused on gender roles, however subtly, because the singer-songwriter felt that within the Chicano community, there existed pervasive injustices.

> INTERVIEWER: Some of your lyrics deal with themes concerning the role of women. Why?
>
> TERESA COVARRUBIAS: What I do as a writer and singer is first of all a statement about women. Our traditional roles as men and women are very unjust. As Chicanos we are oppressed by the society that surrounds us, but in our own homes, the oppression is even deeper with the woman being the victim.
>
> ... In the modern professional world, the sexist attitudes are more subtle. Just working with four men in a band is hell sometimes, ... but I manage. Many are unconscious attitudes that have been socially bred into our culture, ... and I think it's time we weed them out.[53]

By prioritizing lyrics about the subordination of women within the home and community, Covarrubias traces how larger societal structures of oppression such as sexism translate into everyday attitudes, which are "more subtle" forms of silencing. Meanwhile, these more minor forms of oppression beget similar minor forms of subversion. For Covarrubias, attitude acts as a lo-fi avenue of communication where politics are negotiated between persons and families within the everyday and in not-so-obvious ways.

For example, take the titular song "Attitudes" off The Brat's original 1980 five-song EP, *Attitudes*, released by the independent label Fatima Records.[54] The ominous drum and guitar lead breaks with the frenetic opening of the song, which alternates between melodic and cacophonous sounds. Covarrubias's voice somehow virtuosically embodies both a serene composition and an indignant disposition, at the same time. She starts by addressing a presumed woman listener who has once again felt the sting of alienation brought by a sexist encounter: "So you think it starts the day you are born." In an almost Beauvoirian vein, the speaker underscores the ambiguity of such a thought, noting, "Or you think it starts from being torn," a reference to the socially derived cause of felt difference and alienation. (One must recount here Simone de Beauvoir's dictum, "One is not born, but rather, becomes a woman.")[55] Confused as to the cause of alienation, whether beginning from the "day one is born" or to "being torn," the pronoun "he" starts to take a more ambiguous meaning: "He said you'd better change / Your frame of thought / Look at all the trouble / You have brought." "He" signifies both a person and society, broaching the relationship both between two people and between an individual and the community.

As the song revs up, the speaker, in an almost aha moment, switches voices to that of the addressee, proclaiming, "It's just my attitude / It's only attitude / Everything I say is wrong / Everything I do is wrong." One is struck by the marrying of action and speech in the lyrics, whereby the failure to adequately say or do makes present the overdetermining measure by which Chicanas are rendered merely attitudinal. "When everything you say goes wrong," the voice switches back to the initial speaker, "And everything you do goes wrong," she continues: "Say it's your attitude." And almost as if the chorus of feminist listeners has joined in, the song then ends with a reworked-shame-*cum*-declaration: "My attitude." By the end of the song, a particular feminist consciousness emerges, where "nothing more" than "attitude" evidences *an individuated feminist expression of a low fidelity to both the dominant and minoritarian norms.*

Attitudes are akin to "frames of mind" and reflect a certain style in thinking, orienting, and apprehending the world. Attitude works in Covarrubias's lyrics as a stylized discontent, a subtle weeding out of low-key oppressive patterns toward women by reclaiming attitude as a dissatisfied aesthetic expression. Covarrubias's theorization of the bad attitude as a lo-fi feminist expression is in line with Sara Ahmed's thinking of the feminist killjoy, especially evident in songs like "Misogyny," both an ode to feminism and a talking down to patriarchy, or "High School," a song about a disaffected Catholic schoolgirl who "won't dance [and] won't make romance."[56] But a bad attitude begs the question, *Bad* compared to what? In some sense, any acknowledgment of an attitude indicates some fraught expectation, for any "good" or optimistic attitude is no attitude at all; otherwise, it would have never registered as something effectively different. This is why anyone consistently performing a good attitude draws suspicion, since any form of earnestness collapses into insincerity under a paranoid eye. Attitudes effeminize a complaint; they register something off-kilter with norms while expressing some agential, subversive distance from patriarchal expectations.

Attitudes perform critiques of both dominant and minoritarian norms, and Covarrubias's feminist lyricism—her punk ethos—understood and enacted this crucial point. In keeping within a Beauvoirian genealogy, Covarrubias (and the other historical actors presented in this chapter) articulates a very important disagreement in aesthetic philosophy, one where the individuated feminist expression of a low fidelity to norms actively politicizes the experience of artistic production. If popular modernism has all but vanished after the 1980s, the lo-fi aesthetic and its subsequent embodiment as a feminist bad attitude remain some of the most consequential effects of having to make do with what was given. Some early LA punk shows, punk memorabilia, zines like *Slash*, the "terrorist drag" of Vaginal Davis, Alice Bag's punk scream, Covarrubias's lyrics, and the makeshift women of color presses all conjoin politics with aesthetic experience and extend from an underappreciated critique of what is known in aesthetic philosophy as "the aesthetic attitude" leveled by the existential feminist philosopher Simone de Beauvoir.

Beauvoir's short and densely written 1948 volume *The Ethics of Ambiguity* offers an often-overlooked critique of the dominant view at the time (mostly by men) of aesthetic experience. Some strands of aesthetic philosophy posit the aesthetic realm as completely separate from the social-cultural context, which allows for the appreciation of art for its own sake. This frame of mind is known as the aesthetic attitude. The aesthetic attitude requires the cultivation of one's attention to the aesthetic qualities presented to the observer. This can happen in a museum, in a theater, or especially in nature. Without giving much historical context to the concept, Beauvoir describes those who adopt the aesthetic attitude as having "no other relation with the world than that of detached contemplation."[57] For Beauvoir, the aesthetic attitude operates as "pure beholding," an "impersonal" disposition that in effect "equalizes all situations."[58] In a remarkable moment, Beauvoir, aware of her own historical position as a French intellectual at the end of the Second World War, dismisses those who claim to be "outside" a projected future since that is "still a way of living the inescapable fact that one is inside." She goes on, "Those French intellectuals who, in the name of history, poetry, or art, sought to rise above the drama of the age, were willy-nilly its actors; more or less explicitly, they were playing the occupier's game."[59] In referring to the Nazi occupation of France, Beauvoir is keen to show how life is lived as a series of choices, if only toward death. We can glean Beauvoir's suspicion of the aesthetic attitude, though not because of its claim to universality but instead due to its radical nonaction.

Up until this small section on the aesthetic attitude, Beauvoir charts positive ethics of ambiguity. Unlike the aesthetic attitude's negative approach—negative because it inhabits a "position of withdrawal, a way of fleeing the truth of the present"—the positive aspect of ambiguity beguiles any artists, writers, or observers preoccupied with their "pure contemplation" into a "definite project."[60] Here, "project" becomes inflected with an existential definition as both noun and transitive verb, one where action is privileged over passive indifference: "since man never contemplates: he does."[61] Beauvoir is a philosopher of performance, and what concerns her in the midcentury, after the perils of World War II, is the "tragic ambivalence" inherent in conscious life, best captured in the text's opening sentence, quoted from the sixteenth-century French philosopher Michel de Montaigne: "The continuous work of our life . . . is to build death." For Beauvoir, such a claim announces a paradox, a "nontemporal truth," at the heart of human existence: "But between the past which no longer is and the future which is not yet, this moment when he exists is nothing. This privilege, which he alone possesses, of being a sovereign and unique subject amidst a universe of objects, is what he shares with all his fellow-men. In turn an object for others, he is nothing more than an individual in the collectivity on which he depends."[62] The nothingness of existence, which Beauvoir conditionally names "tragic ambiguity" or "tragic ambivalence," composes the moment—the gap between past and future. Ambivalence constitutes the human condition because "one is both subject and object" in the world.[63] Yet in her ethics, Beauvoir claims that such nothingness in fact is experienced as a universally shared exigence: "he must first will freedom in himself and universally; he must try to conquer it: in the light of this project situations are graded and reasons for acting are made manifest."[64] Beauvoir reconfigures the aesthetic attitude into a protofeminist attitude, one where art (and aesthetics generally) ought to move the individual to will freedom in oneself; and importantly for Beauvoir's ethics, this act is also the will for freedom for all.[65] In the encounter with aesthetics, one experiences the disclosure of the world. In facing tragic ambivalence head-on, art can be liberatory because its effects can extend beyond the moment of its experience; it can leap out of the historical moment of its creation and *move* subjects to experience their freedom as infinite choices within the finite condition of life. In other words, one realizes the profound relation constituting existence: "[art] should reveal existence as a reason for existing."[66]

In conclusion, let us turn to Beauvoir's apt description of the characters presented in our study thus far: "It is existence which [the artist and writer] are trying to pin down and make eternal. The word, the stroke, the very marble indicate the object insofar as it is an absence. Only, in the work of art the lack of being returns to the positive. Time is stopped, clear forms and finished meanings rise up. In this return, existence is confirmed and establishes its own justification. This is what Kant said when he defined art as a 'finality without end.'"[67] The material means by which artists and writers create their art are imbued, according to Beauvoir, with an eternal existence. Thus, to define art as a "finality without end" is to understand art as a positive justification to loss, which is a lesson that comes to live beyond the pinned moment of its *naissance*.

Beauvoir's ethics and reconfigured aesthetic attitude enrich our discussion of lo-fi by reframing the aesthetic subjects and objects in this chapter as a world onto themselves. The queer punks of Los Angeles in the 1970s and early 1980s Vaginal Davis, Alice Bag, Norma Alarcón, Poly Styrene, Darby Crash, and Teresa Covarrubias—all spurred to create, to *do it themselves*, and to make do with the given world—rework dispossession into a positive aspect of ambiguity. Lo-fi operates as an aesthetic but becomes embodied as an attitude in the process of reworking life's constitutive lack into a positive aspect of ambivalence. What becomes transmitted is knowledge about the limits of norms, a knowing that escapes the confines of the here and now and that *exists* in the future for others to unforget.

Like the play central to Asco's art-making process underscored in chapter 1, lo-fi attitudes reverberate within the status quo practical lessons about the decline of popular modernism and the continual hunger to create new ways of living life—politically and ethically. When Covarrubias tells her interviewer that she sees "politics in personal relationships," she ascribes an ethics to her attitude and to the people around her. In this light, Lucretian turbulence and declination describe the productive difficulty in existing in a world of pure relation: "The man of good will sees concrete and difficult problems arising in his relations with [others]."[68] Lo-fi attitudes are aesthetic expressions of the difficulty conditioned by a shared tragic ambivalence manipulated by commodity culture into fantasies of the good life. As we venture into the 1980s and the advent of an epidemiological sexual crisis that forwarded questions of desire, death, aesthetics, and politics, we will see how ambivalence, our next stylized discontent, makes prominent the tragedy in having to represent the unrepresentable. Desire takes center stage now when the limits of Chicano identity announce themselves in what "Chicano" will have been.

# 3

## Desiring in the Dark

*Framing Ambivalence in the Works of Gil Cuadros, Ray Navarro, and "Gay Latino Studies"*

No one had ever explained to me that there was going to be light again in the world, and that the whole world wasn't going to be dark. There are many years to come, let's hope, so what the hell, life is worth living . . . isn't it.
—Ray Navarro, in David France's *How to Survive a Plague*

My bones shine in the dark.
—Gil Cuadros, "My Aztlán: White Place"

If something is to stay in the memory, it must be burned in: only that which never ceases to hurt stays in the memory.
—Friedrich Nietzsche, *On the Genealogy of Morality*

A split of sorts emerged in the understanding of Latino identity with the advent of the AIDS epidemic in the United States. The splintering took the form of a scissiparity, a separation that, in turn, (re)produces something. This chapter argues that what is produced by this historically situated fission within Latino identity is a new way of understanding the relationship between embodiment and representation in Chicano/Latino cultural politics. This is because, in ways unthought before, desire became recognizably central in the construction of Latino identity and in an almost antithetical way to an abounding, generalized despair over the lack of any potential government curtailment of the AIDS epidemic in the 1980s. In Los Angeles, this felt particularly acute. After the amplification and circulation of nausea in Los Angeles at the height of the Vietnam War and the coterminous deamplification of identification articulated by Chicana punk feminist attitudes beginning in the late

1970s, AIDS came to complicate nascent identity politics debates intensifying in the 1980s. As the epidemic unfolded, people living with HIV/AIDS across *all* subject positions were faced with a universal imperative: the internal and (un)conscious realization of one's impending death. At the moment of this conscious realization, the subject of loss confronts its finite body—"language in its most recalcitrant, carnal particularity"—whereby the inanimacy inherent within vital life (embodied, no less, in the subject living with HIV/AIDS) becomes imagined, wished, and aesthetically rendered as "infinite spirit" and where "the worldly object is relinquished by being introjected, abbreviated."[1] Embodiment, then, figures as absolute negation (being through nonbeing) in the act of sharing out what cannot be shared any longer. Rebecca Comay reminds us that this process resembles the psychoanalytic act of mourning and Hegel's account of Spirit's (consciousness within time) ascension into Absolute Knowing (knowledge without internal contradiction): "The final achievement of rationality is to pronounce the funeral oration for religious and poetic *Vorstellung* [representation]."[2] A productive tension emerges between embodiment and representation when we consider how the former, whether linguistically or visually rendered, inevitably breaks down the signification of the latter. Embodiment acts as the epistemological limit to representation; whereas representation surrenders "carnal particularity" to memory and imagination. This interplay circumscribes a peculiar desire I am calling ambivalence, which splits identity from within.

Particularly within Latino identity, desire comes to figure as a crisis in representation, where the transparency in knowing that one's body is finite—rationalizing it—reveals the surd kernel of opacity at the heart of Latino identity and its representations. This ineffable irreducibility *causes* desire in the Latino subject by formalizing the gap between image and body, which I later define as the frame. Christina León has theorized opacity as an aesthetic strategy deployed by Latina/o cultural producers, where opacity, as "visual metaphor, gestures toward an *ambivalent* relation to visual culture—with a keen eye to resisting simplistic representations that seek to tell the whole story, or reading practices that demand completeness."[3] I would add that these twin impulses to tell the whole story and demand completeness undergird the false binary choice between pure resistance to oppression and the will to assimilate.

*Dissatisfactions* has been concerned with the misplaced middle range of possibilities found in the gap between image and the (finite) body. Indeed, it is this ambivalent relation to representation where the frame becomes a site for playful manipulation taking shape as various styles of dissatisfactions with the false binary.

Therefore, the first two stylized dissatisfactions deployed by a Chicano and punk counterculture in Los Angeles may be read together as amplifying a structure of feeling (nausea) to create a space for deamplifying identification with dominant and minoritarian norms (lo-fi). The coterminous relationship between these two Chicano styles came to fruition within the historical context of the AIDS epidemic and Reagan's successful ascension from governor of California to president of the United States in 1981. By this point, a third stylized discontent garnered a politically ambiguous force in Chicano countercultural production: ambivalence. This chapter examines how the trope of ambivalence, a particular mixture of nausea and lo-fi, comes to inform the work of two Chicano cultural producers aesthetically responding to the mundanities of living with HIV/AIDS.

Both the writer Gil Cuadros and the video artist and HIV/AIDS activist Ray Navarro inhabit this split in Latino identity. When we attune ourselves to the tension between image and body in their respective oeuvres, the split between latinidad and homosexuality quickly becomes unavoidable. Cuadros and Navarro occupy a fraught, understudied position in current Latino scholarship, mostly because their politics cannot be subsumed under mere identitarianism or understood as pure resistance to state-sanctioned violence and oppression. The minimal treatment of their work in existing literature is symptomatic of a general conflict in the field, one clearly evidenced by the contemporary return in the field of gay Latino studies to the identity politics debates of the 1980s to produce a more positivist and empirical account of the intersection of gay and Latino identities. Most of the essays in the 2011 anthology *Gay Latino Studies: A Critical Reader* accord with the position of its editors, Michael Hames-García and Ernesto Javier Martínez, in their skeptical stance toward what I characterize as the ambivalent politics of queer theory evident in the aesthetics of Gil Cuadros and Ray Navarro. Hames-García and Martínez's anthology attempts instead to *fill in* the fractious split between Latino and gay and consequently pins down these identities and give them a masterful frame. This chapter can be read, then, as a recuperation of this split to render ambivalence as a style that is both a cultural response to specific sociopolitical forces and a subject's willful refusal to be fully knowable and therefore potentially masterable. To begin, I first explicate current arguments and tensions in the purported field of gay Latino studies by engaging parts of Hames-García and Martínez's anthology *Gay Latino Studies*. The chapter then turns to Navarro and Cuadros as examples that undermine the recovery project of a coherent Latino identity that is now (re)calcifying in current Latino studies scholarship.

## The Problem with "Gay Latino Studies"

How is it that we come to know ourselves as Latino or gay? And more importantly, can the (in)coherence of our identities become entry points into larger discussions of justice, freedom, and love (a question haunting many of the social movements of the late 1960s and 1970s)? These queries bring the utopianism of the 1960s into conversation with the contemporary return to 1980s identity politics, as exemplified by the *Gay Latino Studies: A Critical Reader*. In this section, I begin by addressing Hames-García's introductory chapter to this exciting and critically important anthology for both queer studies and Latino studies. After exposing some contradictions and openings in the theoretical framework of the anthology, I switch to analyzing Hames-García's text as an object performing a wounded identity, which, I argue, can tell us something about the frame of ambivalence. This affliction engenders a form of passionate sensuousness, a self-reflexive acknowledgment of one's subjection, that I read as in excess of the body, as a structure of affective dissonance that keeps one from "knowing" in certitude, that is, *objectively*.

In "Queer Theory Revisited," Hames-García stages a polemic against contemporary queer theory's historical self-narrative and its (poststructuralist) critique of identity. His chapter opens with a melancholic gesture to the promise of early queer theory to hold questions of sexuality and desire as central to radical politics, while at the same time enacting critiques of the social that, in the Marcusean sense, "simultaneously negate society as a given and imagine what more liberatory possibilities are being blocked by that given state of affairs."[4] Instead of fulfilling these promises, Hames-García contends, queer theory has failed to provide people of color and other minoritized subjects any *real* liberationist projects with which to positively articulate their identities and their potential to enact social change.

From the outset, then, Hames-García's position appears contrary to the subjects of the present study by articulating a mode of impatience espoused by the canonical, agential subject of resistance. According to Hames-García, queer theory, broadly construed, displaces marginal voices by theorizing the experiences of people of color as outside, rather than internal to, gay, lesbian, and queer debates. He evinces this situation by pointing out dominant queer genealogies that have excluded prominent works on sexuality and desire by people of color, such as the Chicana feminist Gloria Anzaldúa or the queer Black writers James Baldwin and Audre Lorde. For Hames-García, this exclusion performs an "ontological denial" of race specifically and of identity in general.[5] The category of "queer," he argues, is too *incoherent* an identity, one that suspiciously transgresses boundaries and eclipses other identities (such as race, in Hames-García's understanding), resulting in a theory that is too dependent on an unmarked whiteness.[6] In Hames-García's account, queer(ness) more often than not *lacks* an ontological referent and is therefore too ambivalent. In this view, *queer* fails to deliver on its ostensible promise of "avoid[ing] the fixed *exclusions* of other identity labels."[7] Hames-García concludes that the indefinite signifier "queer" problematically obscures the specificities of gender, race, and sexuality, thus enacting/evidencing a form of Eurocentrism. At the same time, he argues against parsing these categories completely separately—even (presumably) in the project of identifying their different positionalities—so as not to undermine "how *aspects* of identity are interrelated."[8] In short, for Hames-García, identities are coherent on their own and interrelate with one another within a completely transparent, knowable, and measurable system; whereas queerness, for the postpositivist realist, obscures the differences *between* identities in the service of whitewashing and flattening their interrelations.

Hames-García's critique is seductive because it posits the subject as a knowing subject, a subject who *possesses* a history. What is compelling to María Lugones, the chapter's respondent in the anthology, and "true" for Hames-García is the idea that "people *have* histories . . . as complex, interrelated beings in multiple relations."[9] And yet, I want to argue here, positing that subjects possess histories foregrounds a certain logic of ownership, sidelining the question of how subjects *come to be* in history, which is to say how a subject enacts or does history. In effect, Lugones via Hames-García reifies history as something fixed, something that can be possessed. Hames-García's provocative assertion begs the question, How is it possible to *know* one's identity (and presumably one's history) or to know those of others within a shifting terrain of relationality? From the vantage of performance studies, a productive entryway here involves a shift from ontologizing history (its reification) to questions about how histories/identities are performed, which should be noted are correlating questions to epistemological issues about *how* one knows something.

*Gay Latino Studies: A Critical Reader* can be considered an extension of an earlier anthology edited by Hames-García and Paula Moya, *Reclaiming Identity: Realist Theory and the Predicament of Postmodernism* (2000), in which some of the early tenets of "postpositivist realism" were applied to Chicano/Latino literary theory.[10] Within the field of gay/queer Latino studies, Hames-García stands as an astute proponent of postpositivist realism, and in engaging with his argument in the context of *Gay Latino Studies: A Critical Reader*, I am attempting to underscore an irreducible contradiction at the center of "gay Latino identity" and its ontological, epistemological, and performative repercussions for latinidad generally. In fact, I am arguing that the desire to know one's own identity or history reflects a sense of injury and resentment implicit in the inexpressible experiences composed under the sign of latinidad.

In Hames-García's analysis and the general theory of "postpositivist realism" that he deploys, the knowing subject is fetishized, reduced to epistemic concerns, and remade as solely a *product* of lived experience, where this commodity object resembles a receptacle of consciously possessed knowledge. Though he begins his chapter indexing a Marxist materialism à la Herbert Marcuse, a materialist analysis would locate knowledge (or ideology) not in the subject but produced and dispelled through social structures that will always already taint any commitment to an "objective" and "knowable" subject. In essence, the critique that Hames-García wields against (white) queer theorists who extract "people-of-color experiences" to justify theories of the social redoubles back to negate itself, almost as if to articulate the author's *unconscious* though unverifiable pleasure in pointing to this extraction. In other words, the problem of fetishizing and commodifying the "knowing person of color"—that is, the attempt to position a subject as a possessor of knowledge so that one can then extract and abstract experiences from them to justify a theory—goes unresolved. Postpositivist realism would rather have people of color extract knowledge and experiences from other people of color than have white theorists do the same. When we follow this argument to its logical end, it seems that the alleged epistemological problem at the heart of queer theory only illuminates the ambiguous reason to reposit a subject outside of ideology in the first place. Postpositivist realism suggests that people of color theorists solely using people of color experiences to justify theories of the lived experience of people of color might potentially be a less problematic way of doing theory. And though I marginally agree with the political staging of this methodology and its legitimate attempt to stave off queer theorists from fetishizing difference to the extent that it makes them white, such a project remains dubious in framing ideology as unidirectional. Contrary to postpositivist realism's desire to position ideology outside and beyond the subject of knowledge, *Dissatisfactions* continues to focus on how ideology constitutes subjectivity by distracting it from coming to terms with its *own* constitutive inadequacy.

### Ambivalence, Resentment, and Wounded Attachments

In the political theorist Wendy Brown's controversial 1993 essay "Wounded Attachments," she uncovers the tears in the fabric of liberal democracy that were produced and extended by politicized identities from the 1960s onward. Essentially, for Brown, politicized identities follow a logic of injury. An affliction occurs at the paradoxical moment when the "I" in the "I am [gay, Latina, a woman, etc.]" is negated by liberal democracy's move to universalize itself in the law: "The abstract character of liberal political membership and the ideologically naturalized character of liberal individualism together work against politicized identity formation in liberal regimes."[11] As a result, the primary affliction felt by minoritized subjects, subjects who are displaced or, as José

E. Muñoz describes, who "fall off the majoritarian maps of the public sphere," is for Brown a feeling of resentment.[12] Following Friedrich Nietzsche's analysis of resentment, which he terms in the French *ressentiment*, she writes, "But in its attempt to displace its suffering, identity structured by *ressentiment* at the same time becomes invested in its own subjection.... Identity politics structured by *ressentiment* reverses without subverting this blaming structure."[13] In other words, the structure of resentment reinforces itself through the reification of blame, which then reproduces the very resentment that feeds it—an insidious cycle that Nietzsche diagnosed, in Eve Kosofsky Sedgwick's words, as a "self-propagating, near universal psychology, compounded of injury, rancor, envy, and self-righteous vindictiveness, fermented by a sense of disempowerment."[14] This may be the case with some affective performances of belonging, and it especially resonates with the important critique that Hames-García and Martinez stage in their chapters and throughout the *Gay Latino Studies* anthology. Arguably, Brown also gives us an apt framework for considering Chicano politics in Los Angeles after the fadeout of the 1968 promise of social change that engulfed many identity-based movements of the 1970s. For instance, the Brown Power movement could be interpreted as an example of the wounded attachment that she is critiquing. However, I depart from Brown's critical application of Nietzschean resentment as self-propagating injury and, thus, separate my own critique from her call for politicized identities' own self-effacement—that is, from the demand to move on from injurious attachments, to let it go, as it were. Instead, politicized identities require us to recognize our relations differently; in violating the limits of identity, queerness establishes the interrelational as conditional to politics.

Sedgwick, in her essay "Melanie Klein and the Difference Affect Makes," presses the reproductive power structures of resentment and searches for an impasse, or an opening, through which to linger in the ambivalence inherent in *ressentiment*. Sedgwick asks, "What is the most defining act, the conclusively diagnostic act of resentment? It is *accurately* accusing *someone else* of being motivated by it. Where then to find a position from which to interrupt its baleful circuit?"[15] Here, Sedgwick underscores how resentment works almost as a contagious element producing through retroactivity a circuitous relationship. The (unconscious) resentment of the speaker is uncovered in the act of "accurately" because necessarily accusing someone else of it. Said differently, to accuse someone else of being resentful is conditioned by the need to have it be true, which is itself an act of resentment. Thus, how to make incomplete this determinate closure initiated by such accusations? I understand Sedgwick's cue as following Brown's disavowal of the injurious affliction, its open attachment to and "intrinsic relationality" with another.[16] In other words, reading Brown with Sedgwick offers us a site for *identification with* the mark of identity's incompleteness, which is to say an identification with the symptom that is not unlike the structure of ambivalence. It is important to remember here that identity and identification, at least in the psychoanalytic literature, are not equivalent. Such work of identification, according to Diana Fuss, "keeps identity at a distance, . . . prevents identity from ever approximating the status of an ontological given, even if it makes possible . . . the *illusion* of identity as immediate, secure, and totalizable."[17]

Ambivalence calls attention to the interruption of an injurious circuit. An example of such a circuit can be found when an implicated reader of Hames-García hears and feels resentment in his tone and at times *might share in* the resentment of being displaced by queer theory's (often white) attempt to "universalize" itself in its account of identity and marginal experiences.[18] Wounded attachments are produced when one feels like one must *externalize* one's pain (similar to how Hames-García displaces his afflictions onto a counteridentification with queer theory and specifically onto a rejection of Judith Butler's and Sedgwick's writings). However, another displacement is at play, one of perverse identification with injury, a furtive pleasure in repeating one's call for recognition. We may begin to ask what happens when one takes pleasure in one's own resubjugation, that is, in sticking a finger in the wound and forfeiting a position of sovereignty, as a political performance in and onto itself.[19] If this is possible, as I will show is crucial to queer latinidad, the injured subject does not own its historical injury; instead, wounding histories possess the subject, and only through identifying with the other's desire can the injured subject disperse a sensuality into the world as a finite body. Contra Brown, I contend that this move does not forgo politicized identities. Like the process of identification, ambivalence internally destabilizes the coherence of identity and, in turn, repoliticizes, reconceptualizes, and reperforms identity differently. Therefore, it becomes important to ask, What would it look like to identify with the wounded attachment engendered by identity's breakdown, and how is this itself a political process? In a sense, what I am arguing is a recapitulation of Fuss's earlier contention regarding identity politics, when she observes that the personal, and thus individuated, lived experience is *not* political "in any literal or equivalent fashion" since this well-propagated mantra—"the personal is political"—oddly depersonalizes the personal experience while voiding any meaning to politics by virtue of its lacking in specificity.[20] As we shall see, politicized identities require us to recognize our relations differently, through other modalities, such as affect and aesthetic experiences, that are not guaranteed so readily by the dominant posture of a "knowing" subject whose desires are made transparent to and for capitalist logics of reproduction and possession.

Resentment's "baleful circuit" opens, or rather the wounded opening of the power structure is felt and sensed, through the aesthetic realm's production of a structured feeling that I am calling ambivalence. If, as Brown rightly claims, identity structured by resentment "becomes deeply *invested* in its own impotence" (note the economic metaphor at play), then that identity is always already failing, queered, and incongruent with illusions of immediacy, security, and totality.[21]

Furthermore, resentment's circuitous function mirrors the relay in the antiquated debates between essentialism and constructivism, which peaked in the 1980s and early-1990s feminist, gay, and lesbian studies discourses and especially heightened with the advent of the AIDS crisis. For, the "versus" of such binary propositions falsely suggests a deadlock between two stable conceptual categories inherent in almost all theoretical frameworks at the time used to address it, while simultaneously struggling "against a very unstable background of tacit assumptions and fantasies about nature and nurture," as Eve Sedgwick outlines in her notable fourth axiom from *Epistemologies of the Closet*.[22] Instead, Sedgwick suggests their mutual imbrication, a relay of commonalities and differences best captured in her alternative formulation of "minoritizing" versus "universalizing," where this "terminological *choice*" (read: style) registers ways for the homo-/heterosexual definitional meaning to be conferred and lived "with continuing centrality and difficulty."[23] This point further substantiates her first axiom—"people are different from each other"—by avoiding the trap of pinpointing a cultural, material, or historical cause to homosexuality and also resisting the dubious search for a cause *within* the "homosexual species."[24] That is to say, in a world where media representations about AIDS fueled the homophobic fantasy of gay "extirpation," one might also see how this homophobic fantasy's flip side contained a "medicalized dream of the prevention of gay bodies," that is, the quest to help people not "turn" gay, as it were, in order to save their lives. To heed Sedgwick's demurral with the "nature versus nurture" debates and its academic equivalent (essentialism versus constructivism) means that questions about the biosocial origins of homosexuality and the contingent meanings of sexual acts derived, or not, from them require analytical finesse and political nuance: "We have all the more reasons, then, to keep our understanding of gay origin, of gay cultural and material reproduction, plural, multi-capillaried, argus-eyed, respectful, and endlessly cherished."[25] This definition of "gay origin," of the impulse to essentialize, indeed minoritize, shares in its construction the same effect as the elusive cause of desire that splits the "homosexual body" from its representation, much in the same way that mainstream narratives around AIDS, in an almost Cartesian frenzy, imaged a body that necessitated its own local extinction: "In this unstable balance of assumptions between nature and culture, . . . under the overarching, relatively unchallenged aegis of a culture's desire that gay people *not be*, there is no unthreatened, unthreatening conceptual home for a concept of gay origins."[26] In fact, the complicated cycle between essentialism and constructivism finds its double in the elliptical structure that style affords; for, as discussed in the introduction to this book, style confounds the arbitrary limit between cultivation (culture) and innate attribute (nature). Style, once again, singularizes the now-universal feeling of dissatisfaction engendered by late capitalism. The irreducibility between representation and the body, which for our purposes here *causes* desire, must be symbolized as the split in Latino subjectivity, the frame of ambivalence as stylized discontent.

Thus, the reader might infer that I depart from Brown on many levels, and they would be correct. But mostly this is because of my animating desire to read the juridical, political, and social injury composing a wounded attachment rather counterintuitively, that is, in the service of a negativity refusing valorization and verification. I ask, What happens if we do not so quickly disavow this wounded opening? What exactly is *queer*, though, without valor at the moment of nonrecognition and material dispossession? It is here that we must return to the split in Latino identity, a split ushered into view by the advent of the AIDS crisis, because such a crisis in ethnic-racialized sexuality emphasized the very "sovereign incalculability" at the heart of the gay Latino subject of knowledge.[27] Certainly, Sandra K. Soto's forceful injunction that we *read* ethnic-racialized desire "like a queer" unearths the ways "sexual desires [are] constrained by race and shaped by shame and humiliation," which in turn understands sexuality as "unexceptional."[28] This is to say, and as this chapter argues, when we move ethnic-racialized sexuality from a minoritarian position to a majoritarian one, we collapse identarian logics into an aperture at the heart of *Latino* identity.

## Desire's Frame

By the late 1980s, media narratives around the HIV/AIDS crisis often foregrounded a white homosexual body as the primary victim of the disease and government neglect. AIDS activist groups such as the Gay Men's Health Crisis and ACT UP, whose members were largely white and gay, contested this narrative framing of the "AIDS victim" and at the turn of the decade sought to revise it into something more hopeful. In 1990, Michael Callen published his book *Surviving AIDS*, introducing a different lens that shifted the predominant victim narrative into the more empowering lens of the "long-term survivor." Along with the writer Richard Berkowitz, Callen developed a new perspective that lifted the (racially unmarked) gay man with AIDS outside the official understanding that they were "as good as dead" and instead offered the promise that they might survive.

I begin this section with Callen because I am interested in how his survivor concept "provided a framework" of hope, acting as a sort of "life raft that kept [Callen] afloat in a sea of doom and gloom."[29] As the narrative frame of the "long-term survivor" developed in HIV/AIDS discourse and policy, it propped up an unmarked—and thus implicitly white—body with HIV/AIDS. The discourse here excludes racialized and politically disenfranchised people who are living with HIV/AIDS and thus left to swim in a sea of despair. This becomes even more evident when we remember, as some scholars of HIV/AIDS have pointed out, that early instances of the disease in the United States, first identified in 1981 and named GRID (Gay Related Immune Deficiency), had already affected many people decades before, especially in drug-using communities in urban cities.[30] In other words, the concept of the "long-term survivor" is nothing new to populations overexposed to extreme conditions of poverty and violence, particularly as the Reagan administration's early policies systemically shrank federal systems of social support in the mid- to late eighties. We cannot understand the AIDS epidemic without accounting for the ethnic-racial logics that undergird the retelling of its history. Debates over such frames of knowledge also carry political and aesthetic implications for our understanding of ethnic-racial differences in an AIDS-stricken United States.

To further investigate the racial underpinnings of HIV/AIDS narrative frames, I turn to the video artworks and writings of Ray Navarro, who, like Callen, was an HIV/AIDS activist concerned with the epidemic's narrative framing. However, unlike Callen, Navarro translates AIDS narratives into visual phenomena. Calling on Navarro's interest in television and video activism, I argue that his work is central to a televisual aesthetics that also prominently emerges in the experimental prose and poetry of the queer Chicano writer Gil Cuadros. By reading Navarro's and Cuadros's work beside each other, we see how the literary comes to inform Navarro's visual work and how the visual structures Cuadros's literature. Both Cuadros and Navarro offer the intersection of HIV/AIDS scholarship and Chicano cultural production a new poetic optics that draws our attention to the very function of the frame—its frame-work, as it were—while suspending questions of what the frame includes or excludes. This optics exposes the frame as a structure of ambivalence lingering in between the dyad of inclusion and exclusion. Where appearance is taken for granted, Cuadros and Navarro stylize a dissatisfaction with the apparent, given world. Navarro and Cuadros both enact an aesthetic that moves us away from victim-survival AIDS narratives and into a more politically ambiguous terrain, where the foretold death of the Chicano body with AIDS implies a body dispersed into the world by the force of loss, rather than solely atrophying in death.

One critical "given" during the AIDS epidemic that many artists and activists sought to undermine was the simple question of whether this crisis was solely about a virus that needed to be treated and cured. Many artists-activists understood that the virus was situated within a larger cultural and historical context, which inevitably meant confronting more abstract social systems, such as media, mass culture, and education. What this yielded was a politics that underscored how activism always carried with it an implicit aestheticization. Style provides a heuristic through which to think about the inconclusive relation between aesthetic abstraction and direct action, since, as the art historian George Kubler argues, style's "ambiguities and inconsistencies mirror aesthetic activity as a whole."[31] Navarro understood how video activism was, however equivocal, both a form of political action and a conceptual endeavor entangled with particular aesthetic concerns.

### Navarro's Queer Televisual Aesthetics

Navarro studied painting and video in Los Angeles before moving to New York City in 1988, where he became involved in AIDS activism. His training in video art at the Otis Art Institute of Parsons School of Design and the California Institute of the Arts proved useful to this activism in New York City, and he became a cofounder of DIVA TV (Damned Interfering Video Activist-Television), an affinity group to ACT UP. For the artists-activists of DIVA TV, video offered an important format for questioning the style of political action, since the medium's own political motivations were always, in some form or another, in question. Responding to the rise of television's importance within youth culture, exemplified by the popularity of the broadcasting channel MTV (Music Television), DIVA TV sought to circulate images of AIDS activism through video and public-access television in order to short-circuit the otherwise banal distraction of pop music videos. Video activism during the height of the epidemic presented a multiplicity of political styles advanced by activist groups, on the one hand, while underscoring how media and culture were always political, on the other.

Video activists like Navarro picked up camcorders to produce their own representations in a do-it-yourself fashion, videotaping their friends as well as demonstrations and community meetings. Indeed, Navarro's education and experience in Los Angeles greatly influenced his aestheticized activism in ACT UP/NYC. One major impulse animating such video activists was the notion of countersurveillance, whereby the DIY strategy of video allowed them to produce images about, by, and for the movement while simultaneously turning their gaze back at the dominant culture. In turn, members of DIVA TV became cultural archivists of the movement, while also circulating images that did not polish, streamline, or censor a fight that was, for many, traumatic and messy.

The DIY attitude undergirding DIVA TV's video activism grew from criticism after a demonstration against the Federal Drug Administration on October 11, 1988, where fellow activists claimed that the media makers involved with ACT UP were just "MTV activists," an insult meant to undermine stylized video activism as superfluous to the more politically efficacious form of direct action. As a result, DIVA TV members such as Gregg Bordowitz, Catherine Gund Saalfield, and Navarro reworked the term "MTV activist," adjusting the acronym to affirm that, in fact, they were "More Than a Virus" activists, since it was more than a virus that was killing them and their friends. DIVA TV strategically recalibrated a response to HIV/AIDS that underscored the ways cultural media, popular rhetoric, and uncritical representations of those who were affected by the virus all fostered the spread of HIV/AIDS. By placing the emphasis on media and culture, DIVA TV demonstrated how images are transformed into stories and how stories are always mediated and thus possess the capacity to be manipulated, altered, and reused. The end result was a mode of activism that made video performative; DIVA TV's work not only represented what was happening but actively spurred others to question the status quo and to act.

This was often achieved through comedic, sometimes campy devices or simply by reflecting and redefining popular culture as dictated by commercial giants such as MTV. Take, for example, the redeployment of Madonna's popular 1989 song "Like a Prayer" as the title of DIVA TV's video documenting the major direct-action protest "Stop the Church" on December 10 of that same year (figure 3.1). The radical promise of such video activism, enabled by the commercial release of affordable handheld cameras in the late 1980s, was that anyone could do it, and so DIVA TV printed and disseminated "Make Your Own Press Pass" fliers that carried instructions on how to produce fraudulent credentials and thus attain the event and institutional access of mainstream media journalists (figure 3.2).[32] DIVA TV's stylized mode of countersurveillance

Figure 3.1. Video still from DIVA TV's "Like a Prayer," featuring Navarro as Jesus Christ (1989).

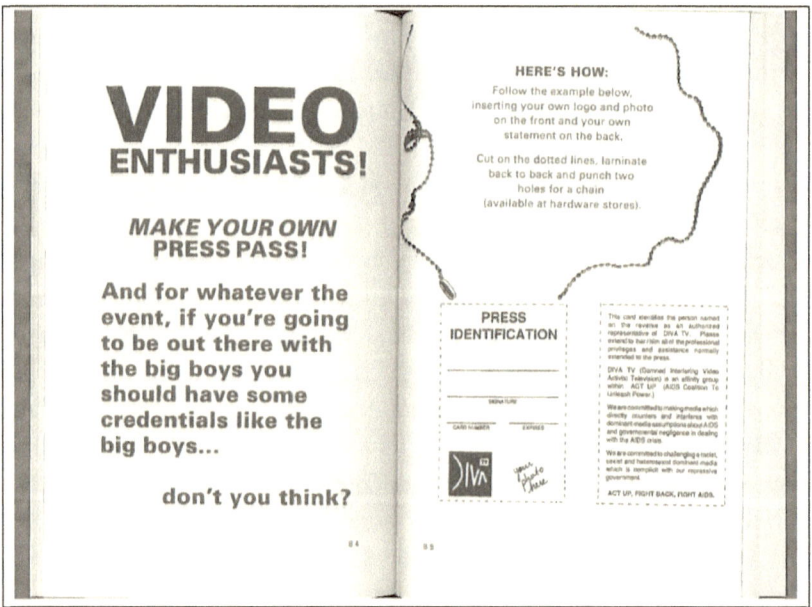

Figure 3.2. Sample of DIVA TV DIY press pass.

differed from that of the polished ACT UP media crew (composed mostly of white men), who were granted access to high-level meetings and negotiations.

Navarro's own documentary style was heavily influenced by his work with DIVA TV. Even after going blind and deaf as a result of AIDS-related cryptococcal meningitis, Navarro continued making video diaries with the help of his mother and friends.[33] By then, most were staged in his room in St. Vincent's Hospital in Greenwich Village, at times an epicenter for the disease in New York City, with over one hundred thousand patients treated at the hospital during the epidemic. One of Navarro's autodocumentary scenes, which David France incorporated in the middle of *How to Survive a Plague*, his 2012 film on the early years of the epidemic, shows Navarro seated in a hospital gown, evincing confusion about whether the camera is even shooting. With the help of his mother, Patricia Navarro, herself a former activist in the Chicano movement of 1970s Los Angeles, Ray Navarro begins to describe his poignant desire to travel to St. Vincent's tenth floor to see the sun. "No one had ever explained to me that there was going to be light again in the world, and that the whole world wasn't going to be dark," he says. Amid visual cuts from Navarro's hospital room to the hallway of the tenth floor and back to the hospital room, Navarro's voice-over suggests that generational challenges punctuate one's life, such that the AIDS epidemic "is the challenge that has been placed in front of [him]" in his twenties. The diaristic tone of Navarro's narration culminates in a seemingly playful remark—"and who knows, little camera?"—after which emerges, cheek by jowl, a verbal expression of hope and a visage of disappointment: "a lot of blind and deaf men have lived happy lives," he ventures. The incongruity of Navarro's affect with this ambivalent hope registers in his use of the present perfect tense ("men have lived"). The artist's heavy reminder posits the question, What happens between hope and disappointment? That is, what *frames* hope and disappointment's perceived difference and cohabitation?

Navarro's mother hovers around the visual frame of the camera, often breaking into it to talk to her son (figure 3.3). This scene suggests something other than an Oedipal narrative when we consider, through the juxtaposition of Navarro's and his mother's bodies, overlaps and differences between Patricia's history with the Chicano movement of the 1970s

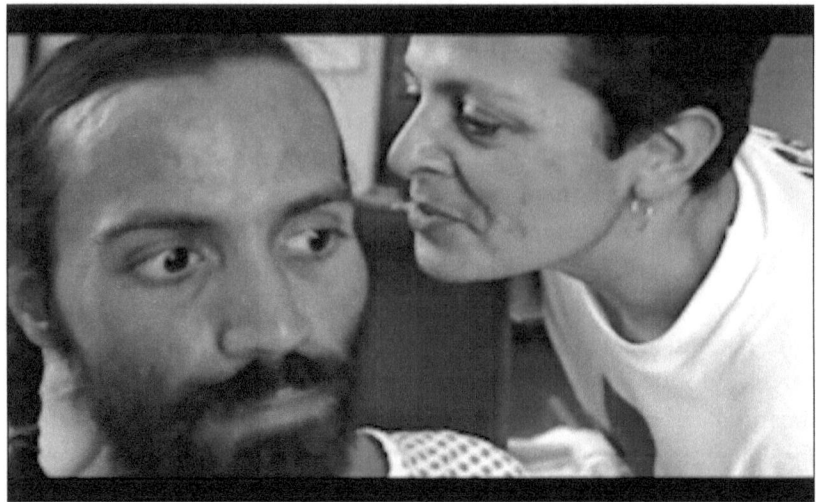

Figure 3.3. Patricia Navarro breaks the visual frame to talk to her son, Ray Navarro, who is becoming deaf. Still from *How to Survive a Plague* (dir. David France, 2012).

and Ray's involvement in AIDS activism with ACT UP and DIVA TV in the late '80s. Patricia's activism called into question a certain framing of Chicano politics that foregrounded themes such as the Chicano family, the importance of labor, and regional and folkloric representations of Chicano history and art. These emphases at times centered the modern Chicano man as key to Chicanismo's legibility. Patricia's appearance in the frame of her son's documentary can be seen to underscore Maylei Blackwell's important reminder that "women were there, too," in the fight for racial and economic justice for Chicanos in the US Southwest and abroad.[34] This feminist undercurrent of the Chicano movement, its Chicana power if you will, is embodied by Patricia, who stands next to her young though physically deteriorating son with AIDS. Patricia does not perform the role of an abundant, supple maternal figure endlessly attending the child in need. Rather, her presence, as a metonym for the unsung gendered consciousness of the Chicano movement, performs an uncanny double to Ray's telling of a neglected, racialized version of AIDS history and thus further politicizes Ray's ambivalence about the past and future, captured in his seemingly flippant remark, "who knows, little camera?"

In a short introductory essay framing a 1990 art exhibition on HIV/AIDS titled *An Army of Lovers: Combatting AIDS, Homophobia, and Censorship*, which Navarro helped to curate, he writes,

> At any rate there is a force within society that cannot be contained. Call it queer theory. Clearly, no one could predict the visual representation of this theory. To maintain that this theory still exists in the modern world, one could only be certain that it [does] not appear in the classical form. Many of these artist[s'] works are not used to being in the gallery context—they are usually on TV, outdoors, being mailed, miniaturized, or just given away. The works seem somewhat resigned, *spread out* like reluctant objects across the plane of the wall—sterilized and punctured—in an attempt to visualize the true situation in which we find ourselves. *The significance of this exhibition is that art cannot be contained precisely to the extent to which the queer community is under siege.* [Art] bursts forth from the edges of its frames and through the gallery doors seeking liberation. It does more than illustrate the crisis, it actually *is* the crisis.[35]

In this short piece of writing, Navarro offers us a way to see the structural impossibility of the frame to contain the aesthetic intensity that he understands as queer art. However, toward the end of the quote, the reader may surmise that Navarro foregrounds the art in the exhibition metonymically for queer theory and *not* as representing queer theory per se. When queer theory comes into contact with visual forms of representation, not knowing in advance what that encounter should look like becomes necessary for understanding its political potential as "[bursting] forth from the edges of its frames . . . seeking liberation." In this way, the impossibility of figuring the force of queer theory, which the art in the exhibition performs for Navarro, persists beyond any intention to "illustrate the crisis," since queer theory becomes the very ontological ground for the crisis itself: "it actually *is* the crisis." This is why Lugones is right to point to Hames-García's "questions of ontological commitment" concerning queer theory, which ultimately leads him to correctly charge queer theory with performing an "ontological denial" of race. With Hames-García in mind alongside Navarro's idea of an uncontainable queer theory breaking forth from the frame *as* crisis, we might imagine this crisis to be the sublimated force of a disavowed racial history of the epidemic. This sublimated "anonymous root of racial identity," to use Joan Copjec's turn of phrase, opaquely grounds the crisis that is queer theory.[36] For Navarro, queer is performative and active, not static, and in this way cannot be fully apprehended in advance by positivist forms of knowledge. This might be frustrating from the position of a postpositivist realist, but, as Navarro reminds us, an impossibility exists here precisely because "the queer community is under siege."

The migratory impulse guiding queer theory, a force highly performative in that it actively seeks liberation from epistemological certitude, also draws attention to Navarro's use of television's broadcasting capacities. Navarro's video activism demonstrates that the crisis of HIV/AIDS is less about the event of the disease and more about the circuits and transmission of racialized and queer modes of sensing the finite materiality of everyday life. Navarro's work shows us how queer Chicanos' violations of (implicitly white) framings of the AIDS epidemic were not only about questioning what gets to be represented within them. Instead, these works suspend and expose the aesthetic frame as a structure of ambivalence that fails to exclude/include ethnic-racial representations of AIDS, regardless of its avowal or denial of racial identity.

In the scene previously discussed from *How to Survive a Plague*, Navarro stages an encounter structured by ambivalence when he stares into the camera, his gaze reflected in both the lens and the viewer.[37] Ambivalence here is read as an interrelation, however tenuous, between the inner life of the Chicano body with AIDS and the social external world engendering such a body. Ambivalence becomes a stylistic construction when Navarro cunningly addresses the inanimate object of the camcorder as a "little camera," endowing it with the capacity for subjective response. Navarro questions the boundaries between object and subject, both by suspending the epistemic demand to know ("who knows") and by disclosing the difference between his own animated, sentimental Chicano body with AIDS and the inanimate video camera that frames, captures, and exposes it. At the same time, by fantasizing about the camera-object as an interlocutor sensitive to both sound and image, Navarro ironically foils his own body's sensory deterioration. The double exposure of Navarro's body to both the deadly virus and the camera's frame foregrounds the inanimacy *within* Navarro: an embodied form of death interior to the body *living* with HIV/AIDS and the cause of his own desire.

## More than a City of Angels: Gil Cuadros's *City of God*

By the time of Navarro's death from AIDS-related illness in November 1990—the same year Callen published *Surviving AIDS*—the queer Chicano writer Gil Cuadros was developing his own literary mode of stylized ambivalence with respect to Chicano identity and the experience of surviving AIDS in Los Angeles. Reading it alongside Navarro's video activism, I argue that Cuadros's writing deploys a televisual aesthetic specifically at moments when Chicano identity grates against the cause of desire, otherwise thought as the embodiment of inanimacy, such as discussed earlier regarding Navarro. In what follows, we will see how Cuadros interinanimates the literary and the televisual to stage a larger, equivocal relationship between the AIDS epidemic and the literary figure of the Chicano body approaching death. After engaging the scarce yet emerging scholarship on the writings of Gil Cuadros, I proceed to closely read two of his short stories to foreground how Cuadros's (literary) body with HIV/AIDS performs the frame that separates the Chicano sexual mainstream from the fantasy of the white AIDS victim.

The impact of the AIDS epidemic on people of color presents a challenge to scholarship committed to dualistic thought. For one, rhetoric of the "passive" receiver of HIV and the agential activist who fights on behalf of those who are infected with the virus structures much of the history of the epidemic, positioning some bodies, particularly racialized bodies, as either victims or transmitters of the disease. A different approach is required if one tries to reach for something unarticulated within the historical narratives of AIDS and its oft-occluded relation to ethnic-racial difference. Literature and the aesthetic realm more broadly allow for a glimpse into how the disavowal of ethnic-racial difference comes to ontologically ground the structure of AIDS narratives and their often-white cultural imprints. Cuadros's AIDS testimonial does not simply attempt to include what is excluded in dominant narratives of living with AIDS (such as the ones we find in the unconsciously whitewashed activism of *How to Survive a Plague*). Instead, I argue, it deploys aesthetic strategies of ambivalence to undermine the very polarity of exclusion/inclusion that such a corrective project of representation would reinforce. Ultimately, I show how Cuadros reconfigures (ethnic-racialized) death as the dispersal of the body into the world in the form of passionate sensuousness, rather than the body's finitude.

Cuadros was a queer Chicano living in Los Angeles until his death from AIDS complications in 1996 at the age of thirty-four. His writing is the first of its kind to explore the impact of AIDS on the gay Chicano community, yet only a handful of scholars have addressed the importance of Cuadros's work on the history of AIDS and Chicano sexual politics.[38] Though he published some short stories and poems in volumes such as *Indivisible: New Short Fiction by West Coast Gay and Lesbian Writers* (1991), *High Risk 2: Writings on Sex, Death, and Subversion* (1994), and *Blood Whispers: L.A. Writers on AIDS*, volume 1 (1994), Cuadros's only published full-length work of fiction, *City of God* (1994), gives us the most compelling glimpse into the material effects of AIDS on the racialized Chicano body.[39]

Notions of death, home, sex, and the mystical operate as themes in Cuadros's writing. Unlike other accounts of AIDS that hover around identifiable feelings, such as Douglas Crimp's militancy and melancholia, Leo Bersani's nihilism, or Lee Edelman's purported antirelationality, Cuadros's writing is permeated by ambivalence, leaving the reader in a hazy realm that renders these themes unknowable to one another.[40] In Cuadros's short story "My Aztlán: White Place," he presents us with a gritty version of Aztlán, the mystical homeland for Chicanos. The story's sick, gay Chicano narrator, a loosely autobiographical avatar for Cuadros himself, recalls the house where he was born, which is "now plowed under" the San Bernardino freeway near Montebello, as "the closest [he] can get to Mecca." Home is deferred, and through the imagery of burial and concealment, "home" figures below history, culture, and family, where language is brought to the threshold of meaning: "Like the house these words spiral in on themselves, stab into the moist earth and rot; the words eat their own."[41] This flushing of meaning mirrors the following image of the speaker: after enacting revenge on his parents "like a disease-ridden blanket," he runs to the toilet to vomit an empty AZT shell that then floats like an evacuated yet (en)capsulated promised futurity of a white place: "another set of pills, what some people call hope."[42]

Cuadros's story performs the dizzying and insecure position of Aztlán for the Chicano imaginary. Yet Cuadros's Aztlán is less myth than the dark reality of living in AZT-land as a gay Chicano with AIDS, an Aztlán that "floats on the water's tension, circles the bowl and disappears."[43] The vertiginous imagery of language eating itself is crucial for Cuadros and suggests inevitable betrayal by the source of knowledge, that fallacy of origin we can call home. The paradox that Cuadros's character confronts in this story lies in this cannibalistic quality of language, which obstructs any communication of meaning, and yet the necessity of writing the experience of living with HIV/AIDS forces the writer to confront language's constitutive betrayal. Cuadros's literary corpus comes to reflect the writer's own corporeality and its atrophying capacity for expression.

The ambivalence of Cuadros's writerly tone surfaces in the grating tensions that the literary figure of a gay Chicano living with AIDS performs. For example, the Latino literature scholar Paul Allatson argues that Cuadros's "autobiographically modulated pieces" in *City of God* emerge as a "textual site for a struggle between mutually affective, and potentially conflictive, identificatory positions."[44] Allatson goes on to argue that Cuadros underscores the mutual entanglement between "Chicano" and "queer" in an effort to disarm and reconfigure "signifying processes and their potential to wreak physical and psychic damage on the Chicano queer subject living with HIV/AIDS."[45] Allatson ends by contending that it was Cuadros's material body that became the "textualized battleground" for "competing graphic modes: Chicanismo and Chicano family patriarchy, Roman Catholicism, white gay exoticization of the 'brown' body, the pathologizing discourse of AIDS, and the power of nation-border logics to produce 'aliens.'"[46]

Meanwhile, the Chicano literary scholar Rafael Pérez-Torres argues that because of these grating identificatory processes inscribed on the queer Chicano body living with and dying from AIDS, Cuadros deliberately refrains from giving voice to the very social transformations that might make possible a place and home for the queer Chicano subject.[47] Like Allatson and Pérez-Torres, Raul Villa understands Cuadros's characters as "doubly displaced."[48] Other scholars such as Julie Minich in her generative essay "Aztlán Unprotected: Reading Gil Cuadros in the Aftermath of HIV/AIDS" argues against reading Cuadros as ambivalently articulating a lost sense of place and home in an AIDS-inflected Los

Angeles. Instead, Minich reads *City of God* as registering "its characters' search for health care and sexual access in a hostile social environment," which in effect reframes Cuadros as actively "claiming space within Mexican and Gay Los Angeles."⁴⁹

Marissa K. López takes an interesting and different approach in *Racial Immanence*, where she makes a larger claim about the limits of Chicano representational practices. López reads Cuadros's writings on HIV/AIDS not as a racial allegory but rather as embodying the chemical process of a wild Mexican yam, *barbasco*. Both espouse a nonreproductive sexuality that shatters any attempt at representing human experience. This innovative reading undergirds López's larger argument that literature does not just represent but can actively create the social world, "iteratively through a recursive return to roots."⁵⁰ By "roots," the author means organic things like *barbasco* and the real, natural world that she argues Cuadros's texts perform a "nostalgic longing for."⁵¹

Considering these incredibly significant contributions to scholarship on Cuadros and HIV/AIDS in Chicano/Latino cultural production, it would seem that the (un)attainable task of finding a "home" for the queer Chicano body with AIDS, which Cuadros's literature symbolizes, plays out in processes of identification "within Mexican and Gay Los Angeles." Such an understanding imagines the Chicano body only as an ethnic-racialized social construction (via access to health care, colorism, and geography) that Cuadros is then able to holistically "represent" through the literary frame. Except in López's interpretation, representation remains central to these scholarly arguments. López gets us to the "racial immanence" that the text performs, and I agree with López to the extent that Cuadros's text indeed longs, not for home *and* nature but for something inarticulable and incommensurate with experience. Thus, I would like to build on these conversations by investigating how the body performs other than as a "textualized battleground" for identificatory processes that come to inform quests for social justice or a return to land/place. Rather, I foreground corporeality as given at the moment the aesthetic realm comes to frame the political itself. This mode of reading allows us, on the one hand, to ask what happens between the body and its image while, on the other hand, outlining a nuanced understanding of how queer latinidad as a social phenomenon and a performative problem emerges at the intersection of the aesthetic and the political. Cuadros reworks the frame and makes the frame labor by foregrounding an ethnic-racialized corporeality of HIV/AIDS deeply rooted in the incongruency between finitude and memory, for "as long as there is something like experience, it is not entirely mine."[52]

Meanwhile, the dominant posture in some queer theory conceives of the body with HIV/AIDS as the abject result of same-sex intercourse, or as harboring the "pleasure of self-shattering" and thus forgoing the social.[53] Cuadros shows how AIDS is *not* the final mark on the queer Chicano body. Instead, the corporeal effects of AIDS undo the body as a set of discursive knots into a looser and dispersed mode of being, a self-shattering exposing the very sharing-out of that which cannot be contained. I am suggesting that readers of Cuadros attend closely to the mechanism by which experience is transformed into a sense, which expands out, not only as an indication of subjectivity, identity, or other products of history or discourse but also as a mode of apprehending the *mere* appearance of ethnic-racialized desire. In Cuadros's writing, these aberrant visual traces of the body resemble the residual glow of a televisual aesthetic and its indexing of what I discuss as nonsubjective memory.

\* \* \*

The first half of *City of God* contains nine semiautobiographical short stories loosely structured around the life of Gil Cuadros. The first three, "Indulgences," "Reynaldo," and "Chivalry," deal with themes of the Chicano family and growing up queer in Los Angeles. The following three stories, "My Aztlán: White Place," "Unprotected," and "Holy," describe the narrator's sexual encounters with men (particularly white men who fetishize brown men), the narrator's eventual contraction of HIV, and his subsequent life with AIDS. The last three stories, "Baptism," "Letting Go," and "Sight," shift in tone, largely because of their explicit concern with death and the atrophying Chicano body. I would like here to look at the last two short stories, wherein we begin to get a sense of how the text performs a very textured relation to material finitude and sense. Though literary in form, this textual relation to finitude also resonates with the televisual aesthetic we saw in Navarro's camcorder scene described earlier.

Cuadros's story "Letting Go" begins with the narrator dressed in all white and standing at the threshold between ocean and land, where, to his astonishment, he is suddenly holding a "thick sea-worthy rope woven of twine," with the other end tied to his ex-lover's foot. They have not had sex in over a year because of the ex-lover's "condition," which we infer is his HIV infection. The speaker's new lover, Rudy, a gorgeous model-like boy wearing shiny trunks that read "Versace," as if to certify his boyish charm, begs the narrator for sex, since he too has not had sex in over a year. We are presented with a triangulated field of desire whereby the reader gets the sense that the speaker is torn between his two lovers. As the speaker attempts to hold and manage the slicing twine, these two grating sexual desires produce a tension that becomes manifest as hemorrhaging wounds on the narrator's hand. Rudy attempts to coax the narrator to let go by offering to bandage his bruised hand. Before the narrator breaks into anger and resentment, priests appear with "lesions cover[ing] what little flesh is exposed." One priest exclaims, "Son, it is time to let go, last rites, you need to live in the city of God." The priests gives the three men trinkets that Rudy then buries in the sand. These surreal images evince a derangement of the senses that eventually culminates in the following televisual moment of the short story:

> I look where I believe the artifacts are buried and can see the sand rises in little dunes. I notice a head growing out of the sand, a young woman with long, black hair. My mother at sixteen. A young man follows her, reaches to hold her hand. By that simple touch, magic, I see her belly swell. There is pain in her eyes, regret for being so young. When I am born, my father dances with me in his arms, drunk. *I smell his love.* My mother pulls me away from him. He begins to strangle her, she won't leave. I want to ask her why, she slaps me. My neck feels broken and she continues to hit me. I grab her hand. I am now grown, masturbating every day in the bathroom, letting the water run to cover the sound. My mother is afraid of what I can do to her. I am sure of my strength, my ability to break her arm. That's when she tells me what a handsome boy I've become. My father turns his back on us, the muscles in his back are knotted. All he says is, "Faggot." My mother wants to hit me but cannot bring herself to do it. I see myself walk away from them alone.[54]

This peculiar paragraph breaks from the rest of the short story in multiple ways, including tone, style, and imagery. But most interesting for this section's discussion of the frame is the paragraph's drastic and uncanny shift in speed. The narration suddenly moves quickly, yet with a slight stutter, punctuating images of lost maternity, heterosexual coupling, the church, reproduction, misogyny, youthful eroticism, homophobia, and alienation, all of which are situations, images, and experiences of life.

This fantastical scene's obvious Oedipal narrative appears to mirror the triangulated same-sex desire between the narrator and his two lovers. That is to say, Cuadros stages in this scene the drama of triangulated framing—"my mother pulls me away from him"—embodied in and performed through the gay Chicano, a figure composed of "mother," "me," and "him." But somehow the tension and speed of Cuadros's prose contradict the promise of harmonious mediation, where the normative Mother/Father dyad might cohere into the birth of a synthesized Chicano subject: "A young man follows her, reaches to hold her hand. By that simple touch, magic, I see her belly swell." If there is a televisual aesthetic at play in this scene, who is the implied viewer?

Attending closely to Cuadros's stuttering prose, one realizes that the speaker is split into two positions, *watching himself* as these scenes unfold. Cuadros's story foregrounds the family drama in Chicano cultural production. But most Chicano scholarship, however unconsciously, relies on and reifies the Oedipal frame in order to construct a notion of family that either homophobically enacts uplift ideologies of respectability or couches a "queer Aztlán" in a landscape of resentment. The state becomes the reason for the cut corner in the former, whereas activism and recovery are the "solutions" for the corner's absence in the latter. *Dissatisfactions* has been attempting to illuminate the middle range between these opposing choices.

As in "My Aztlán: White Place," the sequence of the dream-like images in "Letting Go" is activated by a gesture of burying and covering something over (the trinkets), as if to countervail unconscious pangs of betrayal, illustrated by the narrator's memory of his father calling him "faggot" or his mother's being "afraid of what [her son] can do to her." Such dynamics indicate how the Chicano family homophobically hails the queer Chicano body while recoiling from it. In this scene, however, the speaker is forced to internalize *the cut corner of the frame*, the vectors of desire knotted like "the muscles in [his father's] back" that paradoxically come to frame the Oedipal narrative. Yet, as it turns out, the analytic structure between utterance and action stages the provisional singularity of a body fully "sure of [its] strength" against the background of its own difference, "alone" and *without* a frame of reference, which is to say, as the very crisis of reference itself—its orphanic function. This internalization is one of inscrutability and ambivalence insofar as it blurs the delineation between form and content, on the one hand, and calls attention to the narrative frame at the expense of content, on the other.

We can think about Cuadros's insistence on the televisual as a way to escape dominant frames of knowledge production such as the Oedipal narrative. Aesthetically, this scene performs the mundane act of channel surfing, which by the late 1980s and '90s structures a wider disenchantment with Reagan's individuating America. We can imagine a less activism-inclined Navarro sitting at home, clicking a remote, and finding images that speak to the plight of people suffering and living with AIDS, or a Cuadros, alienated in his room as a young boy, searching for a televisual snapshot of a desire unsanctioned by the Chicano family. Such speculative scenes manifest themselves in the lapses in Cuadros's rapid sequence of images. The strobing intensities of the televisual, interrupting the darkness of a room in which one aimlessly flips through channels, come to structure the choppy flow of Cuadros's narrative voice. The televisual makes visible the structure of ambivalence suturing the Oedipal desire to cut its fourth corner, a suturing that happens within the narrator and within the attuned reader.

Yet I invoke this scene in "Letting Go" for a second reason: it allows us to let go, as it were, of the fantasy of the agential Chicano subject. Readers of Cuadros's writing must attune themselves to his act of suspension, or what Barbara Johnson calls the "textual drifting" of the frame, which unfolds as the "remarkable ellipses" between these images.[55] The scene's vertiginous *mise en abyme* structure forgoes any possibility of analytic mastery over the representative function of the gay Chicano with AIDS. One is tempted to read these images—the father's turned back, knotted with muscles; his uttering "Faggot"; the fearful and vengeful mother—as representing social relations of systemic violence like homophobia and misogyny. However, the "impotence" of such a reading (to echo Wendy Brown from earlier in the chapter) arises at the intervallic jolt between the fading in and fading out of the story's images. The dissolve between images, which the speaker witnesses and the reader experiences, draws attention to the narrative function of suspension. I want to argue against the presumption that this interrupted sequence, which resembles the well-known convention of "your life flashing before your eyes," illustrates a subjective, relational scene filled with moments of identification, however desirable this reading may be. Instead, the passage's performative breaks, which we hear mostly in the sequencing of first-person pronouns "I" or "my," interfere with any attempt to impose a narrative flow on this collection of memories. Where perhaps the reader is tempted to project a narrative (maybe an Oedipal one), the text resists the reader's attempts to stitch together its fragments. The speed is too fast; the flow is too intense for a triangulated field of relation to emerge uncompromised.

The scene's disruptions effect a turbulent testimonial style evidenced in repeating, flashing moments of recognition, which are dependent on a certain mode of misrecognition. We can look back to the video scene in which Navarro breaks the frame by exposing it and, in so doing, also calls attention to the fraught relation between exposure and blindness. Cuadros's own televisual prose aligns the two cultural producers in their drive to trace and mobilize the aesthetic ambivalence of the (dis)figured gay Chicano with AIDS. In Cuadros's disjunctive passage, the reader asks themselves, What happened between one scene and the next? How did we end up here? What was left out or forgotten? The repetitive function of this paragraph *suspends* linkages between the images. In short, the narrator's active suspension of connectivity displaces the agential Chicano subject while foregrounding the work that the frame performs.[56]

This is perhaps why the closing short story of *City of God* ends in darkness, almost as if to linger in the nonsubjective break between the images in "Letting Go." "Sight" tells the poignant story of a man, the narrator, going blind from AIDS complications. Curiously, at the doctor's office, where the narrator realizes he can no longer make out the words on a page, he begins to "see that everything, everyone in her office has a glow around their bodies, some with colors more distinct, others thin and wavering."[57] The apparent contradiction between going blind and being able to see things that are not usually seen again demonstrates Cuadros's dispersive understanding of finitude. Death is not equated with the depletion or evacuation of sense but rather with an altered vision that allows for a different account of the sensible (to paraphrase another late queer poet).[58] Cuadros writes, "My peripheral vision diminishes, the crest of my forehead, the crown of my head seems to ignite. My other senses revel in new-found power, guiding me through a maze of streets, using the scent of jacarandas and freshly cut, large-leaf philodendrons, the feel of the bumps on the road, the dampness along my arms that means I've come into my underground parking space."[59] In this way, a heightened perception activated by the very loss of visual faculties of recognition enables the speaker to navigate a familiar world made all the more familiar with a difference: "The dampness along my arms that means I've come into my underground parking space."

What I have been attempting to sketch thus far is another level on which to think of a dissatisfied ethnic-racialized body with AIDS, articulated in the suspension of knowledge and representation. Suspension has as much to do with the mechanisms of ethnic-racial difference and their relation to the structure of AIDS as does any serious history of its cultural impact. Exposure's remarkable capacity to disclose and yet withhold, through blotting out and saturating an object with too much knowledge, rhetorically drives the narrative of Cuadros's stories and constitutes their particular ambivalent aesthetic.

"Sight" ends like this: "I have come to the end, thoughts of the world seem woven of thread, thinly disguised, a veil. I let the angels consume me, each one biting into my body, until nothing is left, nothing but a small glow and even that begins to perish."[60] As the small glow begins to perish, a televisual aesthetic serves as a reminder of the overexposure to violence and oppressive systems that queer people of color endure, specifically the exposure of Cuadros's brown body to the virus and his underexposure to effective treatment. The too-quick speed that pulled his body toward death is heard within the stutters and fissures of meaning in *City of God*. It is for this reason that the reader is *with* the narrator when he says that his "bones shine in the dark," since his writing pulls us to imagine ways to see the unseen and to feel it differently so that we may come to know our relations to the world and each other otherwise.

## Desiring in the Dark

What Cuadros leaves us with in "Sight" is a method by which to ambivalently read interracial desire without the metaphor of disease and infection. In "My Aztlán: White Place," interracial desire is manifest as an internalized vector of identification, troubling the coherence of the Chicano body with AIDS within a confusing and precarious social world that desires its premature death. The short story opens with the speaker's description of his venture into West Hollywood, a destination for men cruising for gay sex:

> I am stinking drunk, driving down the wrong freeway back to my place. My eyes, which are getting bad, now blur the large green exit signs, reflective dots that spell City Terrace Drive. Hours in Rage, Revolver, Motherlode, and Mickey's have made me wish for my childhood home. I don't know why I am attracted to those West Hollywood bar types—blond hair, blue eyes—who twist my gold chain with a wedding ring on it. Their fingers are pale compared to my darker skin. They run them down my neck, under my lapel. They ask where I am from, disappointed at my answer, as if *they* are the natives.[61]

In this opening scene, we are introduced to a speaker inundated with inebriated perceptions. His intoxication only amplifies the incapacity of his eyes, "which are getting bad" due to the disease. The speaker's eyes, seemingly failing or inoperative, "blur" direction and location, leaving him vulnerable to his drive to find his "childhood home" in "West Hollywood bar types." The racial markings of blond hair and blue eyes do more than just contrast the speaker's skin tone. The question of belonging emerges through the affective vehicle of the speaker's disappointment, wherein white men who have sex with (brown) men displace the speaker from his mythical homeland of Aztlán, "as if *they* are the natives."

However, the text performs a double displacement. Neither the blond-haired, blue-eyed men nor the "darker skin[ned]" bodies in an AIDS-inflected Los Angeles *belong* anywhere. On the level of interracial desire, the act of "driving down the wrong freeway back [home]" showcases the speaker's drive toward difference and estrangement from oneself. The speaker's ambivalent desire for white "dick" clogs his perception, thereby confusing the relationship between cause and effect and complicating any wish to maintain a unidirectional mode of desiring another. Did the speaker end up in West Hollywood because he by happenstance took the wrong freeway, or did he desire to end up in West Hollywood to get his gold chain twisted by the same consuming (white) bodies who cause him to get "stinking drunk"? These contradictory ligaments of desire entangle themselves in the minute gesture of white men twisting the speaker's gold chain with their pale fingers, an act of (mis)recognition, almost as if to communicate, "Why are you confused that you are here, since we all know where we are?" Yet this tacit locus of desire never materializes in the text; instead, it registers as a shared moment of collective disappointment.

This baneful disappointment calls on, once again, a family romance that is never really about the family to begin with. When the disoriented speaker confronts his disappointed mother, blabbering on about his childhood home, she dismisses him, blaming the virus for his "ramble" and thus his longing to belong. The narrative of the short story personifies the virus as the very impossibility of communication between the Chicana mother and her son, a son longing for home and a mother confused and threatened by his guilty desire for *his* own Aztlán, a white place: "She questions me about what my doctor has said, ignores my response when I say I'm just lonely. She doesn't want to think about the white man who infected me. 'He might as well have shot you,' she said once. My mother let me know that she turns in her sleep, sick at the thought of his dick up my ass or in my mouth. A milky white fluid floats in my body's space, breaks into the secret bonding of her sex, my father's sex, and the marriage of the cells."[62] Interracial desire floats and fails to socially mix like the image of milky white fluid of infected semen. The rupture of familial lineage, embodied by the figure of the homosexual's vexed relationship to reproductive inheritance, makes fatal the act of interracial desire, here particularly a queer Chicano's desire for whiteness. For the speaker's mother, and implicitly for the speaker's own conflicted consciousness, to desire whiteness is to desire death: "He might as well have shot you." And this existential problem structuring the sense of feeling alone is figured in the presence of the Chicana mother, who effectively embodies the speaker's own ambivalence toward himself. But at the same time, the existential paradox of searching for intimacy in the vicinity of death need not equate easily to a nihilistic understanding of desire, however seductive the antirelational paradigm may seem for disparaged (homophobic) Chicana mothers and disaffected white gay men desiring brown boys alike. Desiring whiteness is also to desire a relation to death, which might be finding pleasure, if only momentarily, in the internal contradiction of the speaker's perverse relationship to *being* a brown object of desire in West Hollywood, where "they said stuff like, 'Hot latin, brown-skinned, warm, exotic, dark, dark, dark,' buried under their bodies' weight, dirt and asphalt, moist skin, muscle and blood": "I beat off to their memories."[63] The obfuscatory trajectories of desiring whiteness leave a queer Chicano body with AIDS textually suspended, longing to find meaning, a condition reflected by the failure of the poetic prose of "My Aztlán: White Place" to actually name and give a place, a home, to its speaker, whether it be West Hollywood, East Los Angeles, or even in death: "I can feel my body becoming tar, limbs divided, north and south."[64] The coordinates of west, east, north, and south foreground the literary frame's ability to divide and confuse hope, which culminates in the speaker's whisper in the story's last paragraph: "My belief, when my skin is oiled up, is that I won't be in so much pain afterwards.... I will come home."[65]

And yet West Hollywood is hardly home for anyone living with HIV/AIDS during the epidemic. Populated at this historical juncture by middle-class white men cruising brown and Black bodies that come from South or East Los Angeles looking for interracial sex, the neighborhood occupies a contentious space within the history of HIV/AIDS. In fact, in an interview with the AIDS historian Sarah Schulman, Patricia Navarro, Ray Navarro's mother, speculates about *where* Navarro might have contracted HIV:

SARAH SCHULMAN: Now did he join ACT UP before he realized he was infected, or after?
PATRICIA NAVARRO: He didn't know he was infected until after [his lover] Anthony got sick in June of 1988.
SS: Okay. So, he was already in ACT UP, right?
PN: No.
SS: No?

PN: Around—I mean—first of all, *we don't know* when they got infected. He was probably infected when he was 15 years old, because he wasn't gay in Simi Valley; he was gay in West Hollywood.

SS: Right.

PN: Okay? That was the time, probably in 1986 and '87, he went to West Hollywood, and according to him, had as much sex as he could possibly want. And that's how he says he got infected.

SS: Okay.

PN: Unprotected sex, I should say.

SS: Right.

PN: So, he probably got infected then. He was not diagnosed with AIDS until January of 1990. But Anthony became ill first, because they went up to Montreal.[66]

Patricia cannot exactly pinpoint where or when Navarro might have contracted the virus, but we do know "he wasn't gay in Simi Valley; he was gay in West Hollywood." The cultural signifier of "gay" is reworked, in Patricia Navarro's recounting of her son's sexual history, from an identity marker into a performative force, an act that is constituted by, rather than represented by, a place. Simi Valley, where Navarro grew up and also the affluent city to which the O. J. Simpson trial was notoriously relocated, negates the act of being gay; instead, this identity emerges in the same place that Cuadros's speaker confusingly finds himself looking for sex. Like the speaker of "My Aztlán: White Place," Navarro found in West Hollywood "as much sex as he could possibly want." In his mother's reflection on or fantasy of her young and sexually promiscuous son, West Hollywood promises differing and abundant sexual encounters for young, queer Chicano men. But in the same breath, Patricia delivers the B-side to this narrative—that is, collective disappointment: "And that's how he says he got infected." Somehow the spectacle of revealing the origin story of when ("probably in 1986 and '87"), how ("Unprotected sex, I should say"), and where (not Simi Valley but maybe West Hollywood) one contracted HIV—a naggingly persistent pursuit that plagued most people who were (inter)personally affected by the virus—betrays the primary epistemic disturbance governing the ambivalent search for truth during the AIDS epidemic. As Patricia Navarro emphasizes, "first of all, *we don't know* when they got infected," because those who were infected early on generally could not possibly know with certitude, let alone what it could mean. Yet, sex figures as a dispersing force connecting all players in this drama around a shared disappointment with sputtering fantasies about penetration and infection.

Passionate Sensuousness

We have seen how a certain antagonism toward queer theory emerges in current Latino scholarship. This antagonism in return unearths the equivocal nature between representation and experience, especially since such ambiguity evidences the excessiveness of race/ethnicity, gender, ability, and class when framed by sexuality. However, Ray Navarro's anticipation of this critique at the height of the AIDS crisis is formalized in his ambivalent style. The artist's televisual aesthetic is a primary example of how this ambivalence is made into the material and visual ground for the debate about how to frame the queer Chicano (with AIDS) in the first place. Cuadros emphatically draws on a similar force in his literary writings, whereby ambivalence characterizes the very confusing road of desire and sensation, two important tropes that haunt the history of AIDS as it comes into opaque contact with the queer Chicano body. Therefore, I would like to conclude by rereading Hames-García's essay as a literary object in and of itself, one that performs a passionate sensuousness when framed by Cuadros's and Navarro's work. As a reader of theory after Navarro's protoqueer theory and Cuadros's ambivalence-ridden literature, I find (a shared) pleasure in Hames-García's extravagant passion, reaching out of its pages, as if with a desire to afflict his imagined reader. It is a passionate excess of something else, of something brown and of something queer.[67] Its anachronistic quality allows us to return to Marcuse once again, to find what was already there. In the passage from Marcuse that Hames-García deploys in order to discredit a certain genealogy of queer theory, the notion of critique that Marcuse sought is predicated on a wounded attachment to a new form of consumer capitalism. For Marcuse, to enact critique is to perform an affliction, to formalize the contradiction between an intensifying US consumer culture (more owning, more possessing, more consuming) and the need for recognition mediated by commodities (objects). Marcuse brings us back to the intricacies of the subject of desire caught in a web of capitalist reproduction, where one cannot ignore Marx's early humanism if they wanted to.

In Marx's critique of Hegel, he talks about the suffering of human beings:

> To say that man is a corporeal, living, real, sensuous, objective being with natural powers means that he *has* real, sensuous objects as the objects of his being and of his vital expression, or that he can only express his life in real sensuous objects. To be objective, natural and sensuous, and to *have* object nature and sense *outside* of oneself, or to be oneself object, nature and sense *for* a third person is *one and the same thing*. . . . To be sensuous is to suffer (to be *subjected* to actions of another). Man as an objective, sensuous being is therefore a suffering being, and because he *feels* his suffering, he is a passionate being.[68]

In this passage from his 1844 manuscripts, Marx elaborates on an early theory of alienated labor. His use of hyperbole, however, should not deter us from noting the possessive language at work here. A worker under capitalism, in all his vitality, relates to objects that express or are expressive of life in themselves; to exist under such conditions means to be in material relation within and without—"to *have* object nature and sense *outside* of oneself"—and to be both an individual and a member of society. Consequently, to possess an object means to be possessed by it. Objectively sensuous, modern man feels his suffering (the primary affective condition under capitalism) because he is a passionate, corporal being "subjected to the actions of another." And yet, in this dialectic, something hardens through the very claim to universality under the heading of "Man." Without saying too much about the obvious occlusion of chattel slavery, imperial genocidal expansion, and Marx's expulsion from France a year later in 1845, what these omissions animate is how the absolute nature of "Man" is one of lag, where corporeality is catching up to its suffering, running, as it were, behind the amorphous cloud of his own alienated desires. And yet even this young Hegelian's humanist drama is too much for a more mature, scientifically minded Marx, who will come to refashion this proposition when examining more closely the production and mystification of commodities in early capitalist economies, best exemplified in *Capital* and the *Grundrisse*.

Considering our discussion of Navarro and Cuadros, I offer this reflection: if we take the logic of Marx's passage seriously, the split between corporeal being and passionate being is, in one blow, ethnic-racial difference and sexual difference (slavery, dispossession, and Marx's later shattered utopian dreams all in one). By this, I mean the suffering subject, alienated from its labor in being subjected to the actions of another, finds itself entangled within the excluded vectors of ethnic-racialized sexuality, subjugation's disavowed though all the more material components. When suffering ends, which is to say when subjection ends, the "corporeal, living, real, sensuous, objective being" logically comes to a close. What remains after such closure, indeed what challenges the finitude of such ontological closure, is the life of the excluded elements of ethnic-racialized sexuality as such, much like the optical traces that Cuadros's speaker witnesses in "Sight." Or better yet, what remains after Man catches up to his suffering is the trace of his warped desires, warped, that is, through the prism of ethnic-racialized sexuality. One productive way to approach such a speculative argument is to reverse engineer its claim, by starting from the end. This provocation falls in line with other scholars of minoritarian aesthetics who seek to reframe the aesthetic as an excess of sensation. Amber J. Musser essentially translates Marx's passionate sensuousness into what she calls "brown jouissance." Brown jouissance, the "expressiveness of excess flesh" that Musser understands as the aesthetic, collapses the object/subject binary.[69] In so doing, the foreclosure to an origin of Being (the outside of Being and thus the end of suffering) and "abjection," "itself . . . a condition of foreclosure in relation to subjectivity," forwards the body as object and abject.[70] This excess, I suggest, indexes a failure in identity and suggests a latinidad operating as what Leticia Alvarado argues is an "abject otherness."[71] But latinidad's abjection does not have to be ugly, per se, but does shatter a sense of life in a subtler, more minor, and, as Musser would contend, more empathetic style.[72] Thus, in closing, I offer one last aesthetic example to help explicate the final major point of this chapter regarding passionate sensuousness and the ambivalent framing of the Chicano body with AIDS: the artist Laura Aguilar's altar to her close friend Gil Cuadros, titled *Gilbert's Altar* (2001).

The altar is displayed as a suitcase of ephemera, and one cannot ignore the Benjaminian overtones of a melancholic's flee from fatal despair. The suitcase's worn brown leather opens onto its internal, historical world. Petit fours of remembrance, the collected objects showcase a life lived in various modes: friendship (photographs of Aguilar and Cuadros posing by statues in a garden), activism (an image of ACT UP's Los Angeles chapter surrounded by Queer Nation buttons), writing (a photograph of Cuadros reading from *City of God*), sickness (a pill box shaped like a gingerbread man and filled with its own cocktail of medications), exuberance (a valentine from the cartoon *Captain Planet* reading, "You make this planet a better place," juxtaposed with a figurine from *A Nightmare before Christmas*), and faith (happy Buddha and guardian angel figurines). The most striking image in this assemblage is a centered black-and-white photograph of Cuadros on his deathbed, presumably having passed, which is animated by surrounding color photos of him posing and cooking. Aguilar's careful curation underscores for the observer how one is remembered in death by the objects and images left behind, scattered "capsules of desire" collected and displayed as an unveiling, open casket.[73] We witness through this artwork how the devastating blow of AIDS disperses the material remains of sexual and ethnic-racial difference, imagined as an interiority brought to the fore by a desire to share-out something incommensurable, something as brown as the leather case and as queer as the punctum of the altar, to which I now turn.

Roland Barthes described the punctum of a photograph as a wounding detail, the subjective relation of the photo-as-object to the viewer.[74] In the altar at hand, we find the punctum in a small photograph of Cuadros taken by Laura Aguilar. This queer photograph displays the *belle âme* in pure awe: an upward-oriented angle captures Cuadros in reverie, mouth agape, against a deep indigo background, surrounded by swirling pigments of color. Here, we witness a soul anticipating its dispersal amid the dream of its arrival, suitcase in hand; here exists a passionate sensuousness withdrawing into the altar and bursting forth from its frame. The altar's punctum interinanimates the other objects collected and re-membered in *Gilbert's Altar* and exemplifies the depressive anxiety of having to frame the queer Chicano body. As I have been arguing in this chapter, such a project betrays the very capacity of a frame to capture what it sets out to foreground.

Building on the work of the psychoanalyst R. D. Hinshelwood, Eve Sedgwick describes depressive anxiety as "the crucial element of mature relationships, the source of generous and altruistic feelings that are devoted to the well-being of the object."[75] Only through this position, according to Sedgwick, can one move toward assembling a sense of wholeness—a provisional assembly akin to that of an altar. However, this sense of wholeness does not signal a disavowal of loss but rather a working-through of such a loss, reparative to be sure. Yet, this project is never completed and in fact constitutively cannot be completed, because the work is done in excess, as the passage from Marx curiously underscores and which Cuadros demonstrates in both "Sight" and "Letting Go." This form of laboring and remembering in excess might rather be understood as a labor of *unforgetting*, a performance that "'carries' our dead with us."[76] The act signals an ontological failure of identities to ever contain all the feelings, histories, and knowings that afflict and pass through an "objective being." Most importantly, the altar-turned-aesthetic-object, framed in the display case in a gallery, collapses form and content in its very attempt to show and hold something incalculable and in excess of ownership.

In attuning to this excess, which I have been calling passionate sensuousness, in turn making ambivalent the frame's representational capacity, this chapter's aim has been to show how queerness is deeply shared and intimately relational, especially when one attempts to unforget a (tragic) loss. For if Nietzsche is correct in the epigraph of this chapter ("If something is to stay in the memory, it must be burned in: only that which never ceases to *hurt* stays in the memory"), then we must learn how to inhabit our internal gaps as a modality of never forgetting how to remember: "I beat off to their memories," writes Cuadros.[77] In this chapter, I have sought to read Hames-García's essay and Aguilar's altar as aesthetic objects that perform passionate sensuousness. These examples exceed the white normative demands to remain in *ressentiment* by putting pressure on the mark of loss and making it work, indeed, by coming to identify with this loss in remembrance.

Similarly, Cuadros and Navarro together articulate a dissatisfied style that deploys and negotiates the formality of the frame as a failed promise of partition. Their work both *inhabits* and *embodies* a split in

Latino identity, where formalized ambivalence registers discontent with the status quo and the desire to represent the Chicano body. The incongruities between blindness and insight, in the capacity to feel otherwise while one's survival is obstructed by a homophobic and racist world, require an analytic that does not determine what it seeks to find in advance. The project of representing and framing the Chicano body with AIDS, particularly for Cuadros and Navarro and for Aguilar in *Gilbert's Altar*, was one tethered to the insuperable obstacle of knowing what this body might signify for others. Therefore, in response to a key question posed at the beginning of this chapter—"How is it possible to know one's identity and to know those of others within a shifting terrain of relationality?"—Barbara Johnson gets us closest to the answer my analysis offers: "This story of the self's difference from others inevitably becomes the story of its own unbridgeable difference from itself. Difference is not engendered in the space between identities; it is what makes all totalization of the identity of a self or the meaning of a text impossible."[78] This impossibility configures Cuadros's and Navarro's ambivalent style, staging the "unbridgeable difference" within their work as the very ground for the project(ion) of their own remembrance. The frame makes palpable a struggle for attaining meaning and knowledge, whereby the *existence* of the gay Chicano with AIDS foregrounds the fallacy in distinguishing aesthetics from politics, content from form, thus calling us to remain in the dysphoria of our own desire to know latinidad.

4

## Twilight of the Idlers

*Gregg Araki, Felix Gonzalez-Torres, and the Aesthetics of Malaise*

Thinkers of desire, of force, of radical negativity, they do not *believe* in the promising animal, but, blasé, they continue nevertheless to desire, to promise, to commit their naïveté.
—Shoshana Felman, *The Scandal of the Speaking Body: Don Juan with J. L. Austin, or Seduction in Two Languages*

L.A. 1990. Yes, it was very depressing, and very hard to sustain any sense of hope in such a bleak social landscape. How is one supposed to keep any hope alive, the romantic impetus of wishing for a better place for as many people as possible, the desire for justice, the desire for meaning, and history?
—Felix Gonzalez-Torres, "1990: L.A., 'The Gold Field'"

And that behind Orpheus's laments shines the glory of having seen, however fleetingly, the unattainable face at the very instant it turned away.
—Michel Foucault, *Maurice Blanchot: The Thought from Outside*

Through aesthetic modes dissonant with the dominant Chicano and mainstream cultures, queer Chicanos in Los Angeles from the late 1960s up until the advent of the AIDS crisis skillfully interrogated the tension between complacency and social change. This book has analyzed two stylized discontents characteristic of this period, nausea and lo-fi. By the peak of the AIDS epidemic in the 1980s, Chicano counterculture turned its critical optics inward to apply a structural ambivalence to the project of documenting the queer Chicano with AIDS. These internally contradictory dynamics within queer Chicano cultural production—manifesting themselves as functions of the literary-visual frame—repoliticized the definitional and representational crisis inherent in Chicano culture. When the AIDS crisis broke, an irresolvable tension emerged within queer Chicano culture in Los Angeles over the decision either to collectivize or to withdraw into the perverse pleasure of desiring that thing that might hurt you.[1] This shift in sexual politics occurred in typical Los Angeles punk fashion, as a flirtation with the razor's edge between annihilation and creation. What ensued was a cultural moment that radically opened the meaning of what and who could be "called" Latino, whereby those who were attuned to the minor-within-the-minority, a minority self-generating its own internal difference, manifested an "inoperative community" along with others who refused to collectivize under the ethnic and sexual signifiers of Chicano and gay.[2] Chapters 1 and 2 drew on non-Chicano cultural producers and thinkers such as the LA punk band X, the British punk rock singer Poly Styrene, and the philosophers Jean-Paul Sartre and Simone de Beauvoir, with the aim of articulating an alternative style politics to Chicano identity. Chapter 3 traced the split between Chicano and gay identities while questioning the political potential of identitarian categories to capture the material reality they sought to represent at the height of the AIDS crisis. Such a crisis of loss begets a crisis of categorization. Extending from this point of indeterminacy, this chapter stages an encounter between two seemingly non-Chicano queer artists—Gregg Araki and Felix Gonzalez-Torres—in order to make a larger argument about queer Latino cultural politics, namely, that by the early 1990s, the coherency of Chicano identity diffused at the historical moment that a market geared to "Latinos" was beginning to take hold, and this had a profound impact on queer aesthetics.

For example, reflecting on the political and cultural milieu of Los Angeles in 1990, Gonzalez-Torres writes, "Already ten years into trickle-down economics, a rise in cynicism, growing racial and class tension, and the widening gap between the very rich and the rest of us. [This is] L.A. before the riots of 1992." Setting the historical tone for the cultural production at the center of this chapter, Gonzalez-Torres evokes a palpable, mounting pressure, to the extent that the artist cannot unyoke the determinate-future (the Rodney King race riots) from the moment on which he reflects. Gonzalez-Torres continues, waxing cynical on the year 1990, "A time of defunding vital social programs, the abandonment of the ideals on which our country was supposedly founded. The erasure of history."[3]

The artist evokes the bleak economic legacy of the Reagan era, which had concluded just a year prior with George H. W. Bush's ascension to the White House. Just months after the latter's inauguration, a new historical flash point shocked the global stage. The fall of the Berlin Wall in November 1989 signaled the end of the Cold War, leaving US capitalism as the world's only viable economic system as the twentieth century neared its end. During the summer of 1989—which Joshua Clover describes as "the second summer of love" in UK popular culture—the US economist Francis Fukuyama published his controversial essay "The End of History?" in the conservative magazine *National Interest*. In this essay, which was subsequently turned into a book published in 1992 as *The End of History and the Last Man*, Fukuyama argued that the fall of the Berlin Wall signaled "the triumph of the West, [and specifically] of the Western idea," confirming that at the end of the Cold War, "a future that is not essentially democratic and capitalist" was no longer imaginable.[4] For Clover, Fukuyama's "tragic claim" illuminates other geopolitical happenings clustered around the year that the essay was published; considered together, they constitute what Clover calls "the long 1989," a historical year turned concept.[5]

Clover connects Fukuyama's contention about the end of history with Fredric Jameson's argument earlier in the decade, in his influential 1981 book *The Political Unconscious* and 1984 essay "Postmodernism, or, the Cultural Logic of Late Capitalism," that the logic of late capitalism is predicated on a series of announced finalities. "Premonitions of the future, catastrophic or redemptive," Jameson asserts, "have been replaced by senses of the end of this or that (the end of ideology, art, or social class; the 'crisis' of Leninism, social democracy, or the welfare state, etc., etc.)."[6] Jameson locates the beginning of "postmodernism" in 1973, a year that inaugurated a period of economic instability in the West that lasted the rest of the decade, mirroring the "image-defeat of the Vietnam War," otherwise understood as the US empire's *spectaculum* of failure.[7] Coincidentally, this was also the year that George Lucas released his ironically nostalgic film *American Graffiti*. The film is set in Eisenhower-era Los Angeles, and its "aesthetic discourse," Jameson says, articulated the retrospectively "mesmerizing lost reality" of 1950s pax Americana as seen two decades later.[8] What was also lost during this period was the unawareness, if not blatant ignorance, of countercultural motivations, which will later take hold at the end of the decade. But exactly what would take hold were political impulses around sexual and ethnic-racial differences contrasted against the nuclear, white, and heterosexual middle-class suburban American family best exemplified in the 1957 sitcom *Leave It to Beaver*. Thus, it would not be a stretch to similarly consider as an analog to the loss of the idealized American family the sexual politics around AIDS in the 1980s, crystallizing around images of direct action and aesthetic responses to a crisis of loss. As explored in chapter 3, this activism, informed by the self-conscious realization of the impending end of one's life due to the government's homophobic neglect, demonstrated that the need to imagine an alternative to the status quo was an urgent reality for certain portions of the population. However, the need to imagine other futures failed to materialize precisely because of the crisis of loss compounding from the 1950s up to the melancholy initiated on the left after 1968. Though these are different political losses, the yield is the same: the failure inherent in idealization.

Meanwhile, the fall of the Berlin Wall, what Clover astutely describes as an "image-event," or the spectacle of a happening, represented the "absolute metonymy" of the end of the Cold War and subsequently produced its own structures of feeling in tandem with the emergence of a new ideology. The immediate period after Reagan's presidency—1988–1991—occasioned a "surplus of emergence" at the level of popular culture, to the extent that we might characterize this period as "an emergence of emergence," according to Clover. What the cultural scholar means by this is simply that during this short span of three years, many US popular cultural feats first appeared as emerging phenomena, only to then later become dominant styles. Clover reminds us to think of how novel the 1980 hip-hop track "Rapper's Delight" by The Sugar Hill Gang seemed to popular audiences, just as "Rock Around the Clock" by Bill Haley & His Comets did in 1955.[9] Except in this short period, popular culture was dominated by emerging sensibilities. In other words, when attending to what appeared as an emergent style in the past, one tends to notice how that style was always already capable of becoming dominant later. The temporality espoused here is one of anachronism conditioned by culture's capacity to mediate understanding, much like the way Cuadros and Navarro in chapter 3 retooled the indeterminacy at the center of their style politics as a limit to Chicano representation and identity.

Therefore, a reader who has ventured this far into *Dissatisfactions* will easily notice that Clover's time period corresponds to the exhaustive fight for adequate medical care for people living with HIV/AIDS and the dissemination of accurate information on how to prevent contracting the virus. The "long 1989," with its image-event of the fall at the end of Reagan's presidency, signifies the privatization of the public sphere, the retrenchment of social and artistic resources, and unending waves of deaths from AIDS, which, on the one hand, exhausted subcultures' imaginative possibilities and, on the other hand, fueled them with a diffused mediating force. This is to say that while capitalist realism was intensifying, subcultural production also had to account for the way politics, or that dynamic tension between the individual and a community, was increasingly sexualized and racialized, thus subsequently altering the way politics *appeared*. In short, an exhausted cultural sensibility whose articulation requires an equivocal political position because splayed through the prism of racialized sexuality came to have a profound impact on queer Chicano style politics at the end of the decade.

Los Angeles presents a complicated picture of how to make meaning of the long 1989, which initiated a pessimism contrasting sharply with the propagated "economic boom" of the era. The city where Jameson first famously theorized "postmodernism" (in the Bonaventure Hotel in downtown Los Angeles) met "the end of history" after the end of everything but capitalism itself. With growing race tensions, mistrust in the police, and the lack of government action for millions of young people dying of AIDS (Gonzalez-Torres included), some artists sought to aestheticize a diffused yet ubiquitously palpable cynicism. This form of discontent can be described as a social malaise, manifested in a loose gathering of subjects and objects who perform a politics of withdrawing from the political realm as such.[10] This is a contradiction: How to articulate the ambivalent collectivity of subjects who both fall out of the majoritarian sphere *and* suspend, if only momentarily, the political meaning of such a social exile?

In the next section, I turn to two pillars to help set up the trajectory of our final theme: the etymology of malaise, on one side, and three short video art pieces created in 1995 by Laura Aguilar. I then turn to the aesthetic objects central to this chapter's argument: Gregg Araki's film *Totally F\*\*\*ed Up* and the art of Felix Gonzalez-Torres. These cultural producers stylize ambivalence by articulating a sense of malaise after Fukuyama's "end of history."

## "Confessions of a Knife"

One year before Laura Aguilar's best friend, Gil Cuadros, passed away from AIDS complications, she ventured into a relatively new medium: video.[11] With the help of her assistant, Becky Villaseñor, Aguilar created a total of five video pieces in 1995 alone and three between 2005 and 2007. Three of the 1995 pieces, *Talking about Depression* (six minutes), *Talking about Depression 2* (eighteen minutes), and *The Knife* (six minutes), are hauntingly beautiful meditations on loss, depression, alienation, and suicide, in which the confessional mode of each video evidences the queer Chicana artist's general dis-ease. I now turn to these pieces to open our discussion of the structural vagueness that constitutes malaise.

*Talking about Depression* acts almost as a prelude to the much longer *Talking about Depression 2*. The first video piece, shot on June 14, 1995, opens with Aguilar striking a pink punching bag, which immediately contrasts with her black gloves and the white background. Before she situates herself in frame, the camera wavers between framing her face and cropping it out to focus on her body. (The artist's novice grasp of videography is evident throughout: Aguilar and her assistant constantly adjust the camcorder, trying to figure out the right angle, and at times even seem to forget that the tape is recording.) Meanwhile, the viewer cannot help but notice that Aguilar's rose-pink shirt matches the punching bag. The artist confirms the connection between the bag and her body when she begins to repeatedly hit herself, as she recounts debilitating thoughts about how self-harm minimally alleviates internal pain. However, Aguilar confesses that no matter what she does, she cannot hit herself "hard enough or long enough."

*Talking about Depression 2* was shot the following day, on June 15, 1995. In a mode of free, indirect discourse, the thirty-six-year-old queer Chicana artist paints us a picture of her humiliating childhood and the suffocating depression she suffered since she was twelve years old, the first time she felt suicidal. Aguilar grew up with an acute form of auditory dyslexia, causing her to be constantly misunderstood in school at an early age. According to Aguilar, her teachers, growing more and more frustrated with their inability to make out what a young "Laurie" was trying to say, would ask her peers to translate for Aguilar, leaving her feeling socially invisible and mute. Silenced, erased, and perpetually misunderstood, Aguilar graduated high school not knowing how to read, "because [she] did not want to cause any trouble." Meanwhile, at home surrounded by her family, Aguilar explains how she developed a deep shame for feeling *in general*, which served as an unacknowledged obstacle to talking about her feelings. The household mantra "I'll give you something to cry about" ought to be read as what Shoshana Felman calls a "negative promise"—a threat that patriarchally manages not only bodies but also discourse itself.[12]

"I've been standing on the edge for so long," Aguilar ambivalently confesses in *The Knife*, another short VHS recording taped in 1995. "The edge is safe. . . . I hate the edge 'cause of what it means, but it's been my home for so long." Accompanying such poignant and haunting narration, the camera, homed in on Aguilar's hands as they caress a knife, captures the artist's ambivalent play with the razor's edge. Imagining her suicide, Aguilar laments that she cannot bring herself to ever accomplish the act. Lightly though ever so determinedly, she stabs her hand while exclaiming with frustration, "Why . . . can't . . . I . . . do . . . this?" In *talking* about depression, Aguilar brings the viewer to the knife's edge, the supposed cure to the impervious depressed body, where we find, like the pink of both the artist's shirt and the Everlast punching bag, a minor inflation of beauty. This beauty is evacuated of Romantic overtones to suggest something different: in talking about depression, the artist successfully makes the viewer feel depressed, showing the superfluidity of this mental, if corporal, state. Beauty, thought as the collapse of object/subject difference, does not romanticize depression but instead (and just like beauty's conventional definition as an aesthetic judgment that must be shared) reminds us of the sociality afforded when forgoing the object/subject divide. For this reason, the loss of the distinction between the viewer and the depressing/impressing object in Aguilar's artwork stings of beauty, whereby the prick of beauty offers a trace of the artist's sublimated creative output, namely, the Freudian "destination of the drives" retrospectively revealing the pull toward self-annihilation.

Let us turn to another example where Aguilar makes do with loss, through something like a feminist act of sublimation. In *Talking about Depression*, Aguilar explains how "art helped [her] survive the depression," pointing to her 1993 series of black-and-white photographs titled *Don't Tell Her Art Can't Hurt*, which depicts the artist inching a revolver closer to her mouth until the last photograph, where we see her with mouth agape, eyes closed, and both hands holding the chamber of the gun, the shaft resting on her bottom lip as if she were about to pull the trigger. Written at the bottom of each of the four photographs is a narrative in the artist's handwriting about a T-shirt she sports in the first two photos, which read, "Art can't hurt you." The text's linear narrative corresponds to the sequential unfolding of the photos. They describe an artist whose "problem" is in believing in art *too* much and eventually recognizing that the art world had alienated people of color who chose to use art "to give voice, to show the positive" of their cultures. Under the penultimate photograph, the artist writes, "How do the bridges get built if the doors are closed to your voice and your vision?" She responds in the final photograph: "So don't tell her art can't hurt, she knows better. The believing can pull at one's soul. So much that one wants to give up." Aguilar gives language to her malaise in the form of written confessions below her images. As in her video pieces, images and words formalize her depression into the very unbridgeable gap that *pulls* the viewer into something like an enveloped discontent. Depression, then, for Aguilar is socially contagious and conveyed to the viewer through the artwork. Thus, Aguilar's *Don't Tell Her Art Can't Hurt* series shows how the cure to depression might be its nonexistence. At the end of Freud's 1930 book *Civilization and Its Discontents*, he makes a small confession regarding the "talking cure" that is psychoanalysis. Freud explains how the cure for the neurotic, the representative of "civilization," can never really be attained since they are situated in a community that causes in perpetuity their very symptom. No cure can exist for having confused the equivocal limit between individual and community. At this limit is where we find discontent (another word for malaise) as the limit to the project of psychoanalysis itself. In the same text, Freud also offers a social theory founded on the impossibility of love. Recalling the Christian injunction "Love thy neighbor as thyself," Freud argues that "the commandment is impossible to fulfill" since such "inflation of love only lowers its value."[13] Jacques Lacan famously reinterpreted this proposition counterintuitively, arguing that Christ's injunction was ironic since people actually hate themselves (however unconsciously), thus proving Freud's gloomy assessment of civilization as the very impossible project of universal love.[14] I have more to say later in this chapter about these consequences regarding one's relationship to neighbors, or to the neighborhood of objects constituting malaise's aesthetic composition. But first I further unfold the meaning of malaise and its relationship to discontent, arguably the general aesthetic heuristic of this book and its negative limit.

## Latinidad's *Unbehagen*

Rei Terada, in her exquisite study of the interplay between phenomenality and dissatisfaction, begins with the relationship between dissatisfaction and Freud's concept of *Unbehagen*, translated as "'discontent' or 'malaise.'"[15] Terada pinpoints how, in *Civilization and Its Discontents*, *Unbehagen* appears highly social—much in the way style has been theorized throughout *Dissatisfactions*—which adds an "extra layer of frustration" since malaise is "stronger in social than in solitary settings; bearable and nontragic, yet relentless."[16] In this way, malaise is similar to the minor affect of nausea that we saw in chapter 1, in that malaise mirrors an ongoing feeling of discontent with virtually everything. But unlike nausea, malaise is not ironically amplified but saturated with a flattening indifference. This might suggest a turning away from sociopolitical strife, but the indifference explored in this chapter is of a different kind, one that questions both the presupposed community posited by disinterested aesthetic judgments and the demand to respond to such an imagined community—a general refusal of both separatism and assimilation.

In the etymology of "malaise," *mal-* and *aise* both derive from Old French, meaning "bad" (as in Spanish) and "ease," respectively. *Aise* (ease) itself derives from the original Latin *adjacens*, meaning "lying close by" something else, while *jacere* in Latin means to "lie down." What does this etymology tell us about the spatiality of malaise? For one, it illuminates malaise's infrastructural gathering of intertextual singularities *around* and *beside* one another; indeed, it traces a sociality of objects and subjects in loose relation to each other. In addition, malaise implies an aesthetic judgment about this plane of relationality, the problem that is its *negative* structure. The story of malaise is one of the immemorial gatherings of radically relational singularities, akin to how Eve Sedgwick describes that queerness is as "antiseparatist as it is anti-assimilationist.... Keenly, [queer] is relational, and strange."[17] There is something queer about malaise, perhaps in its accentuating the dis-ease with and of gender (recalling here that gender and *genre* share an a priori synthesis of the categorical), in all its immanent incoherence. Finally, the social economy of malaise recasts civilization's problem as sociality as such and regards the *constituted* gap between identities (the siloing effect, the atomizing effect, the breaking-up blow of alienation) as the flip side to the *constitutive* gap *within* the subject of desire, that is, the subject of loss.[18] In other words, discontent emerges from the fact that such a gap connects but fails to unify. Indifference, then, is best understood as a being-in-difference, a critical difference to be sure, where its singular-plural form mirrors that of malaise. Malaise is both a qualitatively bad aesthetic judgment and indifferent, and its negativity registers the subject's desire as caused by malaise's diffused and skewed structure. Malaise minds the gap and thus makes loss relational as a style.

Meanwhile, malaise retains a minor aesthetic quality just like the previous three stylized discontents, except that malaise involves a blasé effect, in turn, indexing this stylized discontent under the aesthetic category of beauty. I should reiterate the operating definition of "minor" here as referring not merely to size or solely to minoritarian subjects. Instead, I follow Hentyle Yapp's definition of the minor as a method highlighting "epistemological assumptions and ontological conditions that uphold the order of things."[19] In bringing the norm to focus, malaise's minor quality registers "tensions across universalization and cultural particularity, since minor subjects and objects are often either enfolded into universal discourses or rendered singular for purposes of liberal consumption."[20] We should addend Yapp's definition by suspending the moral oppositionality in favor of a more dynamic relation between universalism and particularity; for it is precisely these tensions that make malaise appear social and beautiful.

Leticia Alvarado's work on the aesthetic politics of abject performances in Latino contemporary culture has been animating many of the arguments made thus far in *Dissatisfactions*, though one significant point of departure involves Alvarado's privileging of the sublime, as philosophized in the history of aesthetics, over the beautiful. This makes sense since Alvarado traces abjection and its performative effects of "dissolution and formlessness" occasioned by the displeasure in encountering the limits of the imaginary.[21] But, since *Dissatisfactions* concerns the noncathartic elements of political life, beauty registers more conservatively in the political imaginary. As opposed to the cathartic overload of the sublime, beauty's more minor quality registers an affliction of loss, namely, a loss of a shared (imagined) community. Quite counterintuitively, beauty appears universal because the loss suffered cannot be communicated as such, whereby the incommunicability of a suffered loss predicates aesthetic judgments of artistic beauty. In other words, the aesthetic judgment of beauty is one made ex nihilo, and as a result, its formal effect is subsumed within the aesthetic structure of malaise, as a connecting gap that mediates any sense of unity. Much like the way this book's previous stylized discontents formalized constitutive contradictions at the center of subjects of desire, which a new post-Fordist form of capitalism sought to mystify, malaise will extend the very *Unbehagen* constitutive of modern "civilization," as Freud argued. Except, when examined through the lens of queer Chicano cultural politics, as this book has been demonstrating, one where the ethnic identity marker "Chicano" inexorably fails to represent those who are afflicted by its sign (as we shall see), this expanded dis-ease comes to figure as an impossible unity, a structure of determinate contradictions, where irresolvable logical disjunctions are but the expression of a desire for desire itself. This, we might as well call *queer latinidad*.

By the end of this chapter, we will have moved from examinations of queer Chicano style politics to a theory of queer latinidad as a collection of antinomies, incommensurate with experience and subjectivity. This analytical move, from a specifically defined ethnic identity (Chicano) to an inconclusive social phenomenon dialectically reversing into a specified nonspecificity, reveals something about the relationship between history and consciousness. I argue that queer latinidad *is* the minor form of an engendered social body retroactively congealing under capital realism as residue from global '68. For instance, throughout Ronald Reagan's presidency, the AIDS epidemic echoed but could not mimic the collectivizing force of global '68 and, in so doing, revealed the "lying close" of its historical unfolding. AIDS activism's lack of equivalency with the social movements of 1968 and the early 1970s occasions a suspension of the political itself so as to decenter consciousness, or rather to express the loss of the future within the here and now. Therefore, malaise ought to be understood as both a characteristic of the aesthetic objects curated in this chapter and their (shared) interinanimation, a common singular-universal quality that tells us something about how a novel, though inadequate, concept such as "queer latinidad" hinges at the height of the AIDS epidemic on a historical split in Chicano identity, as chapter 3 argued.

If the comedown of our study on stylized discontents and their constitutive relation to a queer Chicano politics appears diffused, suspended, and undefined, it is to show how these aesthetics infiltrate the work of two cultural producers who are adjacent but not entirely aligned with the identity marker "Chicano": the queer, Asian American, punk filmmaker Gregg Araki and the queer, Cuban-born American conceptual artist Felix Gonzalez-Torres, whose works contributed to the beginnings of New Queer Cinema and the conceptual and minimalist art of the early 1990s, respectively. As *Dissatisfactions* demonstrates, moving away from the representational and identitarian politics plaguing much of Chicano cultural production in the latter part of the twentieth century might actually free up minor chords of affective, sensual, and aesthetic forms of belonging that are not quite identifiable as Chicano or even Latino forms of sociality. This is important: Gonzalez-Torres's and Araki's works are the final objects in a politically ambiguous archive of an understudied and undertheorized region of queer latinidad that, in turn, causes latinidad to appear ubiquitous yet undefinable. In this chapter, I consider the residue of the collective comedown from the 1960s promise of social change that I have been calling Reagan's America. Such residue tells us something about the "brown study," that enigmatic "state of whirring, blooming confusion," congealing around the high stakes of

Brown Power and the movement's materialized loss at the turn of the decade and after the height of the AIDS epidemic.[22] The goal here is to show how a spatialized relation to loss—what will take the shape of the "beside"—forms the last style of discontent in our study: malaise.

## Felix Gonzalez-Torres and Time

Felix Gonzalez-Torres is one of the most lauded minimalist and conceptual queer artists of the late twentieth century. In fact, he is often described in relation to the AIDS crisis and recognized for creating art about same-sex desire without overtly representing normative visual cues regarding sexuality, the epidemic, or especially race and ethnicity. For this last reason, Gonzalez-Torres is usually not considered within a Latino paradigm. Even the artist's foundation, which is charged with monitoring the afterlife of Gonzalez-Torres's work and estate, insists that the artist never identified as Latino, only used diacritical marks in the spelling of his name within Spanish-language contexts, and preferred to be referred as "Cuban-born" American—not Cuban or Latino. These preferences came from the artist and are reiterated by his foundation for any printed scholarship. However, they also create obstacles for talking about, theorizing, and entertaining the notion that his work might be *about* latinidad.[23] But Gonzalez-Torres's stubbornness, his categorical refusal of ethnic identification, corresponds with a cultural, political, and aesthetic phenomenon that also refuses completeness and definitional coherence.

Gonzalez-Torres was born in Cuba in 1957. At the age of fourteen, he and his sister were sent to Puerto Rico via Madrid to live with their uncle. Gonzalez-Torres went to art school at the University of Puerto Rico from 1976 to 1979. In his last year of undergraduate studies, he returned to Cuba to visit his parents after eight years of separation, a very poignant trip that the young artist then made sense of through his newfound interests in video, photography, and performance art. In a rarely exhibited and analyzed 1979 video performance piece titled *Non-Work* formerly titled: *Autorretrato 3*, created after his trip to Cuba, Gonzalez-Torres describes his farewell to his mother. This *Non-Work* almost feels like a lecture on semiotics, which is no surprise considering that Gonzalez-Torres was an avid reader of philosophy and literature in college.[24] The video begins with Gonzalez-Torres writing on a chalkboard in Spanish the word *recuerdo*, which can mean "memory" or "I remember," followed by his drawing a box around the word *madre* (mother), only to anxiously erase these signs and start again. In the next round, the artist boxes in the word *aeropuerto* (airport) and then crosses it out and erases it (figure 4.1). In the final round, Gonzalez-Torres inscribes the words *recuerdo*, *aeropuerto*, and *madre* within the same box, communicating a fragmented thought: "I remember the airport and mother." The young artist proceeds to write in Spanish, "ten hours, ten years, ten mothers," as if these phrases correlated to the previous three words, to suggest that memory is like ten hours, the airport makes ten hours feel like ten years, and one (Cuban) mother is the equivalent of ten "regular" mothers. After erasing this lesson, the artist finally comes into the frame, seemingly exhausted already by the story he is about to tell. He proceeds by explaining in Spanish, "I remember my mother, big, big, big, and strong. In that last hug in that airport that I don't remember—that big and strong airport—where time makes time, where time makes," he says again enthusiastically, "exactly, where time makes time. With every given hug, with a kiss, we say, 'Ciao.' They say, 'Goodbye.' It's like we have a crystal, a fragile crystal—fragile and strong. But no, we do not say good-bye. It is prohibited; it was prohibited—it is or it was. Doesn't matter, it will be. It was prohibited to say good-bye: it was a password to say good-bye."

Though this *Non-Work* was created by a twenty-one-year-old Gonzalez-Torres months before his move to the United States to begin a fellowship in New York City, which would pave the way for his later ventures into sculpture and conceptual art, the video performance captures what, I believe, Gonzalez-Torres spent the rest of his life making sense of. For one, the piece situates the artist as a pedagogue unfolding a lesson about memory, time, and loss through a semiotic vernacular. The artist's constant erasing, crossing out, and writing over connotes a palimpsestic understanding of loss, perhaps inspired by Gonzalez-Torres's newfound interest in critical theory or the subtly queer 1953 piece by Robert Rauschenberg titled *Erased de Kooning Drawing*, which Rauschenberg's lover, the artist Jasper Johns, would later refer to as an example of "additive subtraction."[25] This paradox helps explain how Gonzalez-Torres needs to remember (after forgetting through the act

Figure 4.1. *Non-Work* by Felix Gonzalez-Torres. Former title: *Autorretrato* 3, circa 1979. Description: Black and white, single-channel video. 9 minutes.

of erasing the signifiers "airport" and "mother") in order to forget once again in his autoethnographic account of what happened at that airport. The airport is significant for the artist because it is precisely the place where "time makes time," where time swells, causing its linear structure to crystallize into shards of broken memories and foretellings, encapsulated in his play on the Spanish tenses of the verb "to be": *está, estaba, estará* (it is, it was, it will be).

In other words, Gonzalez-Torres takes up the difficult question of what it means to be, that is, to exist in time, when time seems to be systematically taken away from you. During a period when homosexuals were persecuted in Castro's Cuba, which eventually led many gay Cuban refugees to flee in a mass known as the Mariel boatlift of 1980 (coincidentally, the same year that Gonzalez-Torres's mother fled the island), homosexual desire needed to be "attenuated, diffused and reflexive," like the structurally vague style of malaise.[26] The artist's expression of good-bye to his mother—an acknowledgment of loss—was itself the very ground for their relation, indeed the sensuous formalization of a nonrelation. What José Muñoz called queerness's "arduous modes of relationality" might very well encompass the paradox of "additive subtraction" in Gonzalez-Torres's work and thinking; an aesthetics of redaction will come to characterize much of the artist's oeuvre insofar as his work actively makes loss teachable.[27] And this lesson became all the more important in the two decades that followed Gonzalez-Torres's move to the US, with the government's neglect of an ever-increasing AIDS epidemic—a period in which Gonzalez-Torres fell in love and created art solely for his new lover, Ross Laycock.

Consider first a personal missive from Gonzalez-Torres to his lover Ross Laycock in 1988—only three years before Laycock would die of AIDS complications (figure 4.2). It reads, "Lovers, 1988—Don't be afraid of the clocks, they are our time, time has been so generous to us. We imprinted time with the sweet taste of victory. We conquered fate by meeting at a certain TIME, in a certain space. We are a product of the time; therefore, we give back credit were [sic] it is due: time. We are synchronized, now and forever. I love you." The letter works as a piece of ephemera, as a minimal/conceptual work of art, and as poetry. Through these three modes, Gonzalez-Torres communicates a theory of time that is indicative of a specific and particular form of love—a

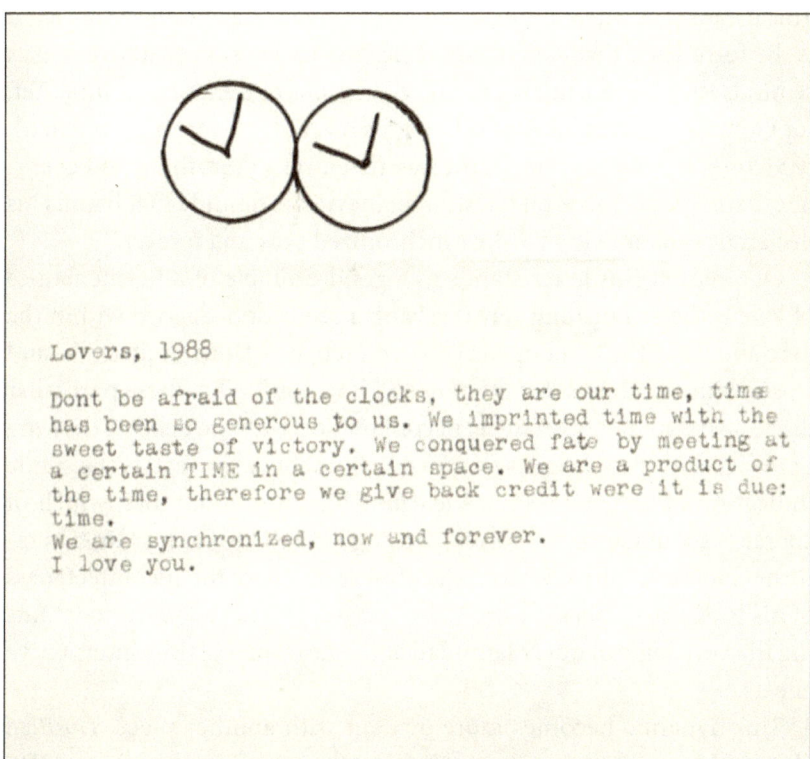

Figure 4.2. Letter to Ross Laycock from Felix Gonzalez-Torres, 1988. Published with special permission in Julie Ault, ed., *Felix Gonzalez-Torres* (Göttingen: Steidl, 2006).

"meeting at a certain time, in a certain space"—that reads as a hermeneutics of love. With this term, I invoke the Chicana feminist theorist Chela Sandoval's explication of "differential consciousness," an intractable feminist consciousness expressed through what Hayden White called "the middle voice," an action-centered as opposed to an object/subject mode of representation, which is central to Sandoval's thinking of a hermeneutics of love.[28] By using the term "love," I want to suggest a particular resistance to the commodification of relation as only a product of history, relation as a teleological end, since to be "a product of . . . time," as Gonzalez-Torres points out, requires *giving back* concern to the place where attention takes the form of an impression or a mold.

This means that where impressions are formed à la an aesthetic object, it is the form itself that concretizes time. The impression that love makes reminds the hermeneutician of the tribulations one endures in time. Yet, for Gonzalez-Torres, who calls upon his lover, this impression is a mark of victory, the overcoming of the fate that awaits everything and everyone, namely, the universal question of inevitable finitude that haunts his declarative statement: "We are synchronized now and forever."

One reason this letter stands as a good example of a hermeneutics of love is the astonishing way it sets up a scene of pedagogy within the here and now. The letter opens with a directive—"Don't be afraid"—and closes with a performative utterance: "I love you." What these particular discursive statements produce, in conjunction with the delicate drawing of two synchronized clocks sketched in blue above the text, is the subtle indication of Gonzalez-Torres *teaching* his lover about loss, which of course is about Gonzalez-Torres teaching himself how to lose Ross in return. Counterintuitively, Gonzalez-Torres lays bare the incompleteness of his love, the implicit failure to be "perfect lovers," a failure constituting the very logic of queer latinidad at the heart of malaise's interpretive effects.

This dynamic becomes more evident with another piece, *Untitled (Perfect Lovers)*, which appeared in 1991, the year Ross died from AIDS complications in Los Angeles. It consists of two store-bought clocks set side by side, touching, with their minute and second hands set in sync and, according to Gonzalez-Torres, "with the understanding that eventually they might go out of sync during the course of the exhibition." What is built into *Untitled (Perfect Lovers)* and anticipated by the letter to Ross is the failure and inadequacy of perfection or completion itself. Though the piece suggests two same-sex lovers in relation, it draws our attention to how no two identical clocks actually keep the same time. There are minuscule, sometimes imperceptible lapses in their mechanisms, and inevitably their batteries will give out on their own. They are then replaced by the museum or gallery per Gonzalez-Torres's instructions, in a representation of the care involved when adequacy fails and equivalency stammers. In other words, *Untitled (Perfect Lovers)* translates Sandoval's "hermeneutics of love" into a stylized malaise, insofar as the revolutionary force of love that Sandoval theorizes in *Methodology of the Oppressed* meets its banal underside in the beauty of dissatisfaction.

Figure 4.3. "*Untitled*" (*Orpheus Twice*), 1991. Installed in *The Work of Mourning*. Bonniers Konsthall, Stockholm, Sweden. September 2– November 1, 2020. Cur. Theodor Ringborg. Photographer: Jean-Baptiste.

Another piece from the same year, Untitled (Orpheus, Twice), displays two identical mirrors set side by side, yet this time with a small gap between them (figure 4.3). There are at least four ways to encounter this particular installation: a viewer stands in front of one mirror and registers the absence of a body in the reflection of the other; two viewers stand in front of each of the two mirrors and notice the double presence of each body, with an unreflected absence in between; a viewer stands in the middle of both mirrors, only to discover a split in their reflection; and a viewer encounters the work from an angle, with both mirrors reflecting only empty space. In all four circumstances, the gap between the mirrors forbids a unified reflection. This phenomenon gives us a way into understanding latinidad, a concept whose structural vulnerability—its inadequacy at capturing the experiences it sets to define—is reflected in artworks developed under the sign of loss.

Gonzalez-Torres's installation underscores what the Latina political theorist Cristina Beltrán calls the "discontinuities inherent in plurality" by refusing to reflect the unified whole promised by liberal inclusion.[29] Beltrán attributes the difficulty of latinidad to achieve any political purchase in electoral politics to such discontinuities. What she terms the "trouble with unity" that conditions Latino democratic politics is in fact, in my view, constitutive of the phenomenon we understand as latinidad in Reagan's America.[30] Once again, I draw the reader's attention to the significant variance among "conditions of possibility" for Latino politics, on the one hand, which are constrained by dissensus according to Beltrán, while emphasizing the importance of the *constitutive* lack of unity in the demographic body. The latter is what Jacques Rancière poetically named "the part of those who have no part," which *Untitled (Orpheus, Twice)* makes operative in its installation.[31] The gap between the mirrors cannot reflect but does affect the positioning and perception of the observer. But perhaps more pertinent to our discussion of malaise is how the gap lays bare the besideness of the mirrors' capacity to represent/reflect. As a result of the gap, the two (perfect lovers) emerge out of nothing, which is to say that the nothingness of the gap makes possible the impossibility of unity, where the resulting loss of unity might be judged as beautiful.

In 1990, while visiting Roni Horn's solo exhibition at the Museum of Contemporary Art in Los Angeles, Gonzalez-Torres and Laycock encountered Horn's work *Forms from the Gold Field* (1980–82).[32] As Gonzalez-Torres coped with his lover's diagnosis and the all-too-certain future of his imminent death (Laycock survived the show by a mere six months), he came across a large rippled sheet of annealed pure gold, forty-nine by sixty inches, displayed by itself on the concrete floor of an all-white room at the Temporary Contemporary, the museum's provisional space at the time. Horn's piece surprised the couple, who "spent every Saturday afternoon visiting galleries, museums, thrift shops, and going on long, very long drives all around L.A., enjoying the 'magic hour' when the light makes everything gold and magical in that city."[33] Momentarily suspended in time, Laycock and Gonzalez-Torres were enmeshed in a new landscape outside the bleak environs of a Los Angeles suffering the lingering effects of what the artist called the "Reagan Empire." Gonzalez-Torres writes of the experience as an encounter with "a possible horizon, a place of rest and absolute beauty."[34] In Horn's *Gold Field*, the artist gazes with his lover down at a horizon of possibility

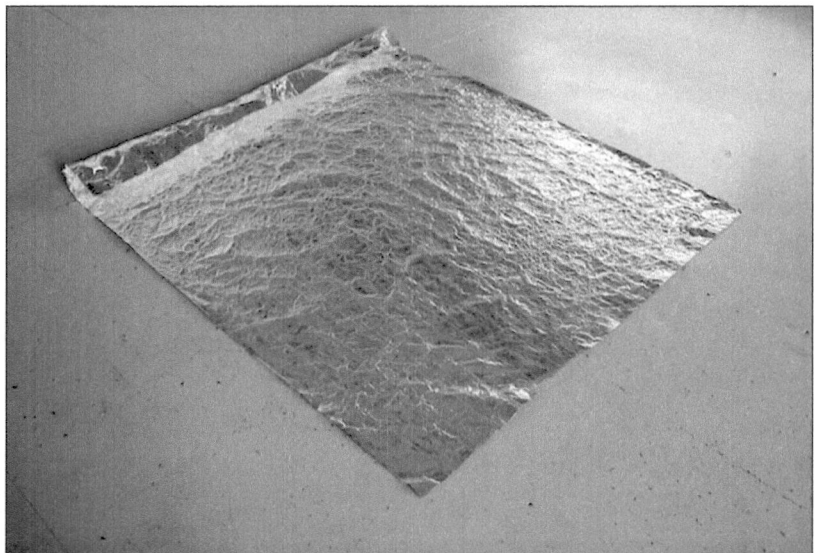

Figure 4.4. Roni Horn, *Gold Field*, 1980–82.

unfolding as the very ground of their relationality, and, like golden sunsets in Los Angeles, "Roni [Horn] had named something that had always been there."[35] We can say that in apprehending the piece's "absolute beauty," Gonzalez-Torres and Laycock experienced beauty as the container for a more disorganizing principle, namely, the way loss formalizes a thought "about the possibility of change." In Gonzalez-Torres's words, "Roni showed the innate ability of an artist proposing to make this place a better place. How truly revolutionary."[36] What appears revolutionary to Gonzalez-Torres in Horn's work involves the way loss mediates the apprehension of any object, a loss that is grounded in historical contexts of social difference such as race, class, sexual orientation, and gender, while also allowing room for desire, memory, and imagination.

Similarly, I want to argue that a sense of beauty emerges, almost paradoxically, in Gonzalez-Torres's own works through their articulation of loss—specifically, the sense of noncoincidence or nonrelation that they elicit. The profound loss emanating from *Untitled (Orpheus, Twice)* does not overwhelm the viewer who stands in front of it. In fact, the installation's subtlety is indicative of much of Gonzalez-Torres's work, whose sheer minimalism or redactive aesthetic counters the cliché notion that

Latino citizen-subjects are excessive and over the top.[37] The refusal of excess in *Untitled (Orpheus, Twice)* is also what makes it anti-sublime, unlike the hypothesized "sleeping Latino giant" voting bloc or consumer market. Indeed, Gonzalez-Torres binds the loss of universal wholeness to the singular Barthesian punctum of its beauty.

In Steven Shaviro's rereading of Immanuel Kant through Alfred North Whitehead, he argues that Kant's theory of beauty "is really a theory of affect and of singularity."[38] Unlike the sublime, which is excessive, disruptive, and immense at the level of scale, beauty appears more conservative, harmonious, and quotidian, much like the moment that Laycock and Gonzalez-Torres encountered Horn's gold horizon. Beauty may not offer many possibilities for change, as the artist confessed in his interpretation of Horn's work, but this is exactly what is contested in *Untitled (Orpheus, Twice)* when read through the structure of malaise. If we can say, following Shaviro, that beauty implies the loss of aura, it is in Gonzalez-Torres's work where loss unfolds on a minor scale, "like a blasé shrug of the shoulders, or like Andy Warhol's bland and oft-repeated judgment: 'it's great.'"[39] For Gonzalez-Torres, this indifference is really about a being-in-difference, as argued at the beginning of this chapter, where the loss of a unifying sameness figures in the singular beauty of clocks, mirrors, and sheets of gold displayed beside one another and beside the viewer. This is not to say that only *one* loss is communicated but exactly the opposite. Loss fails to communicate, and it is in the very lapse of communication that singularity affects the subject; this structural impasse to the subject's own consciousness frees them up to make a judgment. This is why Gonzalez-Torres describes his feeling as having been "lifted" when he encountered the "gesture" of Horn's *Gold Field*, a gesture resembling a Wallace Stevens poem, "precise, with no extra baggage, nothing extra."[40] One is tempted to ask how Gonzalez-Torres's minimal pieces, like Horn's, convey *so much* through minimalism's "precise" because abstracted meaning.

I argue throughout *Dissatisfactions* that stylized discontent formalizes the singular-universal at the core of the Latino subject of desire. This singular-universal quality ties the subject to a lost wholeness that never was. Shaviro points to Kant's "sensus communis," the a priori synthesis of a shared judgment of taste, more recognizable as "common sense," that must presuppose beauty, the inevitable act of sharing this disinterested judgment. That judgment remains disinterested because it is primarily noncognitive, nonrepresentable, and does not seek universalization (even if it is premised on a priori synthetic judgment, unlike the desire for unity in Beltrán's critique of Latino political theory). In this way, according to Shaviro, "sensus communis would be seen as the cultivation and sharing of the highest possible degree of singularity."[41] Kandice Chuh has recently offered a compelling analysis of how Kant's aesthetic philosophy and its positing of a "sensus communis" subsequently shaped the liberal humanisms that were canonized in academic discourse to the exclusion of minoritarian life and aesthetics. For Chuh, Kant's "sensus communis" "refers to a common sense as an invocation of what is presumed to be reasonable" and begs a series of questions that the author homes in on throughout her book *The Difference Aesthetics Makes: On the Humanities "After Man."* Chuh asks, "How is the sensus communis that is the condition and measure of reasonability formed? What are its governing structures, and its sources of authority? How is that knowledge made to stand as a product of reason? By what legitimating authorities? By what right and understanding of reason?"[42]

I find these provocations and Chuh's subsequent argument intellectually stimulating. In addition to these questions, *Dissatisfactions* offers an explanation *to the side* of the conditionality that Chuh brings to the fore, that is, the implicit and particular governing structures and "politics of distribution" at play and positioned as universal in notions like "reason" and "common sense." Stylized discontent acknowledges the conditioning structures of aesthetics and underscores their importance for studies of oppression and struggle. While the politics of aesthetics aims directly at expounding the historical unfolding of sense perception and thus thought, this book seeks to explicate how the aesthetics of politics situates the cause of desire as a heuristic, to understand how dominating structures of oppression persist *despite* the exposure and acknowledgment of their conditional aspects. This process, I argue, is underscored by Gonzalez-Torres's artworks examined in this chapter.

*Untitled (Orpheus, Twice)* refuses to bridge the gap within subjectivity and between singularities. Rather, the work enacts the spatial dimension of malaise by making visible the besideness of contradictory realities, however unified in their shared loss of a historical reason. In this regard, beauty qualifies the inherently deferred desire to define what latinidad might mean *because* of its conditional existence. What we are left with is a dynamic relationship between the blasé and ordinary imprint of beauty, on the one hand, and the discordant notes—the part that has no part to play—in the political structure of latinidad, on the other. Yet beauty, like malaise, is stronger in social moments than in solitary ones, which require (if not demand) a community of difference. Contrasting singularities tell us something about how things and subjects are collectively displaced from the majoritarian sphere. These singular coordinates also revive a sense of beauty in signifying their constitutive loss of belonging but can only accomplish this in a spatial relation of being beside one another, as *Untitled (Orpheus, Twice)* lays bare. This besideness maps an amoral, noncathartic, and indefinable sense of belonging through its incessant demands that the Latino subject *remain* or *be*-in-longing.

The highly queer notion of "belonging-in-difference" seems not so different, now, from the aesthetic and political contours of latinidad that form the implicit focus of *Dissatisfactions*. That is, queer Chicano politics in post-1968 Los Angeles experienced a self-reflexive critique evident in its ambivalent framing of the Chicano body with AIDS, which, when coupled with the aesthetic structure of malaise, allowed it to persist under Reagan's America and its legacies into the George H. W. Bush administration. Political withdrawal from canonical understandings of Chicano culture and politics only invigorated the vital punk force running throughout this book. Though seemingly passive, malaise cunningly confronts the demand to assume an oppositional position. Malaise becomes manifest as an almost faux-sentimental vehicle for infiltrating other forms of cultural production, such as minimalist art and cinema, as we will see. As a queer Cuban-born refugee, Gonzalez-Torres understood this social tactic very well, which he explained in an interview with Tim Rollins: "I love the idea of being an infiltrator. I always said that I wanted to be a spy. I want my artwork to look like something else, non-artistic yet beautifully simple. I don't want to be the opposition because the opposition always serves a purpose: 'Improve your arms against me.' But if you're the spy—always 'straight acting,' always within the system—you are the person that they fear the most because *you're one of them and you become impossible to define.*"[43] What Gonzalez-Torres theorizes here is the cloaking mechanism that a stylized malaise offers for queer Chicano politics. To be an infiltrator or spy is to refuse to be the opposition, since "the opposition always serves a purpose." In Joshua Chambers-Letson's fantastic essay "Contracting Justice: The Viral Strategy of Felix Gonzalez-Torres," he pushes further Gonzalez-Torres's infiltrating motivations by linking the desire to the HIV/AIDS epidemic and astutely diagnoses Gonzalez-Torres's work as effecting a "viral strategy." The author argues that the Gonzalez-Torres's art work calls on "spectators to ascribe meaning to the piece through hermeneutic practices that were attentive to the context and spectator's subjective experience of the artwork."[44] In this way, Gonzalez-Torres's aesthetic process mirrors that of a virus in that like something going viral, it first needs a host; and so "rather than regarding the body's susceptibility to infection as a weakness, Gonzalez-Torres structures his artwork to function as carriers of his viruses."[45] The artist's viral strategy and infiltrating capabilities allow him to subtract the literal body from his conceptual pieces while referencing it "without reinforcing the fixity of identity through bodily representations."[46] Figuration and conceptual pieces become the expression of a viral strategy seeking freedom and relation.

The goal, as we move now to the beginning of New Queer Cinema and an early film by Gregg Araki, is to see how the politics emerging in chapters 1 and 2 of this study—nausea and lo-fi—hit an impasse marked by ambivalence in confronting the phenomenon of AIDS and then were forced to cloak and deface themselves into a seemingly irreverent flat affect, like an infiltrating spy, in order to survive as that undefinable thing "that [the system] fear[s] the most." For "we must be willing to infect the present with the demands of a better future," as Chamber-Letson reminds us after Gonzalez-Torres.[47]

## "The Lifestyles of the Bored and Disenfranchised"

In 1991, the same year Gonzalez-Torres created *Untitled (Orpheus, Twice)*, the film scholar B. Ruby Rich published a groundbreaking article in the *Village Voice*, then the leading New York chronicle of anything subcultural and weird. Her essay "A Queer Sensation" reflects on an emerging trend that Rich terms the "New Queer Cinema" (NQC), characterized by films made by queer filmmakers who are ostensibly dedicated to showing the lives of sexually marginalized subjects on the silver screen.⁴⁸ Prime examples include Derek Jarman's *Edward II* (1991), Jennie Livingston's now-canonical *Paris Is Burning* (1990), and Gregg Araki's second film, *The Living End* (1992). Jarman, who was actively producing films accounting for the equivocal impact of AIDS on queer youth, and Livingston, who housed Ray Navarro and his lover during their time in New York City before falling ill, represent a small cohort of filmmakers who, with Araki, charted new aesthetic territory during the AIDS crisis. As Rich explains, "Definitively breaking with older humanist approaches and the films and tapes that accompanied identity politics, these works are irreverent, energetic, alternately minimalist, and excessive. Above all, they're full of pleasure."⁴⁹

Yet Araki occupied a more precarious spot in this new trend than his fellow white queer filmmakers did. Araki's critical reception came to suffer at the hands of his own "alternatively minimalist" and "irreverent" style in the years after the release of *The Living End*. What was dangerous for Araki as an Asian American filmmaker in the late 1980s and early 1990s was not so much the queer content of his films but his almost desirous way of being marginal and finding pleasure in minor styles of existence. Though this sentiment was shared with early NQC filmmakers, ethnically marked subjects bore more of the burden to represent queer life in a positive and affirmative light. As a result, such filmmakers as Araki are left feeling a bit ambivalent about their positionality. In an interview with Lawrence Chua, a queer Asian American punk filmmaker from Los Angeles, Araki explains how the minor as a form of marginalization might be politically advantageous, despite his hesitation:

> CHUA: Are you satisfied with the placement of your work?
> ARAKI: I realize that my work is bound to be marginalized. Not just because of the queerness of the subject matter, but because of the whole punk thing, which probably much more than being gay or Asian is the biggest cultural influence on me. I don't think marginalization is necessarily a bad thing. Economically it's inferior. Certainly, my level of living is well below anybody who directs commercials in Hollywood, but that's not why I make movies.⁵⁰

Araki distinguishes his queer style from his early punk influences, but most interesting is his sidelining of his ethnic background. Araki inaugurates for queer people of color a style or attitude that breaks with identity politics through its paradoxically excessive minimalism. In light of our discussion of Gonzalez-Torres, we can read Araki's investment in the excess of loss through his minimalist aesthetic as registering, in a punk fashion, his own malaise and general discontent with the burden of ethnic representation.[51] A deeper study of Araki, in tandem with the queer Chicano styles of discontent that *Dissatisfactions* has constellated, shows how NQC is only one particular extension of a postidentitarian Chicano aesthetic. Through strategies of infiltration, under the guise of malaise, Araki's films sneak in remnants of a queer Chicano counterculture.

Let us turn to a film of Araki's released in 1993, one example of Rich's New Queer Cinema. Titled *Totally F\*\*\*ed Up*, this film inaugurated what Araki termed his "Teenage Apocalypse Trilogy," which would later include *The Doom Generation* (1995), followed by *Nowhere* (1997). Araki had been pressured to make a film about queer youth of color after his all-white-male casts in *The Long Weekend (O' Despair)* (1989) and *The Living End* (1992).[52] In a snarky response to this critique, Araki cast a group of amateur teenage actors from a range of ethnic backgrounds in *Totally F\*\*\*ed Up*, his first "big multi-ethnic production."[53] In the interview with Chua, Araki admits that his actors were interchangeable among the film's characters, suggesting that their ethnicities were superfluous to the plot and "like wardrobe, essentially."[54] Thus, the filmmaker tried to prove, through the ambiguously ethnic group of teenagers that constitute the tight-knit family of *Totally F\*\*\*ed Up*, that race/ethnicity was somehow ornamental and "beside the point" to what he was trying to accomplish.

A critical methodology attuned to what Eve Sedgwick describes as the "spacious agnosticism" of the beside allows for an analysis of Araki's films unmoored from symptomatic and reductive critiques that reject a cultural artifact based on its supposed neglect of ethnic-racial difference.[55] Araki's flippant response to solicitations to create a film *about* and *by* people of color allowed him to strategically elide the issue of ethnic-racial particularity by placing it *to the side* of his intentions. For Araki, the para-position of race does not mean it disappears *tout court*. Instead, the displacement at work in Araki's loose attachment to "representing" ethnic-racial difference permits other forms of relation and recognition to emerge that are not necessarily predicated on equivalency and directionality. Perhaps predictably, this strategy has been met with harsh criticism, notably from the British writer Tony Rayns, whose aesthetic critiques of Araki's films seem to always rely on a certain disavowal of his own gay white sensibility. Rayns finds it difficult, for instance, to "keep the solipsistic airhead act that Gregg Araki puts on when he presents his films in public separate from rational appraisal of the films themselves."[56] Rayns's desperate desire for "rational appraisal," that is, an aesthetic judgment based on pure reason, boomerangs back onto the critic's own implicit demand that queer artists of color occupy contradictory roles: on the one hand, Araki as a queer Asian American was expected to produce films that exist outside the purview of normative racial and sexual schemas, while on the other, Araki himself was held accountable to specific nonnormative racial and sexual stereotypes in his own public self-presentations, where explicit references to French New Wave, Andy Warhol, and industrial and shoegaze music felt "elitist." This is perhaps why *Totally F\*\*\*ed Up* reads as one of Araki's most obnoxiously art-damaged films in its outright homage to Jean-Luc Godard's *Masculin Féminin* (1966).[57] Like *Masculin Féminin*, *Totally F\*\*\*ed Up* is divided into fifteen parts, and its nonlinear narrative foregrounds the intertitle technique that Godard mastered in his 1966 film. Araki's 1993 work showcases a group of queer disenfranchised youth and their seemingly boring suburban lives in contemporary Los Angeles. Harking back to Laura Aguilar's poignant mediation in *The Knife*, the film begins with a newspaper report on the surge of teenage suicides in the early 1990s, of which queer and gay teens constituted a startling percentage. From the film's opening frame, viewers infer that it will somehow address the issue of gay suicide within the context of a post-Reaganite industrial Los Angeles—but it never does. Here again, Rayns takes issue with Araki's easy sidestepping of the "sociological questions raised by the newspaper clipping on which the film opens." Rayns finds it too easy that, "as the film goes on, its purported randomness looks more and more like a cop-out, a mask for an underlying (and decidedly un-Godardian) sentimentality."[58] Moving away from Godard's own stylistic intentions, I am interested in how Araki's "mask" for sentimentality echoes the excessive minimalism we find in Gonzalez-Torres's work. Rather than engaging in social realism, Araki's film formalizes a fundamental notion of loss tethered to the question of malaise.

Araki's malaise might be summed up in Rayns's own words: "Araki, himself no spring chicken himself at the age of 35, may pride himself on getting so close to emotionally inarticulate teenagers, but he ought to be experienced enough to know that empathy alone gets you nowhere."[59] It appears as if Rayns understands Araki's stylized discontent, too, as "emotionally inarticulate," a nontragic dissatisfaction that permeates his film through a sentimentality that toggles between redefined notions of solipsism and empathy: for Rayns, Araki appears conflicted between an emotionally naïve understanding that the presence of the self to the self is the only thing guaranteed (solipsism) and a sentimental tendency to hide from oneself in others (empathy). Once again, this point is made clear in the composition and narrative of *Totally F\*\*\*ed Up*.

The beginning of the film introduces a portrait of six queer teenagers: Andy (the ethnically ambiguous object of desire who becomes the film's main character), Tommy (a promiscuous and curious teen whose father disowns him when he comes out as gay), Michele and Patricia (the lesbian couple that occupies an almost ornamental role compared to the gay boys in the clique), and Deric and Steven (an African American and a Chicano, respectively, involved in a tumultuous, unfaithful relationship). Steven is an aspiring filmmaker who, like Araki, insists on visually recording the quotidian happenings of his close circle of friends. The following section attempts to give an account of this queer Chicano drive embedded within a film that questions its own status as an ethnic-racially driven script. Methodologically, this requires attention to the very dynamic that Rayns diagnosed between the contrasting elements of solipsism and empathy. It is my hope to lay out a reading of Araki and his film *Totally F\*\*\*ed Up* that does not emphasize the absence of a Chicano sensibility but rather points to an inarticulate Chicano style that infiltrates the film as the stain of loss itself.

## Between Araki and Steven

*Totally F\*\*\*ed Up* vacillates between the director's cinematic shots and moving images that are captured by Steven's lo-fi camcorder. The film's heavy use of a camcorder aesthetic derives from the DIY subcultures of the late 1980s and early 1990s and is also represented in queer avant-garde art of the time, like Peggy Ahwesh's *Strange Weather* (1993) or the early videos of Sadie Benning. Chapter 2 of this book reminds us that Chicano lo-fi style marks a low fidelity to the reproduction of the norm, whether it be the dominant Chicano nationalist narrative or the towering culture of American consumerism. Additionally, such style reflects what Lucas Hilderbrand terms an "aesthetics of access" unfolding across a variety of analog media, especially VHS tapes, as a particular aesthetics of failure though nonetheless relational.[60] This particular style influences Araki's filmmaking by allowing him to visually exaggerate the camcorder's grainy materiality, which signifies incompleteness and amateurism, on the one hand, while also demonstrating his own personal entanglement with his project, on the other. In other words, despite feeling irreverent about or indifferent to identity politics, Araki is radically attached to his art projects and invested in circulating his own story through a quasi-autoethnographic mode of production. But this aesthetics of access also registers what Sandra Ruiz has beautifully termed an "aesthetics of mediated ontologies." Through the artwork of the late Ryan Rivera, Ruiz surmises that the screen exploits sense and perceptions to the extent that the "dialectic [between subject and object] becomes the scene of the exchange," endemic of the existential weight burdened in the act of waiting, which she understands as having "profound implications" on ethnic-racial and sexualized desire.[61] Thus, in extending the pedagogical scene of exchange inherent within the act of waiting, Araki uses media to, in a sense, ventriloquize experience. The queer director tells his story about loss through the character of a queer Chicano teenager, Steven. Araki's subtle yet persistent attempt to give an autobiographical account culminates in a strategic camouflaging of his authorial voice and directorial gaze through Steven's queer Chicano standpoint.

    I use "standpoint" here to gesture to debates in certain feminist strands of thought over standpoint epistemologies and how they complicate questions of ethnography. Taking as a starting point the importance of the technical substrate of the unconscious, as that "mark of the noncoincidence of subjectivity with consciousness," Patricia Clough has shown how some autoethnographic writing begins with the disavowal of unconscious thought and desire in order to suppose a much "fuller or more accurate or even more ethical" account of knowledge—at best, a self-knowing.[62] By contrast, Clough argues, a political refusal of fullness and accuracy makes room for cross-affiliations enabled by a self-differing, autoaffectionate desire that is not predicated on giving presence to oneself. Autoaffection underscores the unconscious or absent element within a text and identity, rendering meaning, coherency, and authenticity impossible. Araki, by utilizing Steven to tell his story, relinquishes his own voice, displacing it through a queer Chicano sensibility that is doubly disavowed by contemporaneous white queer cinema and the dominant Chicano culture of normative sexuality. It should be no surprise that the queer Chicano character functions as Araki's authorial surrogate in his film, while Araki himself obscures his own voice in public appearances by performing a vacuous personality.

Like Gonzalez-Torres's *Untitled (Orpheus, Twice)*, Araki's film necessitates a reading that displaces the overly fraught binaries between inner and outer and especially between passive and active, in order to read Steven and Araki beside each other. Once again, we encounter the infrastructure of malaise as the very loss of minor voices emerging through the gathering of singular yet contrasting moments of desire. As Araki imagines himself as a brown Chicano living in Los Angeles, disenfranchised, bored, in love, and ambivalent, he creates the narrative of *Totally F\*\*\*ed Up* out of a semiautobiographical story (literally, the narrative of the film begins when Steven stops recording). If skeptical readers are not completely convinced, Araki himself leaves certain clues for his viewers to decipher this punk form of infiltration. Take, for instance, a moment in the film when Steven, wallowing in teenage angst from being torn between two gay lovers, stares up at the ceiling, where the camera is located, and stares back, his gaze lingering in a sort of blasé way (figure 4.5). Steven's brown body lies dazed and confused, confined by his own burgeoning young emotions. He has spent the first half of *Totally F\*\*\*ed Up* filming his friends, even asking them to come in and rehearse tiny snippets of confessional opinions on social problems such as AIDS and safe sex, boredom, and the age-old question about whether love actually exists. These interviews are an effort to document and archive not only his experience as a queer Chicano in Los Angeles but also his queer circle of friends. They are reminiscent of the dramatic

Figure 4.5. Still from *Totally F\*\*\*ed Up* (1993).

confessional culture that MTV's *Real World* later co-opted and commodified as reality TV. But they are perhaps also a response to Andy Warhol's screen tests, if we remember that Warhol too was invested in capturing his circle of friends to then direct them and make them perform for his camera.

In the scene I am describing, however, the camera turns to Steven through Araki's eyes. At this moment, the filmmaker stares at his authorial surrogate through the camera's lens, short-circuiting any easy accusation of narcissism on the part of the filmmaker through the presence of a queer Chicano counterculture embodied in Steven's returning gaze. This scene performs a sort of romanticism that blames the political and economic context of Los Angeles in the early 1990s for the overwhelming nihilism and self-absorption paralyzing youth culture. (Here we can recall a scene in which another character, Andy, wears a T-shirt that reads, "I Blame Society"—an intertextual reference to the malcontent LA punk in the 1984 film *Repo Man*.) However, the gaze connecting Steven with Araki through the proxy of the camera also makes us see how a fundamental failure of meaning is displaced onto the romantic or sentimental subject in order to, as Paul de Man argues, "[retreat] behind a historical scheme which, apocalyptic as it may sound, is basically reassuring and bland."[63] This is to say, in addition to our historical framings and political economic analyses of aesthetic objects, new optics attuned to the style politics between Steven's and Araki's double glance reveal the critical difference operating within Araki's work. In short, if Araki understood the impossible task of representing ethnic identity to be a burden, it was also one of opportunity: a chance to insert a queer Chicano aesthetics of dissatisfaction.

On closer examination of this shot, an intertextual object emerges just *beside* Steven's seemingly thrown body. Floating in the light-blue sea of Steven's bed is a pink book titled *What Is Cinema?* This intertext is, in fact, an early edition of the famous French film critic and philosopher André Bazin's canonical *What Is Cinema?*, volume 1, a series of essays exploring the humanist dimension of cinematic style that were translated into English in 1961. There Bazin argued for long, extended shots to accomplish the mise-en-scène. But, in evoking Bazin, Araki quickly disidentifies with the film theorist by flooding the mise-en-scène with quick flashes of intertextual and cultural paraphernalia. From this book's fleeting appearance on-screen (the shot lasts only two seconds, and we never see the book again), we recognize the personal *attention* that Araki applied to his film through his concern for detail. And it is no coincidence that we find our Chicano beside Bazin, since, like Steven, the French theorist was an avid humanist and idealist. Bazin was an ardent advocate for the mise-en-scène style in cinema, which Araki makes great use of in *Totally F\*\*\*ed Up*. For Bazin, mise-en-scène allowed the director to capture a provisional unity of space that would emphasize the singularity of the objects captured in the frame. The long cinematic takes that this method requires speak to the ongoingness of malaise, if only to have viewers recognize, however briefly, the singularity and beauty of an object through the boredom of having to dwell on its properties.[64] In this case, Araki utilizes the body of a queer Chicano youth in order to illuminate the intellectual and aesthetic influences not only on his own cinematic work but also on the character development of Steven as an aspiring experimental filmmaker.

The spatial confines of this nonoppositional method of contrast-via-affinity remind us that central to the aesthetic agnosticism of besideness is the loss of unity itself. Araki resists many of the conventional theories of film criticism derivative of Bazin. Yet Araki's own ambivalence over Bazin's high status in film criticism does not stop the filmmaker from reworking the mise-en-scène technique into his own stylistic signature. Araki's style marks how a loss of unity only reinforces the aesthetic force of singular objects, not only through varied shots of contrasting texts, objects, bodies, and sounds but also through his films' passionate resistance to narrative completion. Araki's own discontent with cinematic unity indicates the emotional situation of the film's general malaise. In *Totally F\*\*\*ed Up*, Araki's malaise figures as his own loss of commonality with Bazin, and yet this is exactly what makes Bazin operative for a Chicano sensibility embodied in Steven. In short, Araki contrasts Bazin's understanding of the unity of space that the mise-en-scène creates with intertextuals that point to a sensibility escaping the frame, all while underscoring their lying close in relation—a continuous space created through discontinuous object relations.

Reflecting on the possible utopian function of an aesthetics of alienation within philosophy, the American philosopher J. M. Bernstein writes,

> To now conceive of a world in which determinate, subsumptive judgment predominates over common sense is to conceive of a world in which the interest in knowledge has come to mean an interest in what things are apart from any other interests. . . . From the perspective of reflective judgment, the attainment of such a world looks like a loss; a loss of commonness and solidarity. Or better, it images a common world without solidarity. . . . In such a world, our world, judgments of beauty are memorial: in making aesthetic judgments we judge things "as if" from the perspective of our lost common sense, a common sense that may have never existed.[65]

This passage could be read as a sentimental comparison of Kant's First Critique (*Critique of Pure Reason*) with his Third Critique (*Critique of Judgment*). What I would like to linger on in Bernstein's discussion is how he figures the world as a sharing of something that might not even exist. Aesthetic judgments are predicated on a negation of a primal unity of things that consequently frees up objects to exist without the obligation of relating to one another. But when we make judgments, we make them under the illusion of having once had knowledge of things, only to encounter the loss of unity inherent in the search for knowledge. Therefore, "judgments of beauty are memorial"; they calcify the very gap that connects objects in common. In a similar way, the stylistic malaise of *Totally F\*\*\*ed Up* minds the gap between seemingly disparate objects in order to cohere a mode of cinematic production that does not easily conform to dominant notions of representational politics, cinematic conventions of narrative, or compositional unity. Instead, contrasting singularities are operative in their inoperativity *as* a community, if only to highlight how malaise appears as the very "illusion" of loss, "'as if' from the perspective of our lost common sense." After all, as Jean Luc Nancy has pithily proclaimed: "The like is not the same."[66] Style also underscores the workings of false likeness, similar to the way Araki links his unlikely Chicano authorial surrogate, Steven, through their common though unsolidified sense of malaise.[67]

Bazin's famous question "What Is Cinema?" opens up another unlikely connection between Araki and Steven by calling into question the stylistic interconnections of film and video. One might be able to ask, "What *is* cinema?" but in posing that question about video, one sees how video exists *with* other media, not outside of them. For instance, Steven's video camera calls to Araki's cinematic lens. However, Araki's desire for filmic realism, articulated by Steven's status as authorial surrogate and his subsequent utilization of a camcorder technique, registers the very impossibility of video to exist just for itself. Attuning to medium specificity through the work of the video scholar James M. Moran offers an analysis of how style is not only determined by the flows of historical change confronting a precarious status quo. Style also unlocks the impasse to self-identity implicated within the ever-changing medium of video.[68]

Dominant paradigms for analyzing video infused with postmodern "pastiche and schizophrenia," qualities typical of *Totally F\*\*\*ed Up* (and other Araki works like *The Doom Generation*, according to the film scholar Kylo-Patrick R. Hart), fail to account for the importance of style as a deferred desire for autoaffection, a critical difference itself, or that absent though nonetheless structuring element within identity.[69] When examined closely, stylized discontents refuse cathartic techniques of representational unity. Let us not forget Jameson's own seemingly categorical conclusion that there will never be a theory of video.⁷⁰ However, for Moran, "video is the medium that seems to have made an *irrevocable difference* in how we theorize about specificity, for its chameleon-like [recall here Felix Gonzalez-Torres's self-description as an infiltrator] interface between film, television, computers, telephones, and even architecture seems forever in flux."⁷¹ Theories of specificity that are loyal to the singularity of the medium encounter a definitional crisis at the level of video production, since "video, in short, never seems present only to itself."⁷²

And though theories of medium specificity should level down to the local dimensions of production, taking into account the social, cultural, and political forces that make sense of a style that *seems* ahistorical or apolitical, these tensions are already made visible and tangible through the interrelation between video and film in Araki's work. Thus, when Araki interjects a title card reading, "another homo movie by gregg araki," the viewer sutures a home-movie experience to that of watching a film; video by the late 1980s and early '90s was the primary medium for home-movie recordings, thereby relegating film to solely a high art medium.

However, *Totally F\*\*\*ed Up* fails to be both a "homo movie" and a movie "by" Araki. Considering the grating linkages between Steven and Araki, perhaps a more apt description of *Totally F\*\*\*ed Up* is a "queer Chicano movie for Araki," because what Moran isolates as video's "irrevocable difference" corroborates how *Totally F\*\*\*ed Up* marks a moment in which queer Chicano cultural production intersects with NQC through the cloak of a punk and DIY style bent on sharing "the everyday hopes and frustrations of a close circle of gay and lesbian teens, as well as their somewhat jaundiced views of the culture on whose margins they find themselves surviving."⁷³ Araki's somewhat sentimental plot posits a community-building function founded on the negation of dominant social forms of desire and belonging, instead suggesting ways of survival enabled by distinguishing the singularities of hope and disappointment. The precarious gatherings of contrasting pleasures that can fill the vacancy of the now inform the style of discontent that this chapter has been tracing. Malaise, then, cannot be understood without the failure of autoaffection, a failure that productively brings into appearance the shared potential of contrasting singularities: Steven with Araki, video with film, subjectivity with the nonsubjective, Chicano with gay. It is not so much that these singularities are equivalent or whole onto themselves but quite the opposite: acknowledging the inconclusive task of ever understanding one without another.

As I have discussed, because Araki refuses to make films about his (ethnic) identity, the settings of his films (Los Angeles) come to stand in for the displaced ethnic subject through the sociological and historical schema shaping much of post-Reagan Los Angeles. It is reassuring to solely blame Reagan's policies for the disenfranchisement of minoritarian populations. But this reduction obscures a deeper problem behind the impasse to self-identity. If Reagan's America mocks the promise of liberation encapsulated by the social movements of post-1968, then in the transition from this landscape to the 1990s, one experiences the unfolding of a promised future denied. Malaise permeates such a phenomenon since this particular style of dissatisfaction rests on the sense that something *still* remains a problem. This slowing down of self-reflection requires a mode of lingering within the meta-structure of self-examination, an examination that occupies the vacant lot where the self once was in order to find itself, once again, sorted out and displaced. In lingering with the problem that remains, disappointment flips into hope and back again. Thus, if mise-en-scène is supposed to draw our attention to the contrasting quality of singular objects (Steven's brown body against the blue bed and pink philosophy book), then malaise needs to also be punctuated with a cluster of singular moments of hope within the clearing enacted by self-examination.

For the queer counterculture in Los Angeles, and specifically in Araki's own biography, ecstasy offered such a promise of escape. Araki's own experience in the growing rave scene of post-punk Los Angeles in the early 1990s mirrors a moment when Steven turns to his camcorder to capture one of the film's most sentimental, if not one of its most romantic, visual moments.[74] In part 3 of the film, a scene depicts six queer adolescents loitering in an empty parking garage while "sorted out," as it were, on ecstasy. Steven tells the camera to "just say go." The film then cuts to what we assume is Steven's perspective through the aperture of his video camcorder. Through Steven's eye, we first see the delicate pills exposed on an open palm in loose relation to one another, each signifying their

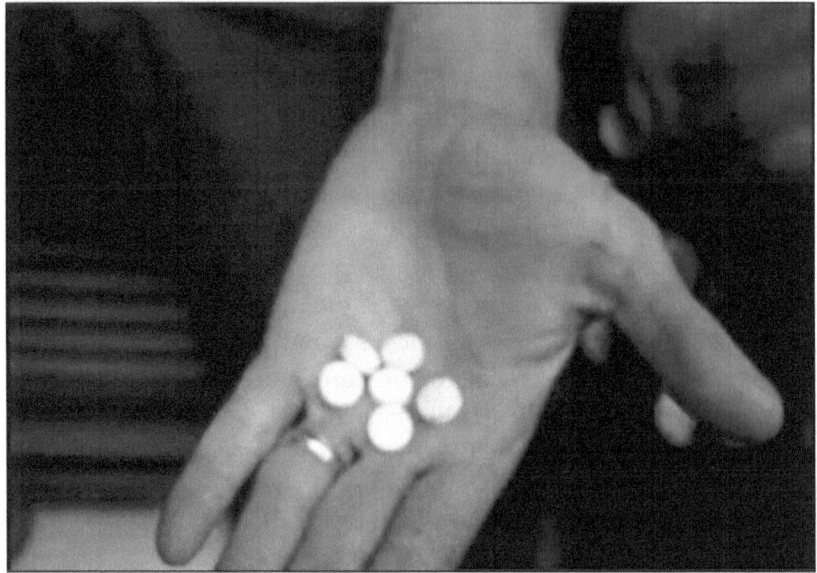

Figure 4.6. Still from *Totally F\*\*\*ed Up* (1993).

singularity, spaced out yet still gathered in a shared plurality (figure 4.6). We see pulsating images of the teens precariously placing the tiny white pills on their eager tongues, twirling around to the industrial music of My Life with the Thrill Kill Kult, falling down, and stumbling around as they drift through the aisles of a 7/11 convenience store, ready to be inspired by some tasty candy bar or midnight snack. The images from Steven's analog camcorder, agitated by his jerky movements, produce a gritty and strobing beat that adds a diaristic quality to *Totally F\*\*\*ed Up*. The autobiographical or autoethnographic drive within queer subcultures at the time, made somewhat easier by accessible technology such as the camcorder, inflected queer cultural production with personal narrative, therefore calling into question the legitimacy and overall stifling distinction between autobiographical content and form.

This documentary *style*, as opposed to the genre of the documentary, also resonates with the ways that Asco, Alice Bag, and the fictional character of Steven created art for their friends. The viewer gleans a similar modesty and innocence from the ordinary moments we see through Steven's video camera in *Totally F\*\*\*ed Up*. This scene is beautiful in its composition and lazy in its affect, that is, swollen with an overwhelming sense of malaise and boredom, as well as with subtle indications of pleasure and escape; we witness an exercise in the strobing intensities that we call freedom and difference.

Seen through Steven's eye, the scene metonymically relates to the autonomous image of freedom that 1968 connotes, almost like a lost future imagined some twenty-five years before the making of *Totally F\*\*\*ed Up*. Araki makes this point through an intertitle citing a line from Christopher Fry's play *Duel of Angels*, which was adapted from Jean Giroudaux's *Pour Lucrèce* (1960), a work Godard wanted to produce into a film but never did. The title card reads, "Purity is not of this world, but every 25 years we see a glimmer, a flash" (figure 4.7). On the occasion of reviewing Fry's translation of Giroudaux, Paul de Man writes of the theme of purity in Giroudaux's plays not as "a prelapsarian childlike innocence" but instead as "the ability to sin gracefully."[75] Araki's queer kids, totally fucked up as they are, gracefully toss themselves around with a certain virtue, akin to what de Man describes as a "sense of style, of detachment, of bright-colored beauty," effectively interilluminating one another like fireflies in a dark field.[76]

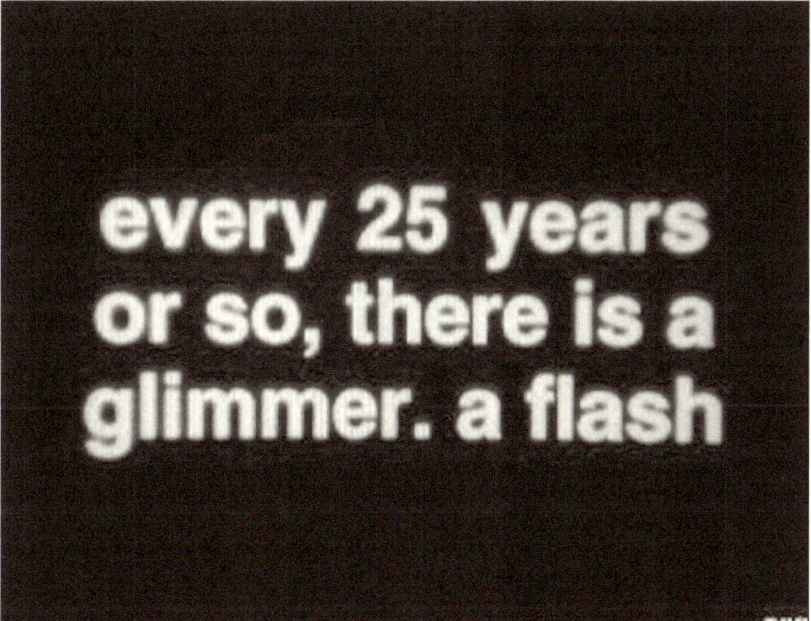

Figure 4.7. Intertitle from *Totally F\*\*\*ed Up* (1993).

The strobe effect from the video camcorder suggests that the twinkling of purity and the ecstatic emerge *with* time, not *as* time. This is to say that both the flash and the glimmer of purity emerge simultaneously, rather than sequentially. The halo of the future and the past, of the tenuous split between "now and here" and "then and there" that José Muñoz draws on in his *Cruising Utopia: The Then and There of Queer Futurity*, resembles the beauty and contrast effect of malaise, since malaise spaces out the highs with intervals like those "25 years" that sort and displace glimmers of purity. Twenty-five years prior to Araki's *Totally F\*\*\*ed Up* was the global '68 image of freedom and difference, denied by a then-parental culture though later sifted out by Steven's queer eye. In Steven's educated gaze, the Chicano authorial surrogate for Araki's queerness, the immemorable lives on in a lazy, ennui-inflected enchantment with disenchantment.

In *Totally F\*\*\*ed Up*, Steven gives us a portrait of his friends, each confessing their personal philosophies and shared ennui.[77] We can argue, then, that Araki presents us with a portrait of portraiture, and one including his own vicariated desires located in Steven. Such fragmented points of view and lack of narrative coherence yield an ununified aesthetic experience; and it is precisely the aesthetic realm that affords an opportunity to linger with the impossibility of unity. Queer latinidad implies attending to the discontinuities that compose such a phenomenon. The scholar Juana María Rodríguez's corpus of work on the matter demonstrates how the discursive configurations of latinidad are indeed malleable but leave those who are afflicted under its sign longing, even sexually longing, for connections that do not add up to something definable, much like the characters in Araki's film.[78] At the same time, Ramon Rivera-Servera claims that queer latinidad is "palpable, even if temporarily, as an affective tie among friends, family members, and even strangers . . . feeling a community in pleasure," a feeling also operative in the film.[79] Without compensating for a loss of a wholeness that never existed, queer latinidad registers an inconclusive discourse and indeed a determinate palpable longing.

*Totally F\*\*\*ed Up* ends with the protagonist, Andy, in a bout of despair, dialing a call to each of his friends to no avail; every call encounters the dreaded busy signal indicative of a failed connection. Despaired,

Andy drinks half a bottle of whiskey laced with cleaning fluids, convulses, and coughs up blood before he falls into the pool and presumably dies by suicide. The shot fades out into a white monochrome screen, and after a momentary pause, Steven's eye returns with a taped recording of Andy sitting on grass nonchalantly smoking a cigarette as the wind blows through his hair, confessing, "All I really want is to be happy for like one second, be able to look around and not to just see shit, say, 'Hey, it's a beautiful day.' [He smirks and takes a drag.] I want to enjoy life while I'm still young enough to appreciate it. I mean, that is what it's all about, right?" The screen then freezes on Andy's ambivalent visage, though still flickering as if a memory, one echoing Aguilar's video art from the beginning of this chapter, Ray Navarro's scene in chapter 3, and Eugene's opening confession in *The Decline of Western Civilization* in chapter 1. Here, though, through Steven's eye, we witness an ambivalent hope presented as evidence of a shared failure. The film cuts away from the home video and spans the group of friends staring at the camera-*cum*-TV-screen: first Steven with a morose and determinate look; then Michelle and Patricia, who look uncomfortable and avoid the camera's eye; next Deric, who looks down in shame; and finally Ian, caressing a manikin head, tracing its eyes and lips as if it were a lover or a friend in a casket. At this moment, the final shot of the film suddenly ends with Steven quickly getting up and, though partially out of frame, clicking off Araki's camera.

In Steven's moving portrait of Andy, he effectively captures the immobile image of loss. Indeed, Araki via Steven catches the gaze of a disappointed object of desire, which in turn tells us something about what *we* expect our objects to do. Antonio Viego, in remarking on the importance of his colleague Robyn Wiegman's provocative monograph *Object Lessons*, cautions,

> As the "desire for critical practice to do emancipatory work," to use the language of *Object Lessons*, more often than not finds some of us disappointed in our objects' inability to do what we keep teaching and being taught they'd do. If you can manage to not catch the gaze of the disappointing objects staring back at you, suggesting you failed them, you might avoid the paralysis that would prevent you from trying to find

ever more new objects in which to be disappointed. This scenario perversely impoverishes the psychoanalytic definition of desire. If desire is the desire for something else, the desire for desire, the desire operative in critical practice is always the desire for something else that's disappointing, something else that fails us. This may help explain why the critique of the institutionalization of "identity knowledges" most often takes the shape of a lamentation that naturalizes sadness, grief and sorrow as the affective properties of the objects and not, as Wiegman argues, "the disciplinary demands that govern what we expect our objects and analytics to do."[80]

I quote this incredibly important passage at length because it offers a larger lesson about the operations of disappointment for critical practice, especially in fields like queer studies and Latino studies, and the significance of loss and desire for these analytics. Intellectual projects such as queer latinidad are usually set up to fail, because any account of it (even in its plurality) fails to cohere at the very attempt at its definition.[81] Like Orpheus's lament, the unattainable face that queer latinidad presents turns away at the very moment of its imagining. However, I would add that in order to understand Viego's and Wiegman's skepticism around identity-knowledge fields and their desire for emancipatory work, one must also account for the fundamental role aesthetics plays in these operations.[82] *Dissatisfactions* has assembled a collection of cultural objects that have *stylized* their discontent with the given world; and *Dissatisfactions* as an intellectual project too has attempted to stylize a critique of certain disciplinary protocols like positivism, coherency, affirmation, and precritical drives toward historical recovery. Such style politics, this book has argued, announce the inexorable disappointment these ideologies produce (indeed, depend on) due to the structural delay in understanding their purported stakes. However, the queerness in identifying with this determinate negation reframes the performance of the everyday or one's way of life (*manera de ser*) into a process of picture-thinking (*Vorstellung*), or in Andy's words again: "... [to] be able to *look* around and not to just see shit, *say*, 'Hey, it's a *beautiful* day.'" For, as Nadia Ellis has beautifully underscored, "failure in queerness is really just a mark of the insufficiency that makes trying necessary."[83]

To try—*that there*—in all its beautiful inadequacies, moves Araki, overwhelms Andy, and holds Steven in a field of malaise, where they desire to "be happy for like one second," to enjoy life while one is still young enough to appreciate it, and where trying is really what stylized discontents are all about.

Right?

## Conclusion

*Dream Damaged, or, A Portrait of Queer Latinidad*
Dream baby dream
Come on and dream baby dream
Forever
—Suicide, "Dream Baby Dream," 1979

The insufficiency that makes trying necessary composes an important aspect of *Dissatisfactions'* lesson and, consequently, calls us to participate in its practice. From the social world of Los Angeles's post-1968 nauseating historical situation, which its queer punk denizen sought to formalize as a style, to the Chicana feminists' lo-fi attitudes and refusal of both the dominant *and* marginal norms, the act of trying only amplified at the onset of the AIDS epidemic in the United States. To be sure, ambivalence and malaise in this study do not evidence some ceding of agency, some romanticized surrender. No. They mark the *need* for better conceptions of political agency in the face of aggression, self-destruction, and catharsis. Beginning with dissatisfaction shows how the labor of imagining and remembering, indeed of dreaming, is what one does when failure is both the condition and the impetus. Thus, in this small attempt at a conclusion, I offer two final artworks by Gonzalez-Torres that push dissatisfaction to the edge overlooking hope.

Consider Gonzalez-Torres's touching piece *Untitled (Portrait of Ross in L.A.)* (figure C.1). Here, the viewer is given over to a pile of individually wrapped candy, each in different cellophane colors, assembled in a corner of a museum space. The participatory installation piece hails museumgoers to take a piece of candy, and as the day goes on, the assembled pile diminishes, with every visitor contributing to the taking of Ross Laycock's figurative body. Gonzalez-Torres insisted that the pile of candy weighed the same as Ross's AIDS-stricken body at the end of his life. The artist also stipulates that the pile be replenished the next

Figure 5.1. "*Untitled*" (*Portrait of Ross in LA*), 1991. Installed in *Felix Gonzalez-Torres*. Luhring Augustine Hetzler Gallery, Los Angeles. October 19–November 16, 1991. Photographer: James Franklin.

day. This signals "hope and regeneration" for Joshua Chambers-Letson.[1] Sandra Ruiz agrees with Chambers-Letson but also sees a "looping ingestion that makes [the spectator] accountable to a diseased life."[2] I am intrigued by the image of temporal looping, which is so central to Ruiz's existential project and her theorizing of endurance in colonial time. For one, Ruiz departs from a dominant strand of Latino studies that privileges space (borders, islands, rurality, etc.) over temporality. Ruiz understands Latino studies' "typical spatial obsession" as neglecting the importance of queer temporality to "antioppressive and anticolonial" performances.[3] And centering temporality would accord with the artwork at hand. Recalling Gonzalez-Torres's lesson to his lover in chapter 4, that "time has been so generous to us," the artist and the participants continuously mold a portrait of a lover, a figurative body that breathes with participation and is made up of the raw materiality of (Ross's favorite) candy, a consumable reminder of innocence. Time affords concern outside the "compressed places of violence" conditioned by colonialism, sexualization, and racialization.[4] But what does this have to do with queer latinidad? And how exactly is this piece a portrait?

I would like to suggest that portraiture helps depict some of the complicated questions that the phenomenon of queer latinidad encapsulates, especially if we consider portraiture's relationship to style's singular-universal quality described in this book's introduction. Chameleon-like in its ability to translate across aesthetic genres such as literature, photography, sculpture, and painting, portraiture traditionally captures a person's attributes and sometimes mood by exhibiting a composed face and/or bodily comportment. Portraiture captures and in so doing reveals a person's essence. If portraiture is to mean a giving-form-to, such as in drawing, or a capturing-of-content, such as in portrait photography, then I want to also suggest that it may be read as an aesthetic judgment, a judgment that is not only historical and social but most importantly pedagogical and, as José Muñoz has advocated, can also be an "educated mode of desiring."[5]

Kaja Silverman's *The Miracle of Analogy* reverses much of the historical understanding of portraiture by linking it to the function of photography's "ontological calling card," which exposes the interconnections and intersubjective relations within a "vast constellation of analogies."[6] Silverman qualifies "analogy" as not meaning "sameness, symbolic equivalence, logical adequation, [or] even a rhetorical relationship."[7] Instead, the author intends "analogy" to signify a structure of the world, indeed of Being, that is authorless, untranscendable, and "give[s] everything the same ontological weight."[8] After quoting a beautiful Walt Whitman passage about similitude, Silverman pointedly contends, "It is only through this interlocking that we ourselves exist. Two is the smallest unit of Being."[9]

Silverman's provocation and rhetorical arithmetic neatly corresponds with other Gonzalez-Torres artworks that posit two as a function of the installation—two mirrors, two clocks, two pools of water, two pillows—to show the intimacy of touch, proximity, and (non)relation.[10] But what of the pile of candy, along with Ruiz's contribution to ontology and the looping structure to Being that she encourages Latino studies to acknowledge? Did we not just end back at the "typical spatial obsession" plaguing Latino studies in foregrounding the besideness explored in chapter 4? Is not the formulation "Two is the smallest unit of Being" positing a spatial understanding of ontology? To escape the trap of mere spatiality, another of Gonzalez-Torres's artworks, when placed beside *Untitled (Portrait of Ross in L.A.)*, remodifies the spatial to account for temporality while foregrounding a contradiction that one astute anonymous reader pinpointed in *Dissatisfactions*' theory of style. To quickly recount, the politics of style hinges on a dialectical relationship between past and present, between the old and the new. Yet, as we saw in chapter 4, bricolage, constellations, and creative assemblage make up *Dissatisfactions*' methodology. The anonymous reader is correct in drawing attention to the contradiction between style's dialectical dynamic and the constellation of singularities/objects as method in this study. But in thinking with queer latinidad, how might we formalize the gap between these two different methodological framings? Taking seriously the anonymous reader's observation, queer latinidad with portraiture helps me understand this theoretical tension, and so I could not escape thinking about *Untitled (Portrait of Ross in L.A.)* alongside Gonzalez-Torres's 1990 installation piece *Untitled (Death by Gun)*.

Another participatory installation, *Untitled (Death by Gun)* is composed of a nine-inch-tall poster stack meant to be depleted and replenished with endless copies (figure C.2). The viewer approaches the stack first as a sculpture, confused as to whether the posters are meant to be taken or left untouched. On closer examination, the black-and-white high-contrast print of the poster lists names of individuals with text and portraits of them, with some shown deceased. The piece appropriates without context a *Time* magazine article titled "7 Deadly Days," which listed the names of 460 persons killed by gun violence in the United States during the week of May 1–7, 1989. Here, Gonzalez-Torres breaks from his other works by presenting a political lesson, what Amanda Cruz has called the artist "at his most didactic."[11] Gonzalez-Torres does not publicly announce his political stance on gun violence in the US but instead visually translates a feeling that is difficult or impossible to share. As the posters endlessly disseminate into the public *and* into the future, we can say that the artist "leaps ahead" of us, like a teacher, to reflect back to us, as in a loop, that thing that we already knew but cannot define. Twenty-seven years after *Time*'s article, I was twenty-eight years old when I woke up to the horrifying news of forty-nine individuals shot

Figure 5.2. "*Untitled*" (*Death by Gun*), 1990. Installed in *Whitney Biennial 1991*. The Whitney Museum of American Art, New York, NY. April 19–June 16, 1991. Cur. Richard Armstrong, John G. Hanhardt, Richard Marshall, and Lisa Phillips.

dead in a mass shooting at a queer nightclub in Orlando, Florida. In no way can one make sense of the senseless, but after the twenty-fifth (and counting) mass shooting in the United States since Orlando, one gets the sickening sense that death by gun has become the norm. Indeed, hope and regeneration would appear to spring forth *after* the return of the Same.

Like a photographic negative ontologically tied to the positive prints of its decedents, how are we to hold similar things at once without collapsing their difference into one? This is a fundamental question in studying queer latinidad. But first, I must concede that queer latinidad does not exist per se, because queer latinidad is part of our cultural imaginary. An ensemble of discontinuities, lapses, differences, incongruities, antinomies, and aporias, queer latinidad would have to be visualized as something like a portrait-of-portraiture, just as *Untitled (Death by Gun)* shows us. And similarly to *Untitled (Portrait of Ross in L.A.)*, queer latinidad's figurative body breathes with love, even when we take from it, or, rather, especially when we take from it. The lesson here reveals itself through analogical thinking, best understood as another way of picture-thinking, snapshots: rewinding the clock with no regrets; finding oneself enmeshed in a constellation of differences; admiring the horizon over which a new dawn fades into the negative.

ACKNOWLEDGMENTS

This book would not have been possible without the sustained love, care, concern, patience, and intelligence that I have been lucky to encounter so early in this journey. Thank you first to Diana Taylor, Karen Shimakawa, Josie Saldaña-Portillo, Licia Fiol-Matta, Barbara Browning, and Ann Pellegrini. Tavia Nyong'o not only saw this project through to the end during an emotionally tumultuous time, but most important to me, Tavia has become a dear friend in the process. Others at NYU nurtured this project and showed me the meaning of community and belonging in difference: Beth Stinson, Alex Pittman, Leon Hilton, Sareh Afshar, Daniel Sander, Jill Lane, Marcial Godoy, Zeb Tortorici, Lisa Duggan, Gayatri Gopinath, Renato Rosaldo, Anna McCarthy, Ana Dopico, and the late Juan Flores and Randy Martin.

Juana María Rodríguez and Deb Vargas animate the project's spirit, and both continue to demonstrate the grace that ought to inhere in mentorship—*gracias*. At Berkeley, when I could not bear thinking about the project due to sheer exhaustion, respite, kindness, and humor unexpectedly found me in conversations with Julia Bryan-Wilson, Poulomi Saha, Damon Young, Stephen Best, Raúl Coronado, and Nadia Ellis. In Northern California, I left the bright-eyed innocence one sheds with the profound privilege of entering the professoriate. Once in Colorado, John-Michael Rivera, Emma Pérez, Nicole Wright, Cheryl Higashida, Seema Sohi, Raúl Melgoza, Hector Ramirez, Jason Gladstone, and Maria Windell provided a deep intellectual community as I entered the track. Thank you to Thora Brylowe for many late-night conversations and for sharing the freedom of the dance floor with me.

Moving to Los Angeles changed everything, including this project. Since I arrived at UCLA, Beth Marchant and Rafael Pérez-Torres have been indispensable to my intellectual, professional, and personal growth; they continue to model for me the centrality of love with wit, intelligence with responsibility, and beauty with grace. I cannot express how humbled I am to be in your lives. UCLA's Department of Gender Studies changed my view of the world through the way my colleagues model collectivity: internal growth with a deep loyalty, bond, and connection in our shared struggles. UCLA is the ideal place for any young scholar setting out to make sense of the larger world. For the small world we have created here, thank you to Uri McMillan, Juliann Anesi, Judy Han, Grace Hong, Zeynep Korkman, Kate Norberg, Rachel Lee, Sarah Roberts, Safiya Nobel, Nancy Mithlo, Shannon Speed, Sharon Traweek, Juliet Williams, Alisa Bierria, Giancarlo Cornejo, Dan Bustillo, Maylei Blackwell, Veronica Terriquez, Carlos Santos, Yogita Goyal, Marissa López, Mitchum Huehls, Sean Metzger, Anurima Banjeri, Danny Snelson, Mishuana Goeman, Purnima Mankekar, Sherene Razack, Laura Gómez, Alex Stern, Abel Valenzuela, Charlene Villaseñor-Black, Jessica Cattelino, Richard Medrano, Van Do-Nguyen, Samantha Hogan, Keith Camacho, Barbara Van Nostrand, Kathleen McHugh, Eleanor Kaufman, Juliana Wang, Leisy Abrego, Vilma Ortiz, Matt Barreto, Alicia Gaspar de Alba, Gaye Johnson, Michelle Carriger, Celia Lacayo, Rebecca Epstein, Eboni Shaw, and Jenna Miller-Von Ah. Thank you to Carrie Hyde and Christopher Looby for allowing me to share this research with the Americanist Research Colloquium and to Suk-Young Kim for inviting me to present research with Theater and Performance Studies. My students have been a dream to work with.

This book includes many voices from friends and colleagues from across the years. I am beyond grateful to Alexandra Vazquez, Ricardo Montez, Jeanne Vaccaro, David Kurnick, Karen Tongson, Lucas Hilderbrand, Beth Freeman, Jennifer Doyle, Laura Gutiérrez, Ann Cvetkovich, Kandice Chuh, Chad Bennett, Zakiyya Jackson, Nao Bustamante, Sandy Soto, Wanda Alarcón, Michelle Habell-Pallán, Eliza Rodriguez, Ramon Rivera-Servera, Xandra Ibarra, Macarena Gómez-Barris, Martin Manalansan, Richard T. Rodríguez, C. Ondine Chavoya, Leticia Alvarado, Malik Gaines, Amber Musser, Homay King, Roshanak Kheshti, Joshua Chambers-Letson, Alberto Varón, Carmen Lamas, Renee Hudson, Julie Minich, Eng-Beng Lim, José Quiroga, Maia Gil'Adi, Eric Stanley, Lakshmi Padmanabhan, C. Riley Snorton, Nancy Mirabal, Larry La Fountain-Stokes, Angie Bonilla, Christine Balance, Erica Edwards, Marcia Ochoa, Ivan Ortiz, Karen Jaime, Roy Perez, Adrián

Flores, Hentyle Yapp, Tatiana Flores, Julian Wong-Nelson, and Patricia Gherovici.

The wild dream of making a life out of teaching, writing, and research was revealed to me in college, where Ricardo Ortíz, Elizabeth Velez, Dana Luciano and Nadine Ehlers first nurtured my craving for critical theory, feminism, and queer life. I owe my academic journey to them.

I am grateful to the Duke Literature Program for allowing me to present my research, and I am deeply indebted to Antonio Viego for his wit, intellect, and scholarship, which continue to motivate my own. I am always in awe of the grace and brilliance of Shane Vogel and Sandra Ruiz, who were the ideal editors for this project, and I continue to be humbled by their belief in me—thank you. Deep thanks to the wonderful team at NYU Press and especially to Furqan Sayeed and Eric Zinner, who has followed this project with an astute editorial eye.

The academic world can be quite lonely at times. So, I know I am beyond lucky to have never felt it because of my friendship with Iván Ramos—thank you for your near-perfect taste in almost everything. Similarly, Christina León was an early co-thinker and fellow shoegazer. Kaegan Sparks, my oldest friend, has stuck by me since we were in the same kindergarten play; childhood neighbors, we clamored for old films to watch and obscure texts to read and struggled through our twenties in New York City. She has read every word of this book since its nascent stage, and I cannot imagine a world without her. Summer Kim Lee is like a second sister to me; thank you for your unwavering closeness and love.

I am lucky to have a small Miami family in Zoilyn Gomez, Hector Gutierrez, Lidice Diaz, Danielle and Chris Solomon, Ana Dorcal, and Elise Muñoz. To my friends who make LA feel like home, my deepest gratitude to Lauren Stephenson, Shannon Davis, Jonathan Brophy, Simon Holguin, Stephanie Castro, Chris Zepeda-Millán, Avi Asher-Schapiro, Kandist Mallett, Aaron Cantú, Mark Huang, Jheanelle Brown, Donna Haratti, Susan and Will Utay, Bill Peris, Roger Henry, David Russell, and Justin Torres.

Pina taught me what unconditional love feels like.

Albert taught me how to be loved.

I thank my parents for their intense and otherworldly support. But above all, I thank them for the gift of reading. Stephanie, Freddie, and

Bobby continue to show me the beauty in difference and give me the will to always search for home. This book is for them—to my family. I love you all.

And finally, José Esteban Muñoz floats through all the pages, ideas, and labor in this book. When I was just beginning my graduate education, the first piece of advice he gave me was to jump into New York City and "get a sense of the world." His mentorship shaped my world, and though he may not be here anymore, he most definitely is a teacher who keeps teaching. I thank José for his love, his wisdom, and these words that reverberate throughout *Dissatisfactions*: "It's not that you have to change. . . . It's the world that must change." This book is also dedicated to him.

# NOTES

## INTRODUCTION

1. The Women's Building was a space where feminists gathered and participated in a host of programs including the Feminist Studio Workshop, the Summer Art Program, performance and gallery spaces, and the Women's Graphic Center, a for-profit arm of the Women's Building offering graphic design services to fund the Women's Building.
2. "Z," "Review of 4-13-79," *Slash* 2, no. 6 (June 1979).
3. Colin Gunckel, "'People Think We're Weird 'Cause We're Queer': Art Meets Punk in Los Angeles," in *Axis Mundo: Queer Networks in Chicano L.A.*, ed. C. Ondine Chavoya and David Evans Frantz (Munich: Prestel, 2018), 275.
4. Mark Fisher, *Ghosts of My Life: Writings on Depression, Hauntology and Lost Futures* (New Alresford, UK: Zero Books, 2014), 25–27.
5. Rubén Salazar, "Who Is Chicano? And What Is It That Chicanos Want?," *Los Angeles Times*, February 6, 1970.
6. José Limón, "The Folk Performance of 'Chicano' and the Cultural Limits of Political Ideology," *Southwest Education Development Laboratory* 62 (1979): 213.
7. Limón, 214 (emphasis added).
8. Sandra K. Soto, *Reading Chican@ Like a Queer: The De-mastery of Desire* (Austin: University of Texas Press, 2010), 96.
9. Theodor W. Adorno, *Problems of Moral Philosophy*, ed. Thomas Schröder, trans. Rodney Livingstone (Stanford, CA: Stanford University Press, 2000), 176.
10. James S. Ackerman, "A Theory of Style," *Journal of Aesthetics and Art Criticism* 20 (1962): 228.
11. Edward J. McCaughan, *Art and Social Movements: Cultural Politics in Mexico and Aztlán* (Durham, NC: Duke University Press, 2012), 102–103.
12. McCaughan, 1.
13. Ludwig Wittgenstein, *Philosophical Investigations: The German Text, with a Revised English Translation*, 3rd ed., trans. G. E. M. Anscombe (London: Wiley-Blackwell, 1991).
14. Michael Hardt and Antonio Negri, *Empire* (Cambridge, MA: Harvard University Press, 2001), 306.
15. José Esteban Muñoz, *Cruising Utopia: The Then and There of Queer Futurity* (New York: New York University Press, 2009), 189.
16. José Esteban Muñoz, *Disidentifications: Queers of Color and the Performance of Politics* (Minneapolis: University of Minnesota Press, 1999), 200.

17 Sandra Ruiz, *Ricanness: Enduring Time in Anticolonial Performance* (New York: New York University Press, 2019), 26.
18 Ruiz, 34.
19 Iván Ramos, *Unbelonging: Inauthentic Sounds in Mexican and Latinx Aesthetics* (New York: New York University Press, 2023), 4.
20 Richard T. Rodríguez, *A Kiss across the Ocean: Transatlantic Intimacies of British Post-Punk and US Latinidad* (Durham, NC: Duke University Press, 2022), 9. For a beautiful meditation on the aesthetic and philosophical consequences of "touch," particularly the (de)linking of body and soul, see Shane Vogel's "Touching Ecstasy: Muñozian Theory and the Extension of the Soul," *Social Text* 32, no. 4 (121) (2014): 47–57.
21 Juana Maria Rodríguez, *Sexual Futures, Queer Gestures, and Other Latina Longings* (New York: New York University Press, 2014), 7–18, 99–103. Another generative queer Latino scholar contributing to anti-identitarian though relational politics is Roy Pérez and his conceptualizations of "proximity," in his beautiful essay on the late Brown queer artist Mark Aguhar. See Roy Pérez, "Proximity: On the Work of Mark Aguhar," in *TrapDoor: Trans Cultural Production and the Politics of Visibility*, ed. Reina Gossett, Eric A. Stanley, and Johanna Burton (Cambridge, MA: MIT Press, 2017), 281–291.
22 See, for instance, Musser's incredible chapter on belonging and Brown jouissance in *Sensual Excess: Queer Femininity and Brown Jouissance* (New York: New York University Press, 2018), 69–94.
23 Leticia Alvarado, *Abject Performances: Aesthetics Strategies in Latino Cultural Production* (Durham, NC: Duke University Press, 2018), 16–17.
24 See Robb Hernández, *Archiving an Epidemic: Art, AIDS, and the Queer Chicanx Avant-Garde* (New York: New York University Press, 2019). Also see the art exhibition catalog C. Ondine Chavoya and Rita Gonzalez, eds., *Asco: Elite of the Obscure: A Retrospective 1972–1987* (Berlin: Hatje Cantz, 2011); and Hernández's field-defining essay "Asco: Ephemera, and Intergroup Exchange in LA," in *Side by Side: Collaborative Artistic Practices in the United States, 1960s–1980s*, ed. Gwyneth Shanks and Allie Tepper, vol. 3 of the *Living Collections Catalogue* (Minneapolis: Walker Art Center, 2020), https://walkerart.org.
25 Ruiz, *Ricanness*, 26.
26 Eve Kosofsky Sedgwick, *Tendencies* (Durham, NC: Duke University Press, 1993), xii.
27 Eve Kosofsky Sedgwick, *The Weather in Proust*, ed. Jonathan Goldberg (Durham, NC: Duke University Press, 2011), 201.
28 Soto, *Reading Chican@ Like a Queer*, 10. Soto's treatise opens with one of my favorite lines in queer Chicano/Latino studies: "The growing *dissatisfaction* over the past twenty-five years with monological and monocausal approaches to subjectivity and power has motivated some of the most powerful experiential creative writings by women of color, such as those included in the edited collection *This Bridge Called My Back: Writings by Radical Women of Color* (1981), and, a range of

interdisciplinary locations, including postcolonial studies, gender studies, African American Studies, and queer theory" (1; my emphasis). Central to the "growing dissatisfaction" is the expansiveness of the analytics offered by women of color and Chicana feminists, which *Dissatisfactions* attempts to extend into the contemporary disciplinary protocols of Latino, queer, and performance studies.

29  Soto, 1.
30  Soto, 6.
31  José Muñoz corroborates this claim in his deconstructive reading of a passage in Arturo Islas's second novel, *Migrant Souls*. Muñoz, *Disidentifications*, 32.
32  Paolo Virno, "The Ambivalence of Disenchantment," in *Radical Thought in Italy*, ed. Paolo Virno and Michael Hardt (Minneapolis: University of Minnesota Press, 1996), 23.
33  Shoshana Felman, *The Scandal of the Speaking Body: Don Juan with J. L. Austin, or Seduction in Two Acts* (Stanford, CA: Stanford University Press, 2002), 104.
34  Felman, 104.
35  David Carroll, *Paraesthetics: Foucault, Lyotard, Derrida* (London: Routledge, 1987), xiv.
36  Tavia Nyong'o, "Brown Punk: Kalup Linzy's Musical Anticipations," *TDR: The Drama Review* 54 (2010): 75.
37  Nyong'o, 75.
38  Nyong'o, 83.
39  Lauren Berlant and Michael Hardt, "No One Is Sovereign in Love: A Conversation between Lauren Berlant and Michael Hardt," NoMorePotlucks.org, accessed March 30, 2015, http://nomorepotlucks.org.
40  Of interest here, however, are recent studies into *minoritarian* conceptions of style that are embedded within a contemporary global political economy emerging from the shift to postmodernism from modernism and that *Dissatisfactions* aligns with, namely, Sean Metzger, *Chinese Looks: Fashion, Performance, Race* (Bloomington: Indiana University Press, 2014); Kareem Khubchandani, *Ishtyle: Accenting Gay Indian Nightlife* (Ann Arbor: University of Michigan Press, 2020); and Madison Moore, *Fabulous: The Rise of the Beautiful Eccentric* (New Haven, CT: Yale University Press, 2018).
41  "Style (n.)," Online Etymology Dictionary, accessed July 9, 2020, www.etymonline.com.
42  Joseph Joubert, *The Notebooks of Joseph Joubert: A Selection*, trans. Paul Auster (New York: New York Review of Books, 1983), 44.
43  Judith Miller, "Style Is the Man Himself," in *Lacan and the Subject of Language*, ed. Ellie Ragland-Sullivan and Mark Bracher (New York: Routledge, 2014), 146.
44  Rebecca Comay, *Mourning Sickness: Hegel and the French Revolution* (Stanford, CA: Stanford University Press, 2011), 90.
45  Miller, "Style Is the Man Himself," 147.
46  Miller, 150.
47  Miller, 151.

48  One such example is as follows: "If money comes into the world with a congenital blood-stain on one cheek, capital comes dripping from head to toe, from every pore, with blood and dirt." Karl Marx, *Capital: A Critique of Political Economy*, vol. 1 (1867), trans. Ben Fowkes (Harmondsworth, UK: Penguin, 1976), 926. Mark Neocleous interprets Marx's use of the metaphor of vampires to demonstrate "the constant sucking of the blood of the Western working class by the bourgeois class." Mark Neocleous, "The Political Economy of the Dead: Marx's Vampires," *History of Political Thought* 24, no. 4 (2003): 668. Jacques Derrida also remarks on Marx's vampire and reads his metaphors as evidence for Marx's spectral position in thought. Jacques Derrida, *Specters of Marx: The State of the Debt, the Work of Mourning, and the New International*, trans. Peggy Kamuf (New York: Routledge, 1994).

49  Mark Fisher, *Capitalist Realism: Is There No Alternative?* (Winchester, UK: Zero Books, 2009), 18.

50  Todd McGowan, *Capitalism and Desire: The Psychic Cost of Free Markets* (New York: Columbia University Press, 2016), 11, 14.

51  McGowan, 11.

52  For a fantastic study of the grounding of Marxist aesthetics to a politics of literary style, see Daniel Hartley's *The Politics of Style: Towards a Marxist Poetics* (Chicago: Haymarket Books, 2017). There, Hartley impressively recuperates Raymond Williams's later writings to offer a systemic analysis of the aestheticization of politics. Through a sustained immanent critique of Raymond Williams, Fredric Jameson, Terry Eagleton, and Karl Marx, Hartley convincingly argues that style is indeed linked to material culture while undergirded with sociopolitical ideologies that tell us something about the "capitalist state's distribution of the means of communication" (9). However, a major limit to Hartley's argument concerns minoritarian life in the United States, since, as *Dissatisfactions* shows, a politics to style must account for the way politics are stylized in response to ethnic-racial and sexual discrimination, dispossession, and prejudices if we are to fully understand the importance of criticism to global politics.

53  Raymond Williams, *Marxism and Literature* (Oxford: Oxford University Press, 1977), 122.

54  Williams, 122 (emphasis added).

55  Williams, 123.

56  Williams, 123.

57  Williams, 125.

58  Williams, 133.

59  Williams, 133–134.

60  Raymond Williams, *Resources of Hope* (Brooklyn, NY: Verso Books, 1989), 86.

61  Samo Tomšič, *The Capitalist Unconscious: Marx and Lacan* (Brooklyn, NY: Verso Books, 2015), 67.

62  Jodi Dean, *Democracy and Other Neoliberal Fantasies: Communicative Capitalism and Left Politics* (Durham, NC: Duke University Press, 2009). Meanwhile, what

came to be known as "intersectionality" is an early theorization of overthrowing this obscuring logic of freedom articulated as the single-axis framework in US law.
63 The act of remembering here is expressed as the act of assembling.
64 Elizabeth Freeman, *Time Binds: Queer Temporalities, Queer Histories* (Durham, NC: Duke University Press, 2010), xvi.
65 Peggy Phelan, *Unmarked: The Politics of Performance* (London: Routledge, 1993); Philip Auslander, *Liveness: Performance in Mediatized Culture* (London: Routledge, 1999); Muñoz, *Cruising Utopia*; Ann Pellegrini, *Performance Anxieties: Staging Psychoanalysis, Staging Race* (London: Routledge, 1997); Diana Taylor, *The Archive and the Repertoire: Performing Cultural Memory in the Americas* (Durham, NC: Duke University Press, 2003).
66 Ann Cvetkovich, *An Archive of Feelings: Trauma, Sexuality, and Lesbian Public Cultures* (Durham, NC: Duke University Press, 2003).
67 Fred Moten, *In the Break: The Aesthetics of the Black Radical Tradition* (Minneapolis: University of Minnesota Press, 2003), 18, 42, 53. Interinanimation might be thought of as a reconstructed dialectic churning within the aesthetic dimension.
68 My hope is that *Dissatisfactions* contributes to recent scholarship on minoritarian performance and art in Los Angeles, best exemplified in works such as Peggy Phelan, ed., *Live Art in LA: Performance in Southern California, 1970–1983* (New York: Routledge, 2012); Meiling Cheng, *In Other Los Angeleses: Multicentric Performance Art* (Berkeley: University of California Press, 2002); Robb Hernández, *Archiving an Epidemic: Art, AIDS, and the Queer Chicanx Avant-Garde* (New York: New York University Press, 2019); Jennifer Doyle, *Hold It against Me: Difficulty and Emotion in Contemporary Art* (Durham, NC: Duke University Press, 2013); and Kellie Jones, *South of Pico: African American Artists in Los Angeles in the 1960s and 1970s* (Durham, NC: Duke University Press, 2017).

## CHAPTER 1. THE STYLE POLITICS OF NAUSEA

*Epigraphs*: I borrow the Merleau-Ponty epigraph from a quote in the concluding chapter of Sara Ahmed's *Queer Phenomenology*, on disorientation, which sparked the theoretical framework for this chapter. See Sara Ahmed, *Queer Phenomenology: Orientations, Objects, Others* (Durham, NC: Duke University Press, 2006).
1 Lauren Berlant, "Structures of Unfeeling: Mysterious Skin," *International Journal of Politics, Culture, and Society* 28 (2015): 191–213.
2 Reyner Banham, *Los Angeles: The Architecture of Four Ecologies* (1971; repr., Berkeley: University of California Press, 2009), 195.
3 Quoted in Banham, 204.
4 Banham, 204.
5 Ahmed, *Queer Phenomenology*, 158.
6 José Esteban Muñoz, "The Wildness of the Punk Rock Commons," *South Atlantic Quarterly* 117, no. 3 (2018): 654.

7   Fred Moten, *Black and Blur: Consent Not to Be a Single Being* (Durham, NC: Duke University Press, 2017), xiii.
8   Mark Fisher, *K-Punk: The Collected and Unpublished Writings of Mark Fisher (2004–2016)*, ed. Darren Ambrose (London: Repeater Books, 2018), 434. Fisher quotes Marazzi from a lecture given in early June 2005 at Goldsmith, University of London, titled "Finance, Attention and Affect."
9   Maria Hynes and Laura Cull are sociologists who have adopted Deleuze's theories of affect to account for resistance and social change in contemporary capitalism. See Maria Hynes, "Reconceptualizing Resistance: Sociology and the Affective Dimension of Resistance," *British Journal of Sociology* 64, no. 4 (2013): 559–577; Laura Cull, "Affect in Deleuze, Hijikata, and Coates: The Politics of Becoming-Animal in Performance," *Journal of Dramatic Theory and Criticism* 26 no. 2 (2012): 189–203. Ruth Leys, "The Turn to Affect: A Critique," *Critical Inquiry* 37, no. 3 (2011): 434–472; Brian Massumi, "The Autonomy of Affect," *Cultural Critique* 31 (1995): 83–109; Patricia Clough, "The Affective Turn: Political Economy, Biomedia and Bodies," *Theory Culture & Society* 25, no. 1 (2008): 3.
10  Sianne Ngai, *Ugly Feelings* (Cambridge, MA: Harvard University Press, 2005), 4.
11  Ngai, 6.
12  Ngai, 12.
13  Ngai, 335.
14  Raúl Homero Villa, *Barrio-Logos: Space and Place in Urban Chicano Literature and Culture* (Austin: University of Texas Press, 2000), 8.
15  Simone de Beauvoir, *The Ethics of Ambiguity*, trans. Bernard Frechtman (1948; repr., New York: Citadel, 1976); Albert Camus, *The Stranger*, trans. Matthew Ward (New York: Vintage International, 1989); Jean-Paul Sartre, *Nausea*, trans. Lloyd Alexander (New York: New Directions, 2013).
16  Kadji Amin, *Disturbing Attachments: Genet, Modern Pederasty, and Queer History* (Durham, NC: Duke University Press, 2017), 14.
17  Ahmed, *Queer Phenomenology*, 162.
18  Ahmed, 163.
19  Neetu Khanna, *The Visceral Logics of Decolonization* (Durham, NC: Duke University Press, 2020), 4.
20  Khanna, 4.
21  Khanna, 5.
22  Khanna, 24.
23  Khanna, 24.
24  Ahmed, *Queer Phenomenology*, 162.
25  Jean-Paul Sartre, *Critique of Dialectical Reason*, vol. 2, trans. Quintin Hoare, ed. Arlette Elkaïm-Sartre (New York: Verso, 2006), 389; Miranda Joseph, *Against the Romance of Community* (Minneapolis: University of Minnesota Press, 2002).
26  Fredric Jameson, *Sartre: The Origins of a Style* (New Haven, CT: Yale University Press, 1961), 184.
27  Andrew Leak, *Jean-Paul Sartre* (London: Reaktion Books, 2006), 25.

28  Richard Howard, foreword to Sartre, *Nausea*, vi.
29  Howard, vi (my emphasis).
30  Alistair Charles Rolls and Elizabeth Rechniewski, "Uprooting the Chestnut Tree: *Nausea* Today," in *Sartre's Nausea: Text, Context, Intertext*, ed. Alistair Charles Rolls and Elizabeth Rechniewski (Amsterdam: Rodopi, 2005), 14–15.
31  Sartre, *Nausea*, 131.
32  D. A. Miller, *Jane Austen, or the Secret of Style* (Princeton, NJ: Princeton University Press, 2003), 7–8.
33  Eve Kosofsky Sedgwick, *Touching Feeling: Affect, Pedagogy, Performativity* (Durham, NC: Duke University Press, 2003), 38; Miller, *Jane Austen*, 8.
34  Leticia Alvarado, *Abject Performances: Aesthetic Strategies in Latino Cultural Production* (Durham, NC: Duke University Press, 2018), 7.
35  For example, see Alvarado's *Abject Performances*, Karen Shimakawa's *National Abjection: The Asian American Body on Stage* (Durham, NC: Duke University Press, 2002), and Darieck Scott's *Extravagant Abjection: Blackness, Power, and Sexuality in African-American Literary Imagination* (New York: New York University Press, 2010).
36  Howard, foreword to *Nausea*, vi.
37  Fredric Jameson argues that *Nausea* can be called many things, from a philosophical novel to a satirical play on the adventure novels of the nineteenth century. Yet it is also "a book of a city: Bouville is one of the main characters, a grotesque image of the absurdities of traditional bourgeois life; and the novel follows the city like a map." What is interesting about Bouville's character development in the novel is the way it is never wholly present and graspable to the reader, "since we always apprehend it through fragmentary parts of it that confront us in the present." Similarly, Los Angeles's topography oddly mirrors that of Bouville, one without a concretized center, a city that sprawls and afflicts a deep disorientation. Jameson, *Sartre*, 98.
38  McCaughan, *Art and Social Movements*, 128.
39  Alvarado, *Abject Performances*, 59.
40  See Richard T. Rodríguez, *Next of Kin: The Family in Chicano/a Cultural Politics* (Durham, NC: Duke University Press, 2009).
41  Grace Kyungwon Hong, *Death beyond Disavowal: The Impossible Politics of Difference* (Minneapolis: University of Minnesota Press, 2015), 7 (my emphasis).
42  Hong, 8.
43  Harry Gamboa Jr., "Light at the End of the Tunnel Vision: In Memory of Gerardo Velázquez and Ray Navarro," in *Urban Exile: Collected Writing of Harry Gamboa Jr.*, ed. Chon A. Noriega (Minneapolis: University of Minnesota Press, 1998), 147. I would like to greatly thank my anonymous reader for drawing my attention to this spectacular quote.
44  Rodolfo F. Acuña, *Occupied America: A History of Chicanos* (London: Pearson Longman, 1981).
45  James Diego Vigil, *Barrio Gangs: Street Life and Identity in Southern California* (Austin: University of Texas Press, 1988).

46  John Baldessari et al., "L.A. Stories: A Roundtable," *Artforum* 50, no. 2 (2011): 245.
47  Christian Marazzi, *Capital and Affects: The Politics of the Language Economy*, trans. Giuseppina Mecchia (Los Angeles: Semiotext(e), 2011), 20.
48  Rei Terada, *Looking Away: Phenomenality and Dissatisfaction, Kant to Adorno* (Cambridge, MA: Harvard University Press, 2009), 174.
49  Maurizio Lazzarato, "Immaterial Labor," in *Radical Thought in Italy: A Potential Politics*, ed. Paolo Virno and Michael Hardt (Minneapolis: University of Minnesota Press, 1996), 142–157. Marazzi borrows the term "communicative action" from Jürgen Habermas's theory of "communicative acting," whereby, in using communication theory, Habermas argues that political tensions within democracies are fundamentally governed by linguistic mediation. Marazzi, *Capital and Affects*, 36. See also Jürgen Habermas, *The Theory of Communicative Action: Reason and the Rationalization of Society* (London: Atheneum, 1986).
50  Marazzi, *Capital and Affects*, 11.
51  Anne-Lise François, *Open Secrets: The Literature of Uncounted Experience* (Stanford, CA: Stanford University Press, 2008), 3 (original emphasis).
52  Villa builds on Albert Camarillo's term and comparative study between Mexican and Anglo communities in the early modern Southern California region. There, Camarillo describes barrioization as the "formation of residentially and socially segregated Chicano barrios and neighborhoods." Quoted in Raúl Homero Villa, *Barrio-Logos: Space and Place in Urban Chicano Literature and Culture* (Austin: University of Texas Press, 2000), 4. For Villa, Camarillo's barrioization could also be "understood as a complex of dominating social processes originating *outside* of the barrios" (4, original emphasis). See also Albert Camarillo, *Chicanos in a Changing Society: From Mexican Pueblos to American Barrios in Santa Barbara and Southern California, 1848–1930* (Cambridge, MA: Harvard University Press, 1979), 53.
53  See Kobena Mercer, "Black Art and the Burden of Representation," *Third Text* 4, no. 10 (1990): 61–78; José Esteban Muñoz, *Disidentifications: Queers of Color and the Performance of Politics* (Minneapolis: University of Minnesota Press, 1999), 181–200.
54  Richard T. Rodríguez, *Next of Kin: The Family in Chicano/a Cultural Politics* (Durham, NC: Duke University Press, 2009); Maylei Blackwell, *¡Chicana Power! Contested Histories of Feminism in the Chicano Movement* (Austin: University of Texas Press, 2011).
55  Sianne Ngai, *Our Aesthetic Categories: Zany, Cute, Interesting* (Cambridge, MA: Harvard University Press, 2012), 35.
56  Muñoz, *Disidentifications*, 189.
57  Muñoz, 187.
58  Muñoz, 189.
59  Martin Heidegger, *Being and Time*, trans. John Macquarrie and Edward Robinson (New York: Harper and Row, 1962); Joshua Javier Guzmán and Christina A. León,

"Cuts and Impressions: The Aesthetic Work of Lingering in Latinidad," *Women & Performance: A Journal of Feminist Theory* 25, no. 3 (2015): 261–276.
60  Mercer, "Black Art and the Burden of Representation," 74.
61  Mercer, 74.
62  Mercer, 78.
63  Mercer, 65, 66.
64  Chon Noriega, "Your Art Disgusts Me: Early Asco 1971–75," *East of Borneo*, November 18, 2010, https://eastofborneo.org.
65  Jessica Nydia Pabón-Colón, *Graffiti Grrlz: Performing Feminism in the Hip Hop Diaspora* (New York: New York University Press, 2018).
66  Randy Ontiveros, *In the Spirit of a New People: The Cultural Politics of the Chicano Movement* (New York: New York University Press, 2013), 201.
67  C. Ondine Chavoya and Rita Gonzalez, eds., *Asco: Elite of the Obscure: A Retrospective, 1972–1987* (Berlin: Hatje Cantz Verlag, 2011), 45.
68  "Interview with Asco," *CALIFAS*, 1983, quoted in Chavoya and Gonzalez, 38.
69  Alvarado, *Abject Performances*, 83.
70  Harry Gamboa Jr., "Past Imperfecto," in *Urban Exile: Collected Writings of Harry Gamboa, Jr.*, ed. Chon A. Noriega (Minneapolis: University of Minnesota Press, 1988), 93.
71  Gamboa, 93.
72  Rodríguez, *Next of Kin*, 83.
73  Rodríguez, 85.
74  Gamboa, "Past Imperfecto," 93.
75  Ngai, *Our Aesthetic Categories*, 34.
76  Ngai, 34.

CHAPTER 2. STRIPPED LIFE

1  One must keep in mind here the constitutive differences between "identity" and "identification." This point is best explored in queer and feminist psychoanalytic theories such as Diana Fuss's *Identification Papers: Readings on Psychoanalysis, Sexuality, and Culture* (New York: Routledge, 1995) and further explored in chapter 3.
2  Kobena Mercer, *Welcome to the Jungle: New Positions in Black Cultural Studies* (New York: Routledge, 1994), 300.
3  Mark Fisher, *Ghosts of My Life: Writings on Depression, Hauntology and Lost Futures* (New Alresford, UK: Zero Books, 2014), 26.
4  Fisher, 26.
5  Tomás Ybarra-Frausto, "Rasquachismo," in *Chicano and Chicana Art: A Critical Anthology*, ed. Jennifer González, C. Ondine Chavoya, Chon Noriega, and Terezita Romo (Durham, NC: Duke University Press, 2019), 86.
6  Ybarra-Frausto, 85.
7  Joan Scott, "The Evidence of Experience," *Critical Inquiry* 17, no. 4 (1991): 777.

8   Simone de Beauvoir, *The Ethics of Ambiguity*, trans. Bernard Frechtman (1948; repr., New York: Citadel, 1976), 74, 75.
9   For more on the relation between fabulation, queer gossip, and Davis's performance practice, see Marc Siegel's "Vaginal Davis's Gospel Truths," *Camera Obscura* 23, no. 1 (2008): 151–159. For more scholarly meditations on Davis's impact on performance, sexuality, and race, see Jennifer Doyle's "White Sex," in *Sex Objects: Art and the Dialectics of Desire* (Minneapolis: University of Minnesota Press, 2006); José Esteban Muñoz's *Disidentifications: Queers of Color and the Performance of Politics* (Minneapolis: University of Minnesota Press, 1999), 93–116; Shane Vogel's "Irrealizing the Queer Harlem Renaissance," in *The Scene of Harlem Cabaret: Race, Sexuality, Performance* (Chicago: University of Chicago Press, 2009); and Michael du Plessis and Kathleen Chapman's "Queercore: The Distinct Identities of Subculture," *College Literature* 24 (1997): 45–58.
10  For more on Vaginal Davis's self-descriptions, see her well-known blog at www.vaginaldavis.com.
11  José Munoz, "'The White to Be Angry': Vaginal Davis's Terrorist Drag," *Social Text*, no. 52/53 (1997): 82.
12  As the queer theorist José Muñoz points out, ¡Cholita! created "socially interrogative performances that complicated any easy understanding of race and ethnicity in the social matrix," thus reinvigorating the punk ethos and tendency of failing to abide by dominant forms of categorization and identification. Muñoz, *Disidentifications*, 97. Many of Davis's performances and collaborations from the 1990s are archived online on platforms such as YouTube. See Davis's briefly talk about ¡Cholita! and her "first trip" to New York City from Los Angeles in a rare clip from the late queer video artist Nelson Sullivan's video recordings here: 5ninthavenueproject, "Fertile LaToya Jackson's First Visit to New York," YouTube, December 12, 2010, www.youtube.com/watch?v=HuC9MxW1xpM.
13  "My Favorite Dead Artist," performed with the exhibition *Nadar/Warhol: Paris/New York* at the Getty Museum in Los Angeles, 1999.
14  Cyrus Grace Dunham, "The 'Terrorist Drag' of Vaginal Davis," *New Yorker*, December 12, 2015, www.newyorker.com; Guy Trebay, "Ready to Fade into Obscurity. Wait, He's Already There," *New York Times*, May 23, 2004, www.nytimes.com. In Berlin, Davis continues to be a prolific artist. As a composer, performer, painter, life curator, band front woman, zinester, video- and filmmaker, cultural critic, and scholar, Dr. Davis is astutely aware of how culture moves and how culture is created. Her ability to antagonize the sedimented norms of today gained her the apt description "organic intellectual" by the late queer theorist and close friend of Davis José Esteban Muñoz. Muñoz writes, "Davis certainly worked to bolster and cohere the L.A. punk scene, giving it a more significant 'homogeneity' and 'awareness.' . . . While Davis did and did not belong to the scene, she nonetheless forged a place for herself that is not *a* place, but instead the still important *position* of intellectual." Davis's invented autobiographies, coupled with her upbringing in a working-poor South Central Los Angeles, lent a queer organizing force to the Los

Angeles punk scene, which also incorporated transgressive artists with whom she often collaborated, such as Glen Meadmore, Rick Castro, Bruce La Bruce, Alice Bag, Fertile La Toyah Jackson, and Bibbe Hansen. The legacy of queer Los Angeles from the 1970s up to the 1990s is due in large part to Davis herself—perhaps her best work of art—that personal canvas she describes as the "indefinite nature of [her] own whimsy." Muñoz, "The White to Be Angry," 87; Hilary E. Macgregor, "Of Dada and Dr. Davis," *Los Angeles Times*, May 2, 2004, www.latimes.com.

15 Vaginal Davis and Lewis Church, "My Womanly Story," *PAJ: A Journal of Performance and Art* 38, no. 2 (2016): 86.
16 Vaginal Davis, *Fertile La Toyah Jackson Magazine*, no. 2 (ca. late 1980s), ONE National Gay and Lesbian Archives.
17 Fisher, *Ghosts of My Life*, 22–23.
18 Sara Ramirez and Norma Cantú, "Publishing Work That Matters: Third Woman Press and Its Impact on Chicana and Latina Publishing," *Diálogo* 20, no. 2 (Fall 2017): 77.
19 Ramirez and Cantú, 78.
20 Ramirez and Cantú, 78. Cervantes's Mango Publications would eventually publish Chicana writers such as Ana Castillo and Sandra Cisneros.
21 Quoted in Jennifer Gilley's "Ghost in the Machine: Kitchen Table Press and the Third Wave Anthology that Vanished," *Frontiers: A Journal of Women's Studies* 38, no. 3 (2017): 144.
22 Gilley, 144.
23 Maylei Blackwell, *¡Chicana Power! Contested Histories of Feminism in the Chicano Movement* (Austin: University of Texas Press, 2011), 156.
24 Alexandra T. Vazquez, *Listening in Detail: Performances of Cuban Music* (Durham, NC: Duke University Press, 2013), 57.
25 Vazquez, 67.
26 Vazquez, 57.
27 Quoted in Vazquez, 259n67.
28 Matilde Martín González reminds us that the large cultural backlash that the Reagan administration brought against the gains of the feminist movement was a crucial background to the rise of alternative feminist presses. See González, "Beyond Mainstream Presses: Publishing Women of Color as Cultural and Political Critique," in *Race, Ethnicity and Publishing in America*, ed. Cecile Cottenet (London: Palgrave Macmillan, 2014), 145–146.
29 Kristine McKenna, "Introduction: Don't Be Afraid to Break Things—An Ode to *Slash*," in *Slash: A Punk Magazine from Los Angeles 1977–80*, ed. Brian Roettinger and J. C. Gabel (Los Angeles: Hat and Beard, 2016), 10.
30 José Esteban Muñoz, "'Gimme Gimme This . . . Gimme Gimme That': Annihilation and Innovation in the Punk Rock Commons," *Social Text* 31, no. 3 (116) (2013): 105.
31 Alice Bag, *Violence Girl: From East L.A. Rage to the Hollywood Stage—A Chicana Punk Story* (Port Townsend, WA: Feral House, 2011), 189. For a detailed review

of the book, see Chris Daley, "Survive: Alice Bag's 'Violence Girl,'" *Los Angeles Review of Books*, June 2, 2012, https://lareviewofbooks.org.

32  Alice Bag, *Pipe Bomb for the Soul* (Los Angeles: Alice Bag, 2015). In 2016, Bag released an eponymous solo album. She continues to be active online, digitally archiving punk women who were involved in the early years of the Los Angeles punk scene. She collaborated with her friend the Chicana punk scholar Michelle Habell-Pallán on the University of Washington's "Women Who Rock: Making Sense, Building Communities" oral history archives, which houses an oral history of Alice Bag's punk career. Habell-Pallán, "'¿Soy Punkera, y Qué?': Sexuality, Translocality, and Punk in Los Angeles and Beyond," in *Loca Motion: The Travels of Chicana and Latina Popular Culture* (New York: New York University Press, 2005), 147–180. Also see Michelle Habell-Pallán's "'Vexed on the Eastside': Chicana Roots and Routes of L.A. Punk," in *Vexing: Female Voices from East L.A. Punk*, exhibition catalogue, ed. Colin Gunckel and Pilar Tompkins (Claremont, CA: Claremont Museum of Art, 2008), 25–29. Some selected exhibitions and a discography include *Alice Bag* (2016), solo album; *Survive* (1978), The Bags album; *Vexing: Female Voices from East L.A. Punk*, Claremont Museum of Art (2008); *All Bagged Up: The Collected Works 1977–1980* (2006), The Bags album; *Disco Is Dead* (2003), The Bags album; "Chicas de Hoy" (1989), ¡Cholita! The Female Menudo album; *Gronk/Dreva: Ten Years of Art Life* (Los Angeles: LACE, 1978).

33  Bag, *Violence Girl*, 103.
34  Bag, 102.
35  Marc Spitz, *We Got the Neutron Bomb* (New York: Three Rivers, 2001), 261.
36  Brendan Mullen, "Annihilation Man," *LA Weekly*, December 27, 2000.
37  Lester Bangs, "Of Pop and Pies and Fun," *Creem*, November 1970.
38  Jean-Luc Nancy, *The Inoperative Community*, ed. Peter Connor, trans. Peter Connor et al. (Minneapolis: University of Minnesota Press, 1991), 3.
39  For more analysis on the relationship between the commons and the phenomenon of punk, see Muñoz, "Gimme Gimme This."
40  It was the US diplomat, ambassador, and economic counselor in London Lawrence P. Taylor who described the two heads of government as such. Taylor, interview by Charles Stuart Kennedy, April 1998, quoted in Association for Diplomatic Study and Training, "The Extra Special Relationship: Thatcher, Reagan, and the 1980s," July 26, 2016, https://adst.org.
41  Karen Tongson, *Relocations: Queer Suburban Imaginaries* (New York: New York University Press, 2011), 23.
42  Tongson, 130; Richard T. Rodríguez, *A Kiss across the Ocean: Transatlantic Intimacies of British Post-Punk and US Latinidad* (Durham, NC: Duke University Press, 2022), 9.
43  Rodríguez, *Kiss across the Ocean*, 9.
44  Elizabeth Freeman, "Packing History, Count(er)ing Generations," *New Literary History* 31, no. 4 (2000): 733. See also Freeman's *Time Binds: Queer Temporalities, Queer Histories* (Durham, NC: Duke University Press, 2010).

45 Jayna Brown, "Poly Styrene, 1957–2011," *Bully Bloggers*, April 26, 2011, https://bullybloggers.wordpress.com.
46 Brown.
47 Mullen, "Annihilation Man."
48 Lucretius, *On the Nature of Things*, trans. W. H. D. Rouse, rev. Martin F. Smith, Loeb Classical Library 181 (Cambridge, MA: Harvard University Press, 1924), 53. "You can find nothing that's composed of atoms of a single kind. There is nothing that does not consist of different seeds combined, and the more powers and qualities a thing has, so we find the more it must contain shapes numerous and diverse."
49 Teresa Covarrubias, "The Brat: East L.A.'s Answer to Modern Music," interview by Salvador Mendez, *Lowrider* 5, no. 3 (1982): 75.
50 Brenda Jo Bright, "Remappings: Los Angeles Low Riders," in *Looking High and Low: Art and Cultural Identity*, ed. Brenda J. Bright and Liza Bakewell (Tucson: University of Arizona Press, 1995), 109.
51 George Lipsitz, "Cruising around the Historical Bloc: Postmodernism and Popular Music in East Los Angeles," *Cultural Critique*, no. 5 (Winter 1986–1987): 174.
52 Covarrubias, "Brat," 75.
53 Covarrubias, 75.
54 Fatima Records was founded in 1979 by Yolanda Comparan Ferrer, Tito Larriva of the Chicano punk band The Plugz, and the Chicano artist Richard Durado, whose print of the band adorns the album cover.
55 Simone de Beauvoir, *The Second Sex*, trans. H. M. Parshley (New York: Vintage, 1989), 267.
56 See Sarah Ahmed, *The Promise of Happiness* (Durham, NC: Duke University Press, 2010), 50–87.
57 Simone de Beauvoir, *The Ethics of Ambiguity*, trans. Bernard Frechtman (1948; repr., New York: Citadel, 1976), 74–75.
58 Beauvoir, 75.
59 Beauvoir, 76.
60 Beauvoir, 76, 77.
61 Beauvoir, 76.
62 Beauvoir, 7.
63 Peg Z. Brand, "The Aesthetic Attitude in *The Ethics of Ambiguity*," *Simone de Beauvoir Studies* 18 (2001–2002): 32.
64 Beauvoir, *Ethics of Ambiguity*, 78.
65 Beauvoir explicitly makes this argument before moving into a discussion of the aesthetic attitude: "To will oneself free is also to will others free. This will is not an abstract formula. It points out to each person concrete action to be achieved." Beauvoir, 73.
66 Beauvoir, 80.
67 Beauvoir, 69
68 Beauvoir, 73.

## CHAPTER 3. DESIRING IN THE DARK

1. Rebecca Comay, "Hegel's Last Words: Mourning and Melancholia at the End of the *Phenomenology*," in *The End(s) of History: Questioning the Stakes of Historical Reason*, ed. Joshua Nichols and Amy Swiffen (London: Routledge, 2013), 146.
2. Comay, 146.
3. Christina A. León, "Forms of Opacity: Roaches, Blood and Being Stuck in Xandra Ibarra's Corpus," *ASAP/Journal* 2, no. 2 (May 2017): 379.
4. Michael Roy Hames-García, "Queer Theory Revisited," in *Gay Latino Studies: A Critical Reader*, ed. Michael Hames-Garcia and Ernesto Javier Martínez (Durham, NC: Duke University Press, 2011), 20.
5. Hames-García, 21.
6. María Lugones, "It's All in Having a History: A Response to Michael Hames-García's 'Queer Theory Revisited,'" in Hames-Garcia and Martínez, *Gay Latino Studies*, 49.
7. Hames-García, "Queer Theory Revisited," 34 (my emphasis).
8. Hames-García, 36 (my emphasis). Eve Kosofsky Sedgwick was aware of this as well: "To use that fait accompli as a reason for analytically conflating sexuality per se with gender would obscure the degree to which the fact itself requires explanation. It would also, I think, risk obscuring yet again the extreme intimacy with which all these available analytic axes do after all mutually constitute one another: to assume the distinctiveness of the *intimacy* between sexuality and gender might well risk assuming too much about the definitional *separability* of either of them from determinations of, say, class or race." Sedgwick, *Epistemology of the Closet* (Berkeley: University of California Press, 1990), 31 (original emphasis).
9. Lugones, "It's All in Having a History," 49 (my emphasis). Hames-García addresses poststructuralist formations of identity as performative, indeterminate, and open to failure through his two examples (posited as evidence) in "Queer Theory Revisited," 34–36.
10. The postpositivist realist approach was first outlined by Satya Mohanty. See Mohanty, *Literary Theory and the Claims of History: Postmodernism, Objectivity, Multicultural Politics* (Ithaca, NY: Cornell University Press, 1997). See also Ramón Saldívar, "Multicultural Politics, Aesthetics, and the Realist Theory of Identity: A Response to Satya Mohanty," *New Literary History* 32, no. 4 (2001): 849–854, http://doi.org/10.1353/nlh.2001.0057.
11. Wendy Brown, "Wounded Attachments," *Political Theory* 21 (1993): 391.
12. José Esteban Muñoz, "Feeling Brown, Feeling Down: Latina Affect, the Performativity of Race, and the Depressive Position," *Signs* 31, no. 3 (Spring 2006): 688; Brown, "Wounded Attachments," 394.
13. Brown, "Wounded Attachments," 403.
14. Eve Kosofsky Sedgwick, "Melanie Klein and the Difference Affect Makes," *South Atlantic Quarterly* 106, no. 3 (Summer 2007): 635.
15. Sedgwick, 635 (original emphasis).

16  Sedgwick, 635.
17  Diana Fuss, *Identification Papers: Readings of Psychoanalysis, Sexuality and Culture* (London: Routledge, 2013), 2.
18  See Joseph M. Pierce, María Amelia Viteri, Diego Falconí Trávez, Salvador Vidal-Ortiz, and Lourdes Martínez-Echazábal, "Introduction: *Cuir*/Queer Américas: Translation, Decoloniality, and the Incommensurable," *GLQ* 27, no. 3 (2021): 321–327. Also see E. Patrick Johnson, "'Quare' Studies, or (Almost) Everything I Know about Queer Studies I Learned from My Grandmother," *Text and Performance Quarterly* 21, no. 1 (2010): 1–25.
19  Here I am referring to Lauren Berlant's theorization of the "nonsovereign relationality." See Berlant, *On the Inconvenience of Other People* (Durham, NC: Duke University Press, 2022), 1–30.
20  Diana Fuss, *Essentially Speaking: Feminism, Nature, and Difference* (London: Routledge, 1989), 101–102.
21  Brown, "Wounded Attachments," 403 (my emphasis).
22  Sedgwick, *Epistemology of the Closet*, 40.
23  Sedgwick, 40.
24  Sedgwick, 22.
25  Sedgwick, 44.
26  Sedgwick, 43.
27  I borrow the term "sovereign incalculability" from the feminist psychoanalyst Joan Copjec, who theorizes the "sexed subject" posited by Lacanian psychoanalysis as a subject defined by its own self-governance. "It is only when the sovereign incalculability of the subject is acknowledged that perceptions of difference will no longer nourish demands for the surrender of difference to processes of 'homogenization,' 'purification,' or any of the other crimes against otherness with which the rise of racism has begun to acquaint us." Copjec, *Read My Desire: Lacan against the Historicists* (London: Verso, 2015), 208.
28  Sandra K. Soto, *Reading Chican@ Like a Queer: The De-mastery of Desire* (Austin: University of Texas Press, 2010), 14. For a discussion of Soto's generative hermeneutics and how racialized sexuality operates as an aperture, see the introduction.
29  Michael Callen, *Surviving AIDS* (New York: HarperCollins, 1990), 6.
30  In fact, current debate around the "first case" of known HIV infection involves Robert Rayford, a sixteen-year-old African American teenager from St. Louis, Missouri, who in 1969 succumbed to pneumonia due to a compromised immune system with rare signs of Kaposi's sarcoma lesions on his body.
31  Kubler goes on to argue that "style describes a specific figure in space better than a type of existence in time." George Kubler, *The Shape of Time: Remarks on the History of Things* (New Haven, CT: Yale University Press, 2008), 3.
32  For a cultural history of video and the rise of home video aesthetics and their relation to popular culture and countercultures, see James M. Moran, *There's No Place like Home Video* (Minneapolis: University of Minnesota Press, 2002).

33 After losing his sight to CMV retinitis, Navarro collaborated with the artist Zoe Leonard on most of these video diaries and on a photographic series called *Equipped* (1990), which has recently garnered scholarly attention and is beautifully explored by Debra Levine, a former friend of Navarro's, in her dissertation titled "Demonstrating ACT UP: The Ethics, Politics, and Performances of Affinity" (PhD diss., New York University, 2012).
34 Maylei Blackwell, *¡Chicana Power! Contested Histories of Feminism in the Chicano Movement* (Austin: University of Texas Press, 2011), 4.
35 Ray Navarro, "Enabling 'Equipped': An Army of Lovers Expanding the Activist Body," in *AIDS in Culture: Aspects of the Cultural History of AIDS 1* (New York: PS 122, 1990), 30–31. *An Army of Lovers: AIDS and Censorship*, curated by Aldo Hernandez, PS 122, New York, NY, 1990.
36 Joan Copjec, *Imagine There's No Woman: Ethics and Sublimation* (Cambridge, MA: MIT Press, 2002), 104–105.
37 For more on the relationship between the sentiment of darkness and ambivalence, see Paolo Virno, "The Ambivalence of Disenchantment," in *Radical Thought in Italy: A Potential Politics*, ed. Michael Hardt and Paolo Virno (Minneapolis: University of Minnesota Press, 2006), 13–36. A queer Chicano reading of darkness breaks from the aesthetic philosophy of Edmund Burke, who posits darkness as an aesthetic category that indicates an emerging and nefarious modernism and comes to mirror the Gothic literary trope of darkness as a signpost for sexual anxiety. See Burke, *A Philosophical Enquiry into the Origin of Our Ideas of the Sublime and Beautiful* (1756; repr., New York: Oxford University Press, 2015); and Eve Kosofsky Sedgwick, *The Coherence of Gothic Conventions* (London: Routledge, Kegan and Paul, 1986).
38 José Monteagudo, "Doomsday Spirituality," *Lambda Book Report* 4, no. 8 (January–February 1995): 34; Rafael Ocasio, "Autobiographical Writing and 'Out of the Closet' Literature by Gay Latino Writers," *Antipodas: Journal of Hispanic and Galician Studies* 3083, no. 11/12 (1999–2000); Raúl Homero Villa, *Barrio Logos: Space and Place in Urban Chicano Literature and Culture* (Austin: University of Texas Press, 2000). More recent scholarship is further discussed in this chapter.
39 Amy Scholder, coeditor of the groundbreaking volume *High Risk: An Anthology of Forbidden Writing* (New York: Plume, 1991), a collection of censored and controversial queer writings on AIDS, helped Cuadros with his book design for *City of God*. Scholder and Cuadros's collaboration makes room to think about the significant rise in cultural and literary queer production around AIDS in the early 1990s and how Chicanos were highly involved in this production, in both literature, as evidenced by Cuadros's writings, and avant-garde video art and photography, as demonstrated by Navarro's expansive oeuvre.
40 See Douglas Crimp and Adam Rolston, *AIDS Demo Graphics* (Seattle: Bay, 1990); see also Douglas Crimp, *Melancholia and Moralism: Essays on AIDS and Queer Politics* (Cambridge, MA: MIT Press, 2002); Leo Bersani, *Homos* (Cambridge,

MA: Harvard University Press, 1995), as well as his famous essay inaugurating what has been termed the antirelational thesis of queer theory, "Is the Rectum a Grave?," in *AIDS: Cultural Analysis / Cultural Activism*, ed. Douglas Crimp (Cambridge, MA: MIT Press, 1988), 197–222. For more on opacity as an aesthetic strategy for Latino culture, see Christina Leon's "Forms of Opacity: Roaches, Blood, and Being Stuck in Xandra Ibarra's Corpus," *ASAP/Journal* 2, no. 2 (2017): 369–394. The writer, media artist, and activist Gregg Bordowitz is also interested in darkness, ambiguity, and the absurd in relation to the AIDS crisis: Gregg Bordowitz, *The AIDS Crisis Is Ridiculous and Other Writings, 1986–2003*, ed. James Meyer (Cambridge, MA: MIT Press, 2006).
41 Gil Cuadros, *City of God* (San Francisco: City Lights, 1994), 54–55.
42 Cuadros, 56. In this passage, the narrator alludes to the use of blankets infected with smallpox that the British disseminated to Amerindians during the French and Indian War, encouraging the spread of diseases to which Europeans were immune but that arguably resulted in the genocide of Native populations. AZT, or zidovudine, is a form of antiviral medication popularly used in the early 1990s to combat HIV/AIDS. AZT features popularly in the cultural psyche around the AIDS epidemic, usually as a simultaneous signifier of both hope and despair, as well as ambivalence about trusting the US government to help treat people infected with the disease.
43 Cuadros, 56.
44 Paul Allatson, "'My Bones Shine in the Dark': AIDS and Chicano Queer Description in the Work of Gil Cuadros," *Aztlán: A Journal of Chicano Studies* 32, no. 1 (Spring 2007): 24.
45 Allatson, 24.
46 Allatson, 46.
47 Rafael Pérez-Torres, *Mestizaje: Critical Uses of Race in Chicano Culture* (Minneapolis: University of Minnesota Press, 2006), 155–156.
48 Villa, *Barrio Logos*, 141.
49 Julie A. Minich, "Aztlán Unprotected: Reading Gil Cuadros in the Aftermath of HIV/AIDS," *GLQ* 23, no. 2 (2017): 169. See also her timely monograph *Radical Health: Unwellness, Care, and Latinx Expressive Culture* (Durham, NC: Duke University Press, 2023).
50 Marissa K. López, *Racial Immanence: Chicanx Bodies beyond Representation* (New York: New York University Press, 2019), 97.
51 López, 96.
52 Avital Ronell, *Finitude's Score: Essays on the End of the Millennium* (Lincoln: University of Nebraska Press, 1998), ix.
53 As Leo Bersani makes clear, the "notion of self-shattering is somewhat a solipsistic view of the sexual" and is tethered to the "primacy of masochism in sexuality." Tim Dean, Hal Foster, Kaja Silverman, and Leo Bersani, "A Conversation with Leo Bersani," *October* 82 (1997): 7.
54 Cuadros, *City of God*, 93.

55 Barbara Johnson, *The Critical Difference: Essays in the Contemporary Rhetoric of Reading* (Baltimore: Johns Hopkins University Press, 1980), 131. Johnson is quoting Jacques Derrida.
56 This is also precisely what the literary critic David Carroll argues in his study on the aesthetic in poststructuralist theory: that any theory of art can only be critical if "it works the frame, makes it work, [and] makes work for it." Carroll, *Paraesthetics: Foucault, Lyotard, Derrida* (New York: Methuen, 1987), 162.
57 Here we can think of the queer filmmaker Derek Jarman's *Blue* (1993) and his book *Chroma: A Book of Color* (London: Vintage, 1994). *Blue* was released just months before Jarman's death from AIDS complications. The film and the book testify to Jarman's aesthetic sensory experiences as he went increasingly blind from AIDS-related causes, which Cuadros also explores in *City of God*.
58 The opening of the first *High Risk* anthology features an image from David Wojnarowicz's *Rimbaud in New York* photographic series, which Cuadros took up in the following volume: *High Risk 2: Writings on Sex, Death, and Subversion*, ed. Amy Scholder and Ira Silverberg (New York: Plume, 1994). The second book was dedicated to Wojnarowicz, who died of AIDS complications in 1992. Thinking about the queer avant-garde connections between Cuadros's writing, Wojnarowicz's work in New York and Mexico, and Arthur Rimbaud's poetry tells us something about the transhistorical, transnational, and interracial artistic implications of the epidemic. As a sixteen-year-old, Rimbaud wrote a letter to his publisher and friend Paul Demeny, proclaiming,

> The Poet makes himself a *seer* by a long, gigantic and rational *derangement* of *all the senses*. All forms of love, suffering, and madness. He searches himself. He exhausts all poisons in himself and keeps only their quintessence. Unspeakable torture where he needs all his faith, all his superhuman strength, where he becomes among all men the great patient, the great criminal, the one accursed—and the supreme Scholar!—Because he reaches the *unknown!* Since he cultivated his soul, rich already, more than any man! He reaches the unknown, and when, bewildered, he ends by losing the intelligence of his visions, he has seen them. Let him die as he leaps through unheard of and unnamable things.
>
> Arthur Rimbaud to Paul Demeny, May 15, 1871, in *Complete Works, Selected Letters*, ed. Jean Nicholas, Arthur Rimbaud, and Wallace Fowlie (Chicago: University of Chicago Press, 1966), 307 (original emphasis).

59 Cuadros, *City of God*, 96–97.
60 Cuadros, 99.
61 Cuadros, 53.
62 Cuadros, 54.
63 Cuadros, 58.
64 Cuadros, 58.
65 Cuadros, 58.

66 Patricia Navarro, interview by Sarah Schulman, July 20, 2007, ACT UP Oral History Project Digital Archive, 30–31 (my emphasis), www.actuporalhistory.org.
67 The same was true for me when I read Scott Herring's *Another Country: Queer Anti-Urbanism* (New York: New York University Press, 2010) and José Esteban Muñoz's *Cruising Utopia: The Then and There of Queer Futurity* (New York: New York University Press, 2009).
68 Karl Marx, *Economic and Philosophic Manuscripts of 1844*, trans. Martin Mulligan (Moscow: Progress, 1959), www.marxists.org.
69 Amber J. Musser, *Sensual Excess: Queer Femininity and Brown Jouissance* (New York: New York University Press, 2018), 17.
70 Musser, 87.
71 Leticia Alvarado, *Abject Performances: Aesthetic Strategies in Latino Cultural Production* (Durham, NC: Duke University Press, 2018), 18.
72 Musser offers a compelling hermeneutic informing the closing of this chapter when she says, "Empathetic reading is a reading practice, a critical hermeneutic, and [a] methodology.... It highlights how we can discern the structure sensation in various texts/performances and it works to give those sensations meaning, which in turn allows us to read difference in a sensational mode." Amber J. Musser, *Sensational Flesh: Race, Power, and Masochism* (New York: New York University Press, 2014), 21–22.
73 For more on this point, see Robb Hernández, *Archiving an Epidemic: Art, AIDS, and the Queer Chicanx Avant-Garde* (New York: New York University Press, 2019), 16–20.
74 Roland Barthes, *Camera Lucida: Reflections on Photography* (New York: Macmillan, 1981), 27.
75 Robert D. Hinshelwood, *A Dictionary of Kleinian Thought* (London: Free Association Books, 1991), 138, quoted in Eve Kosofsky Sedgwick, "Melanie Klein and the Difference Affect Makes," in *After Sex? On Writing since Queer Theory*, ed. Janet Halley and Andrew Parker (Durham, NC: Duke University Press, 2011), 295.
76 Muñoz, *Cruising Utopia*, 46.
77 Cuadros, *City of God*, 58.
78 B. Johnson, *Critical Difference*, 4–5.

CHAPTER 4. TWILIGHT OF THE IDLERS
1 Here, we may also look to Lauren Berlant's excellent study of the impasse of desire in her book *Cruel Optimism* (Durham, NC: Duke University Press, 2011).
2 Jean-Luc Nancy, *The Inoperative Community*, ed. Peter Connor, trans. Lisa Garbus et al. (Minneapolis: University of Minnesota Press, 1990).
3 Felix Gonzalez-Torres, "1990: L.A, 'The Gold Field,'" in *Roni Horn, Earths Grow Thick* (Columbus, OH: Wexner Center for the Arts, 1996), 68.
4 Francis Fukuyama, "The End of History?," *National Interest*, no. 16 (1989): 3; Francis Fukuyama, *The End of History and the Last Man* (New York: Free Press, 1992), 46.

5  Perhaps most important to note here, as Clover does, is the student occupation of Tiananmen Square that started in April 1989 and ended in a massacre of the protestors by Chinese government troops in June. See Joshua Clover, *1989: Bob Dylan Didn't Have This to Sing About* (Berkeley: University of California Press, 2009), 1.
6  Fredric Jameson, "Postmodernism, or, the Cultural Logic of Late Capitalism," *New Left Review*, no. 146 (1984): 188. Here we can also add the notable 2002 conference "End of Theory," in which Jameson gave a keynote talk titled "What Remains of Theory."
7  Joshua Clover, *1989: Bob Dylan Didn't Have This to Sing About* (Berkeley: University of California Press, 2009), 5.
8  Fredric Jameson, *Postmodernism, or, the Cultural Logic of Late Capitalism* (Durham, NC: Duke University Press, 1991), 19.
9  Clover, *1989*, 6.
10  In the introduction to a special issue of *ASAP/Journal* titled "Queer Form," the editors offer a provocative placing of "queer" and "form" beside each other to highlight the "multifaceted materiality" involved in artworks deemed challenging to the visual realm in that they open up equivocally sensuous relations between audience and performer, object and subject, form and content. The editors profess, "Form informs queerness, and queerness is best understood as a series of relations to form, relations not limited to binary and adversarial models of resistance and opposition." Kadji Amin, Amber Jamilla Musser, and Roy Pérez, "Queer Form: Aesthetics, Race, and the Violences of the Social," *ASAP/Journal* 2, no. 2 (2017): 228. Queerness in this vein gives license to a scholar to "set unlikely ideas and objects 'beside' each other and proceed from there (rather than get bogged down in justifying the suitability of cultural material" (230). The editors' thinking of queer form coincides with the operations of malaise's aesthetic structure in that they both share an almost irreverent attitude to normative demands of "making sense," a hermeneutics that makes transparent a hidden logic, an act of disclosure that carries with it racial implications. On this note, another special issue emerged soon after "Queer Form," titled "Surface Aesthetics: Race, Performance, Play," edited by the queer performance scholar Uri McMillan, in *Women and Performance*. In his introduction, McMillan notes that surface aesthetics theorizes "the sensuous ways of knowing marshaled by racialized subjects." Uri McMillan, "Introduction: Skin, Surface, Sensorium," *Women and Performance* 28, no. 1 (2018): 4. McMillan pushes against a general suspicion of surface historically driving studies of ethnicity, gender, class, and sexuality, where ideology, obscured logics, and nefarious intentions are believed to brew deep below the surface, where "critical" work means uncovering the "deeper meaning" of a text, performance, object, etc. Therefore, queer scholarship on race, McMillan argues, needs a retheorization of the surface, "propel[ing] us to consider the fecund potentialities inherent in . . . surface, particularly as an instrument of multisensory perception" (2). In light of these two special issues and their provocative theorizing of queer aesthetics as implicated in racialization and thus informed by form and surface,

the spatial structure of the beside, indicative of a stylized malaise, avoids the trap of such "hermeneutics of suspicion" that both special issues put suggestive pressure on. In other words, the besideness structure of malaise, its diffused style that comprises its form, makes visible the gap—that indeterminate space where ideology hides, though brought to the fore and turned visible on a plane of plain sight. By circumscribing the depth/surface dyad along with structure/event (with which the editors of "Queer Form" repeatedly expresses concern), malaise propels us into an understanding of the structural negative *holding* in *laying bare* the sensual materiality composed of racialized existence.

11  This section's title is a reference to the title of the second studio album of the Chicago electronic industrial band My Life with the Thrill Kill Kult, a group prominently featured in the soundtrack to Greg Araki's 1993 film *Totally F\*\*\*ed Up*, discussed later in this chapter.

12  Shoshana Felman, *The Scandal of the Speaking Body: Don Juan with J. L. Austin, or Seduction in Two Languages* (Stanford, CA: Stanford University Press, 2003), 13.

13  Sigmund Freud, *Civilization and Its Discontents*, trans. James Strachey (New York: Norton, 1961), 90.

14  In a very telling moment in his seminar "The Ethics of Psychoanalysis," Jacques Lacan remarks that "*jouissance* is evil" or, put differently, that enjoyment is suffering, where *mal* in the French also connotes suffering as much as evil, which gives us a more complex definition of "mal-aise." He goes on to say, "it is suffering because it involves the suffering for my neighbor." Lacan then responds to Freud's interpretation of the Christian injunction: "We can found our case on the following, namely that every time that Freud stops short in horror at the consequences of the commandment to love one's neighbor, we see evoked the presence of that fundamental evil which dwells within this neighbor. But if that is the case, then it also dwells within me. And what is more of a neighbor to me than this heart within which is that of my *jouissance* and which I don't dare go near? For as soon as I go near it . . . there rises up the unfathomable aggressivity from which I flee, that I turn against me, and which in the very place of the vanished Law adds its weight to that which prevents me from crossing a certain frontier at the limit of the Thing." Jacques Lacan, *The Ethics of Psychoanalysis 1959–1960*, ed. Jacques-Alain Miller, trans. Dennis Porter (New York: Norton, 1992), 184, 186.

15  Rei Terada, *Looking Away: Phenomenality and Dissatisfaction, Kant to Adorno* (Cambridge, MA: Harvard University Press, 2009), 24. Almost comically, Judith Butler's field-defining 1990 book *Gender Trouble* was translated into German a year later as *Das Unbehagen der Geschlechter*, replacing the more tense "trouble" with "unease."

16  Terada, 24.

17  Eve Kosofsky Sedgwick, *Tendencies* (Durham, NC: Duke University Press, 1993), xii.

18  I borrow this helpful distinction from Samo Tomšič, who, in his *The Capitalist Unconscious*, explains, "Here it makes sense to repeat the distinction between

constitutive alienation—alienation that is equivalent to structure—and constituted alienation—for instance, commodity fetishism, which follows from the misperception of the relation between the appearance of value and the structure that causes this appearance. . . . Constituted alienation functions as a mask or a mystification of the constitutive alienation." Tomšič, *The Capitalist Unconscious: Marx and Lacan* (Brooklyn, NY: Verso, 2015), 224.
19 Hentyle Yapp, *Minor China: Method, Materialism, and the Aesthetic* (Durham, NC: Duke University Press, 2021), 5.
20 Yapp, 5.
21 See Leticia Alvarado *Abject Performances: Aesthetic Strategies in Latino Cultural Production* (Durham, NC: Duke University Press, 2018), 14–16.
22 Tavia Nyong'o, following José Muñoz's use of the term in his posthumously published *The Sense of Brown*, defines "brown study" as such, and he locates it in some contemporary Black speculative performance. Nyong'o, *Afro-Fabulations: The Queer Drama of Black Life* (New York: New York University Press, 2019), 192. Also see José Esteban Muñoz, *The Sense of Brown*, ed. Joshua Chambers-Letson and Tavia Nyong'o (Durham, NC: Duke University Press, 2020).
23 For a critique of the domesticating logics of disciplinarily, or the restrictions embedded in "about-ness," see Kandice Chuh, "It's Not about Anything," *Social Text* 32, no. 4 (121) (2014): 125–134.
24 For a fascinating account of how Gonzalez-Torres's study of language and semiotics armed the artist with a keen eye for the written legal contract and how he deployed contract language to advance artists' rights, see Eduardo M. Peñalver and Sergio Muñoz Sarmiento, "Law in the Work of Félix González-Torres," *Cornell Journal of Law and Public Policy* 26, no. 3 (2017): 449–457.
25 Jasper Johns, *Paintings, Drawings, and Sculpture 1954–1964* (London: Whitechapel Gallery, 1964), 27.
26 Terada, *Looking Away*, 23.
27 José Muñoz, "Theorizing Queer Inhumanisms: The Sense of Brownness," *GLQ* 21, nos. 2–3 (2015): 210. Joshua Javier Guzmán and Christina A. León, "Cuts and Impressions: The Aesthetic Work of Lingering in Latinidad," *Women & Performance: A Journal of Feminist Theory* 25, no. 3 (2015): 261–276.
28 Chela Sandoval, *Methodology of the Oppressed* (Minneapolis: University of Minnesota Press, 2000), 3; Hayden White, "Historical Emplotment and the Problem of Truth in Historical Representation," in *The History and Narrative Reader*, ed. Geoffrey Roberts (London: Routledge, 2001), 383.
29 Cristina Beltrán, *The Trouble with Unity: Latino Politics and the Creation of Identity* (Oxford: Oxford University Press, 2010), 139.
30 Beltrán, 9.
31 Jacques Rancière, *Dissensus: On Politics and Aesthetics*, ed. and trans. Steven Corcoran (London: Continuum, 2010), 70.
32 The exhibition was on display from April 22 to July 22, 1990.
33 Gonzalez-Torres, "1990: L.A, 'The Gold Field,'" 68.

34 Gonzalez-Torres, 68.
35 Gonzalez-Torres, 69.
36 Gonzalez-Torres, 68.
37 José Esteban Muñoz, "Feeling Brown: Ethnicity and Affect in Ricardo Bracho's 'The Sweetest Hangover (and Other STDs),'" *Theatre Journal* 52, no. 1 (2000): 67–79.
38 Steven Shaviro, *Without Criteria: Kant, Whitehead, Deleuze, and Aesthetics* (Cambridge, MA: MIT Press, 2009), 1.
39 Steven Shaviro, "Beauty Lies in the Eye," in "Practicing Deleuze & Guattari," ed. Jeffrey R. Di Leo, special issue, *Symplokē* 6, no. 1/2 (1998): 99.
40 Gonzalez-Torres, "1990: L.A., 'The Gold Field,'" 69.
41 Shaviro, "Beauty Lies in the Eye," 105.
42 Kandice Chuh, *The Difference Aesthetics Makes: On the Humanities "After Man"* (Durham, NC: Duke University Press, 2019), 23.
43 Felix Gonzalez-Torres, interview by Tim Rollins, April 16 and June 12, 1993, in *Felix Gonzalez-Torres*, ed. Bill Bartman (New York: Art Resources Transfer, 1993), 5–31, accessed January 6, 2022, www.felixgonzalez-torresfoundation.org (my emphasis).
44 Joshua Chambers-Letson, "Contracting Justice: The Viral Strategy of Felix Gonzalez-Torres," *Criticism* 51, no. 4 (2009): 560.
45 Chambers-Letson, 561.
46 Chambers-Letson, 561.
47 Chambers-Letson, 582. I would be remiss if I did not also mention Joshua Chambers-Letson's important book *After the Party: A Manifesto for Queer of Color Life* (New York: New York University Press, 2018), in which he offers a more detailed analysis of Gonzalez-Torres's oeuvre and its (possible) relation to Marxism. There, Chambers-Letson foregrounds minoritarian performances, following José Muñoz's use of the terms, to "describe a communism of incommensurability made up of the often fractious and incommensurable, but no-less necessary alliances forged between people of color and especially women, queers, and trans people of color" (15). He quickly qualifies the term by linking it to Du Bois's conception of the "dark proletariat," which underscores the positionality of the subject's relation (or proximity) to "empire, nation capital, power and the entanglement of these systems with white supremacy" (16). This proximity to domination and extinction, for Chambers-Letson, *necessitates* a will to "More Life," which he capitalizes. This vitalism is not contingent or by happenstance but rather constitutive and fundamental to minoritarian performance, perhaps one can even say ontological to Chambers-Letson thinking of (minoritarian) performance. Chambers-Letson's necessary and constitutive vitalism that inheres in minoritarian performance stands in contrast to the constitutive lack to the subject of desire that this book has been tracking and, as I argue, that is determinate of minoritarian aesthetics.
48 For more on the genre of New Queer Cinema, see B. Ruby Rich's *New Queer Cinema: The Director's Cut* (Durham, NC: Duke University Press, 2013);

Michele Aaron, ed., *New Queer Cinema: A Critical Reader* (New Brunswick, NJ: Rutgers University Press, 2004); and Rich's groundbreaking article where the term originally appears, "A Queer Sensation," *Village Voice*, March 24, 1992, 41–44.

49  B. Ruby Rich, "New Queer Cinema," *Sight and Sound* 2, no. 5 (1992): 32.
50  Lawrence Chua, "Profiles and Positions: Gregg Araki," *BOMB* 41 (Fall 1992): 26.
51  For more, see Kobena Mercer's chapter "Black Art and the Burden of Representation," in *Welcome to the Jungle: New Positions in Black Cultural Studies* (London: Routledge, 1994), 233–258.
52  Chua, "Profiles and Positions," 26.
53  Chua, 26.
54  Chua, 27.
55  Eve Kosofsky Sedgwick, *Touching Feeling: Affect, Pedagogy, Performativity* (Durham, NC: Duke University Press, 2003), 8.
56  Tony Rayns, "Review of *Totally F\*\*\*ed Up*," *Sight and Sound* 5, no. 2 (February 1995): 56.
57  We should also recall Vaginal Davis, another Angeleno punk and self-identified Chicana, and her tribute to *Masculin Féminin* in her film *Designy Living* (1995).
58  Rayns, "Review of *Totally F\*\*\*ed Up*," 56.
59  Rayns, 56.
60  Lucas Hilderbrand, *Inherent Vice: Bootleg Histories of Videotape and Copyright* (Durham, NC: Duke University Press, 2009), 3–32.
61  Sandra Ruiz, *Ricanness: Enduring Time in Anticolonial Performance* (New York: New York University Press, 2019), 147.
62  Patricia Clough, *Autoaffection; Unconscious Thought in the Age of Teletechnology* (Minneapolis: University of Minnesota Press, 2000), 17.
63  Paul de Man, *Blindness and Insight: Essays in the Rhetoric of Contemporary Criticism*, 2nd ed. (London: Routledge, 1983), 18.
64  For more on André Bazin's theorization of the relationship between style and cinema, see his two-volume book *What Is Cinema?*, vol. 1, trans. Hugh Gray (1967; repr., Berkeley: University of California Press, 2004); *What Is Cinema?*, vol. 2, trans. Hugh Gray (1968; repr., Berkeley: University of California Press, 2005).
65  J. M. Bernstein, *The Fate of Art: Aesthetic Alienation from Kant to Derrida and Adorno* (University Park: Pennsylvania State University Press, 1992), 59–60.
66  As Nancy states regarding the question on being (*Dasein*) in the world with others, "A like-being resembles me in that I myself 'resemble' him: we 'resemble' together, if you will. That is to say, there is no original or origin of identity. What holds the place of an 'origin' is the sharing of singularities. . . . We are alike because each one of us is exposed to the outside that *we are for ourselves*. The like is not the same [*le semblable n'est pas le pareil*]" (emphasis in original). Jean-Luc Nancy, *The Inoperative Community*, ed. Peter Connor, trans. Peter Connor, Lisa Garbus, Michael Holland, and Simona Swahey (Minneapolis: University of Minnesota Press, 1991), 33.

67 In Jonathan Flatley's fantastic study and reexamination of Andy Warhol's art outside the lens of "the homo/hetero oppositions so central to modern ideas of sexual identity," he argues for a serious consideration of Warhol's use of the performative utterance "like," in "I *like* him or that," to avoid categorically collapsing everything and everyone into sameness or difference. Instead, Flatley shows how Warhol's unique aesthetic judgment, however quotidianly practiced, "dramatizes a mode of attraction based not on lack but on accumulation and plenitude." Flatley, *Like Andy Warhol* (Chicago: University of Chicago Press, 2017), 6.
68 James M. Moran, *There's No Place like Home Video* (Minneapolis: University of Minnesota Press, 2002), xii–xvi.
69 Kylo-Patrick R. Hart, "Auteur/Bricoleur/Provocateur: Gregg Araki and Post Punk Style in The Doom Generation," *Journal of Film and Video* 55 (2003): 37.
70 Jameson makes a distinction between film and video, where the latter, unlike film, represents postmodernism par excellence in its structural capacity to bar any memory or afterimage of itself after a viewing experience of it. Jameson writes, "But memory seems to play no role in television, commercial or otherwise (or, I am tempted to say, in postmodernism generally): nothing here haunts the mind or leaves it's afterimages in the manner of the great moments of film. . . . A description of the structural exclusion of memory, then, and of critical distance, might well lead on into the impossible, namely, a theory of video itself—how the thing blocks its own theorization becoming a theory in its own right." Fredric Jameson, *Postmodernism, or, the Cultural Logic of Late Capitalism* (Durham, NC: Duke University Press, 1991), 70–71.
71 Moran, *There's No Place Like Home Video*, xiii (emphasis added).
72 Moran, xiii.
73 James M. Moran, "Gregg Araki: Guerilla Filmmaker for a Queer Generation," *Film Quarterly* 50 (1996): 20.
74 Martin Heidegger's *Augenblick*, or the "glance of the eye," affords a mediation on the importance of queer culture's attempt to capture personal experience, where the experiential not only comes to evidence some proprietary or individuated knowledge but also melds the future, past, and present together within the intensity of a moment. Martin Heidegger, *Being and Time*, trans. John Macquarrie and Edward Robinson (New York: Harper and Row, 1962), 328. I will note that while *Dissatisfactions* does not deploy Martin Heidegger's phenomenology in the service of its larger argument, I find Heidegger's turn to Nazism horrific and view it as a political failure. In this regard, I follow my mentor's methodology of utilizing theory against itself as a form of breathing life into otherwise-deadening ideas. He says, "Although I take great disdain for what Heidegger's writing became, I nonetheless look on it as failure worth knowing, a potential that faltered but can be nonetheless reworked in the service of a different politics and understanding of the world." Muñoz, *Cruising Utopia*, 16, 15–17.
75 Paul de Man, "Giraudoux," *New York Review of Books*, November 28, 1963, www.nybooks.com.

76 Man.
77 For a compelling discussion of the tone and generally flat affect to Araki's films, see Lauren Berlant, "Structures of Unfeeling: Mysterious Skin," *International Journal of Politics, Culture, and Society* 28 (2015): 191–213.
78 See Juana María Rodríguez, *Queer Latinidad: Identity Practices, Discursive Spaces* (New York: New York University Press, 2003); and Juana María Rodríguez, *Sexual Futures, Queer Gestures, and Other Latina Longings* (New York: New York University Press, 2014).
79 Ramon Rivera-Servera, *Performing Queer Latinidad: Dance, Sexuality, Politics* (Ann Arbor: University of Michigan Press, 2012), 3.
80 Antonio Viego, "The Nightgown," *New Centennial Review* 3, no. 3 (2013): 337.
81 Frances Aparicio has generatively argued for not one but many iterations and forms of "latinidades." See her important study on the matter, *Negotiating Latinidad: Intralatina/o Lives in Chicago* (Urbana: University of Illinois Press, 2019). The inconclusivity of latinidad does not stop some scholars from claiming to *know* what it is. Tatiana Flores's provocative essay "Latinidad Is Cancelled" argues that latinidad (and the "Latin America" it signifies) is an imagined community that excludes African diasporic histories and thus operates as a Eurocentric, whitewashed concept. Flores, "'Latinidad Is Cancelled': Confronting an Anti-Black Construct," *Latin American and Latinx Visual Culture* 3, no. 3 (2021): 58–79. Although I do think the author underscores an incredibly important genealogy that centers Blackness in Latin American and Latino visual culture, the way *Dissatisfactions* approaches queer latinidad is first not to claim to know what it is but instead to apprehend what it does, the main enactment being a failure to cohere into anything operative for a community, although unfolding within experience, consciousness, and subjectivity as a determinate contradiction.
82 For more on "identity-knowledges" and critical practice, see Robyn Wiegman, *Object Lessons* (Durham, NC: Duke University Press, 2012).
83 Nadia Ellis, *Territories of the Soul: Queered Belonging in the Black Diaspora* (Durham, NC: Duke University Press, 2015), 4.

CONCLUSION

1 Joshua Chambers-Letson, "Contracting Justice: The Viral Strategy of Felix Gonzalez-Torres," *Criticism* 51, no. 4 (2009): 562.
2 Sandra Ruiz, *Ricanness: Enduring Time in Anticolonial Performance* (New York: New York University Press, 2019), 151.
3 Ruiz, 29.
4 Ruiz, 29.
5 José Esteban Muñoz, *Cruising Utopia: The Then and There of Queer Futurity* (New York: New York University Press, 2009), 1.
6 Kaja Silverman, *The Miracle of Analogy: or The History of Photography, Part 1* (Stanford, CA: Stanford University Press, 2015), 11.
7 Silverman, 11.

8 Silverman, 11.
9 Silverman, 11. The following passage from Whitman's "On the Beach at Night Alone" is quoted by Silverman:
 A vast similitude interlocks all, / All spheres, grown, ungrown, small, large, suns, moons, planets, / All distances of place however wide, / All distances of time, all inanimate forms, / All souls, all living bodies though they be ever so different, or in different worlds, / All gaseous, watery, vegetable, mineral processes, the fishes, the brutes, / All nations, colors, barbarisms, civilizations, languages, / All identities that have existed or may exist on this globe, or any globe, / All lives and deaths, all of the past, present, future, / This vast similitude spans them, and always has spann'd, / And shall forever span them and compactly hold and enclose them.
10 I have written elsewhere on the aesthetic work of Felix Gonzalez-Torres for queer latinidad. See Joshua Javier Guzmán and Christina León, "Cuts and Impressions: The Aesthetic Work of Lingering in Latinidad," *Women and Performance* 25, no. 3 (2015): 261–276.
11 Amanda Cruz, "The Means of Pleasure," in *Felix Gonzalez-Torres*, ed. Julie Ault (Göttingen: Steidl, 2006), 17.

# INDEX

Page numbers in *italics* indicate Figures.

Ackerman, James, 10
ACT UP, 122, 124–25, 143–44, 148
Adorno, Theodor, 10, 58
aesthetic attitude, 79
aesthetic gestures, 14–15
aesthetic responses, 32–33
aesthetics: art and, 16; of beauty, 157–58; counter-cultural, 33; as cultural response, 57; desire and, 48, 109; of discontent, 18; DIY, 2, 54, 80–81, 94, 99, 125; of Gonzalez-Torres, 195–200, *196*, *199*; hi-fi, 76; lo-fi, 82–83; of malaise, 35, 151–56; minoritarian, 4, 7; in musicology, 21; of nausea, 72–73; negative, 18–19; in performance studies, 19–20; performativity and, 134–35; philosophy, 206n20; politics and, 134–35; of pragmatism, 16–17; queers and, 220n37; televisual, 124–25, *126*, 127–31, *128*, 140
aesthetic theory, 45
Afro Sisters, 79–80
Aguhar, Mark, 206n21
Aguilar, Laura, 34–35, 147–50, 156–59, 178
Ahmed, Sara, 41, 48, 105–6
Ahwesh, Peggy, 180
AIDS: activism, 7–8, 10, 34, 124–25, *126*, 127–31, *128*; aesthetic responses to, 32–33; ambivalence about, 175; Chicanos and, 123–24, 130–31, 150–52; crisis, 120, 122–24, 129–30, 163, 195–97, *196*; in culture, 144–45, 176; death from, 34–35, 155, 166–68, *167*, 219n30, 222n57; epidemic, 9–10, 35; history of, 145–50; homophobia from, 121; in LA, 131, 133–34, 141–44; in media, 72; people of color and, 131–32; politics of, 154; queer Chicanos and, 162–63; in queer theory, 134–35; for Reagan, 10, 34, 113, 162, 174; symptoms of, 132–33; in US, 111–12, 123–24
Alarcón, Norma, 9, 82–85, 108
Alice Bag, 34
alienation, 101–2, 104
Allatson, Paul, 133–34
Alvarado, Leticia, 15–16, 51, 53, 69, 147, 161
ambivalence: about AIDS, 175; in film, 111–14, 131–40; in Gay Latino studies, 111–14, 122–24, 141–45; malaise and, 33, 35; queers and, 114–17, 145–50; resentment and, 117–22
*American Graffiti* (film), 153–54
Amin, Kadji, 47
Anaya, Rudolfo, 65
Angelo, Nancy, 1
Anger, Kenneth, 80
anti-feminism, 2–3
Anton, Susan, 75–76, 99–100
Anzaldúa, Gloria, 9, 115
Aparicio, Frances, 230n81
Araki, Gregg, 34–35; Gonzalez-Torres and, 151–52, 156, 162–63, 175–77, 181, 186; malaise and, 177–81, *182*, 188–92; Navarro, R., and, 191; Shaviro and, 182–87. See also *Totally F\*\*\*ed Up*

233

*An Army of Lovers* (Navarro, R.), 129
art: aesthetics and, 16; artists, 14, 54, 79, 123–24; Benjamin on, 32; California Institute of the Arts, 124; Chicanos and, 11–12, 59–60, 63–64; in East Los Angeles, 60–64; feminist performance, 33; from Gonzalez-Torres, 34–35, 152–53; of gossip, 80; history, 23; LA art scene, 10–11; LACMA, 32–33, 53–54, 63–64; memory in, 164, 166; of mis-en-scène, 183; modernism in, 7; Museum of Contemporary Art, 170; Otis Art Institute of Parsons School of Design, 124; philosophy and, 163–64, *165*, 166–75, *167*, *169*, *171*; Schein, 58–59; social change in, 67–68; spaces, 205n1; writing and, 108. *See also specific art*
Asco: art-making process of, 109; attachment genealogy of, 47; for Chicanos, 34, 52–59, *53*, *56*, 69, 77; cultural politics of, 58–66, *65*, *66*; in Latino studies, 52–53; at Los Angeles County Museum of Art, 53–54; politics of, 32–34, 48; reputation of, 73; Sartre and, 66; style of, 67–74, *68*; violence for, 55–59, *56*; X and, 37, 45, 47, 71–72
*Asco* (Gonzalez and Chavoya), 54
attitude, 79, 100–102, *103*, 104–9
*Attitudes*, 104–5
Aunt Lute Press, 86
Auslander, Philip, 31
*autopia*, 40, 42
Aztec imagery, 102

*Baby Kake* (video art), 69–74
"Babylonian Grogon," 90
Bag, Alice: career of, 88–92, 94–100, 216n32; reputation of, 34, 76, 79–80, *89*, 106, 108, 188–89
The Bags, 6, 75–76, 90–91, 94–98
Baldwin, James, 115
Bangs, Lester, 93
Banham, Reyner, 40

"Baptism" (Cuadros), 13
barrios, 55–59, *56*, 63–64, 212n52
Barthes, Roland, 148
Bazin, André, 183–85, 228n64
Beat, Nicky, 90
beauty, 157–58, 172–73
Beauvoir, Simone de, 46–47, 52, 66, 79, 105–8, 152, 217n65
Being, 49, 147, 197–98
Beltrán, Cristina, 169–70, 173
Benjamin, Walter, 31–32, 57–58, 147–48
Berkowitz, Richard, 122
Berlant, Lauren, 19
"Berlin Redhead," 2
Bernstein, J. M., 184–85
Bessy, Claude, 92–93
Bill Haley & His Comets, 154
"Black Art and the Burden of Representation" (Mercer), 61–62
Black Power movement, 7
Blackwell, Maylei, 9, 85
Black Youth, 7
*Bless Me Ultima* (Anaya), 65
*Blood Whispers* (anthology), 132
*Blue* (Jarman), 222n57
Bowie, David, 90, 100
The Brat, 100–102, *103*, 104–5
Bright, Brenda Jo, 102
Brown, Wendy, 117–22
Brown people, 14–15, 133, 142–43, 147, 206n21
Brown Power movement, 7, 9, 73, 101
Buffon, Georges-Louis, 22–23
Burke, Edmund, 220n37
Bush, George H. W., 153, 174
Butler, Judith, 119

California, 7, 72, 84, 113, 124. *See also specific cities*
Callen, Michael, 122–23, 131
Camarillo, Albert, 212n52
Camus, Albert, 46–47
Cantú, Norma, 9, 83–84

*Das Capital* (Marx), 23–24, 146
capitalism, 23–25, 120–21, 146, 208n52, 226n18; in modernism, 35, 45; in US, 30, 43
*Capitalism and Desire* (McGowan), 25
*The Capitalist Unconscious* (Tomšič), 226n18
*Captain Planet* (cartoon), 148
Carlisle, Belinda, 90
Carrasco, Barbara, 69–70, 72–74
Carrillo, Sean, 80, 100
Carroll, David, 18, 222n56
Carter, Jimmy, 42–43
Castration Squad, 91
Castro, Fidel, 166
Cervantes, Lorna Dee, 84
Chambers-Letson, Joshua, 175, 196, 227n47
Charles, Ray, 80
Chavoya, C. Ondine, 53–54
Chicanismo, 12, 59–60, 77, 79, 128
Chicano movement, 18, 127–28
Chicano nationalism, 32–33, 46–47, 69, 73
Chicanos: AIDS and, 123–24, 130–31, 150–52; art and, 11–12, 59–60, 63–64; Asco for, 34, 52–59, *53*, *56*, 69, 77; barrios, 55–59, *56*, 212n52; in Brown Power movement, 9; in California, 7; after Cold War, 34–35; community for, 95, 104; cultural politics of, 58–59, 69–70; desire and, 13–17; family for, 136–37, 142–43; feminism for, 66, 95–96; identity of, 35, 62, 109, 152; in LA, 32–33, 155, 195–200, *196*, *199*; live representation of, 59–66, *65*, *66*; lowrider cars, 101–2; Marxism and, 8–9; as minorities, 60–61, 91–92; normative Chicano culture, 100–101; Oedipal narratives for, 127–28, 137–39; paternal authority and, 70–71; patriarchy with, 74; in performance studies, 15–16; politics of, 8, 44, 50, 91, 102, 104; punk rock for, 11, 41–42, 111–14; scholarship on, 65–66; stereotypes of, 105; style and, 179, 185; style politics of, 161–62; in video art, 67–74, *68*; in Vietnam War, 56–57; women of color and, 83. *See also* queer Chicanos
Chicano studies, 9, 17, 132–40. *See also* specific topics
China, 224n5
"Chivalry" (Cuadros), 13
Cholita!, 80, 91, 214n12
Christianity, 159
Chua, Lawrence, 176
Chuh, Kandice, 173
La Cicciolina. *See* Davis, Vaginal
Cisneros, Sandra, 65
*City of God* (Cuadros), 34, 111–14, 131–40, 220n39
*Civilization and Its Discontents* (Freud), 158–59
class, 62–63, 152–53
*clinamen* (inclination), 94–100
Clough, Patricia, 180–81
Clover, Joshua, 153–55, 224n5
Cold War, 34–35, 153–55
Comay, Rebecca, 21–22, 30, 112
commodities, 25
communism, 227n47
Compton, Candace, 1
consumerism, 29–31, 145–46
Copjec, Joan, 130, 219n27
counter-culture politics, 9, 40
Covarrubias, Teresa, 34, 100–102, *103*, 104–6, 108–9
Coward, Noel, 80–81
Crash, Darby, 90, 93, 98–99, 108
*Creem* (magazine), 93
*Critique of Judgment* (Kant), 184–85
*Critique of Pure Reason* (Kant), 184–85
*Cruising Utopia* (Muñoz), 13, 190
Cuadros, Gil, 13, 34, 111–14; Aguilar and, 156; in Gay Latino studies, 131–40; Hollywood for, 141–43; Navarro, R., and, 111, 113–14, 123, 139, 145–50, 155; Scholder and, 220n39, 222n58

Cuba, 162–64, 166, 174–75
Cull, Laura, 210n9
cultural history, 31–32
cultural politics, 58–66, 65, 66, 69–70
cultural production, 20, 134
cultural studies, 29
culture. *See specific topics*

darkness: desire and, 141–45; in Gay Latino studies, 131–40
Davis, Vaginal, 79–84, 91, 106, 108, 214n9, 214n12, 214n14
*Dead Subjects* (Viego), 13–14
Dean, Jodi, 30
declination, 94–100
*The Decline of the West* (Spengler), 93
*The Decline of Western Civilization* (Spheeris): legacy of, 72, 90–93, 99, 191; motivation for, 37–38, 39, 40, 44, 52
decolonization, 47–48
*Decoy Gang War Victim* (photograph), 55–59, 56, 67, 71–72
Deleuze, Gilles, 44, 210n9
Demeny, Paul, 222n58
depressive anxiety, 149
*Design Living* (Coward), 80–81
*Designy Living* (Davis), 80–81
desire: aesthetics and, 48, 109; alternative, 5–7; of artists, 79; Chicanos and, 13–17; darkness and, 141–45; desire's frame, 122–24; ethnic-racialized, 33; networks of, 96; by people of color, 115; in performance studies, 85–86; political, 20, 82; in psychoanalysis, 22–25, 29, 73–74, 76; romantic, 43; sensation and, 145; women of color and, 98–99
*The Difference Aesthetics Makes* (Chuh), 173
Dinah Cancer, 91
*Disidentifications* (Muñoz), 13
disinformation, 71–72
dispossession, 23
dissatisfaction. *See specific topics*

DIVA TV (Damned Interfering Video Activist-Television), 124–25, 126
do-it-yourself (DIY): aesthetics, 2, 54, 80–81, 94, 99, 125; culture, 77, 91, 100, 108
dominant culture, 26–27
*Don't Tell Her Art Can't Hurt* (photograph collection), 158–59
*The Doom Generation* (Araki), 177, 185–86
*Dot* (Coward), 80–81
"Do the Gestalt," 2
"Dream Baby Dream," 195
Dreva, Jerry, 90
*Duel of Angels* (Fry), 189

Eagleton, Terry, 208n52
East Los Angeles, 1–4, 7–9, 52–57, 60–64, 68, 90
*Edward II* (Jarman), 176
Edwards, Brent Hayes, 85–86
Eisenhower, Dwight, 154
electropunk music, 6–7
Ellis, Nadia, 192
emergent culture, 26–27
*The End of History and the Last Man* (Fukuyama), 153, 156
ennui, 52
*Epistemologies of the Closet* (Sedgwick), 120–21
epistemology, 15–16; of knowledge, 79–86, 116–17, 173
*Equipped* (Leonard), 220n33
*Erased de Kooning Drawing* (Rauschenberg), 164, 166
*The Ethics of Ambiguity* (Beauvoir), 106–7
ethnicity, 16, 20, 47, 51
etymology, 21–22
Eugene (sic), 37–38, 39, 40, 72, 191
existentialism, 14, 44, 48, 52, 55

Falcon Cable Television, 73
*Falling Down* (film), 40
Fanon, Frantz, 47–48, 66
Fatima Records, 104–5

Felman, Shoshana, 18, 151
feminism: anti-feminism, 2–3; art spaces for, 205n1; for Chicanos, 66, 95–96; in lo-fi performance, 90–93; makeshift presses, 79–86; Nervous Gender and, 1–2; psychology and, 118–20, 213n1; punk rock and, 74, 104; for queers, 71; for Reagan, 215n28; Sandoval, C., on, 167; Sedgwick and, 51; stereotypes in, 105–6; women of color and, 13, 78–79
feminist critiques, 9
feminist of color presses, 84–86
feminist performance art, 33
feminist print culture, 75–79, 86–89, *89*
feminist theory, 82–83
*Fertile La Toyah Jackson* (zine), 79–82
Fisher, Mark, 4, 6, 24, 77, 82
Flatley, Jonathan, 229n67
Ford, Gerald, 43
*Forms from the Gold Field* (Horn), 170–71
Foucault, Michel, 151
Foxx, John, 4
France, 22, 33, 49, 107, 146
France, David, 127–28
Freeman, Elizabeth, 31, 97
Freire, Paulo, 66
French New Wave, 178
Freud, Sigmund, 31, 35, 158–63, 225n14
Friedan, Betty, 66
Fry, Christopher, 189
Fukuyama, Francis, 153, 156

Gallimard, Gaston, 51–52, 59
Gallimard Press, 49, 51
Gamboa, Harry, Jr., 52, 55, 57–58, 60, 67, 69–70. *See also* Asco
gangs, 55–59, *56*
gay identity, 17–18, 33, 152
Gay Latino studies: ambivalence in, 111–14, 122–24, 141–45; Brown in, 117–22; Cuadros, Gil in, 131–40; Navarro, R., in, 124–25, *126*, 127–31, *128*; passionate sensuousness in, 145–50; problems with, 114–17
*Gay Latino Studies* (Hames-García and Martínez), 113–17
gay liberation, 9–10, 18
Gay Men's Health Crisis, 122
The Germs, 90, 98
Geza X, 79–80
*Gilbert's Altar* (Aguilar), 147–48, 150
Gilley, Jennifer, 85
Giroudaux, Jean, 189
Godard, Jean-Luc, 80–81, 178–79
González, Matilde Martín, 215n28
Gonzalez, Rita, 53–54
Gonzalez-Torres, Felix: aesthetics of, 195–200, *196*, *199*; Araki and, 151–52, 156, 162–63, 175–77, 181, 186; art from, 34–35, 152–53; influence of, 226n24; Marxism and, 227n47; time and, 163–64, *165*, 166–75, *167*, *169*, *171*
gossip, 80
Graciela Grejalva. *See* Davis, Vaginal
Grant, Toni, 2–3
Gronk. *See* Nicandro, Glugio Gronk
*Gronk/Dreva* (art exhibition), 90
*Grundrisse* (Marx), 146

Habermas, Jürgen, 212n49
Hag Gallery, 81
Hames-García, Michael, 113–17, 119, 129–30, 145–46, 149, 218n8, 218n9
Hansen, Bibbe, 80
Hart, Kylo-Patrick R., 185
Hartley, Daniel, 208n52
Hebdige, Dick, 10–11
Hegel, Georg Wilhelm Friedrich, 112, 146
hegemony, 10–11, 62–63
Heidegger, Martin, 229n74
Herrón, Willie, III, 52, 66. *See also* Asco
hi-fi aesthetics, 76
*High Risk* (Scholder), 220n39, 222n58
*High Risk 2* (anthology), 132

Hinshelwood, R. D., 149
historical materialism, 47
history. *See specific topics*
HIV. *See* AIDS
Hollywood, 38, 55, 141–44
*Hollywood Babylon*, 80
"Holy" (Cuadros), 13
*Home Girls* (anthology), 84–85
homophobia, 121, 135–39
Hong, Grace, 54, 64
Hong Kong Café, 75–76
Horn, Roni, 170–72, *171*
*The House on Mango Street* (Cisneros), 65
Howard, Richard, 49, 51
*How to Survive a Plague* (France), 127–28, *128*, 130–31
Hunt, Annette, 1
Hynes, Maria, 210n9

Idár, Jovita, 83–84
identity: aspects of, 115–16; of Chicanos, 35, 62, 109, 152; epistemology and, 15–16; gay, 17–18, 33; group, 95–96; identification and, 213n1; LA and, 187; Latino, 111–14, 122, 149–50; lesbian, 61–62; of minorities, 131–32; ontology and, 149; politics, 91–92, 117–22; queer latinidad as, 161–62
ideology, 21, 24–25, 32–33, 61, 116–17
Iggy and the Stooges, 93
*Imperfecto* (video art), 69–70
inauthenticity, 14–15
inclination, 94–100
*Indigo, Sassafras and Molasses*, 79–80
individuality, 94–95
*Indivisible* (anthology), 132
"Indulgences" (Cuadros), 13
*Instant Mural* (performance piece), 64–65, 68
intersectionality, 208n62
*In the Spirit of a New People* (Ontiveros), 65–66
intimacy, 96

Islas, Arturo, 207n31
Italian *Operaismo*, 26

The Jam, 100
Jameson, Fredric, 48–49, 153–54, 208n52, 211n37, 229n70
Jarman, Derek, 176, 222n57
John, Elton, 90–91
Johns, Jasper, 164, 166
Johnson, Barbara, 138, 150
Johnson, Lyndon, 56
Joubert, Joseph, 22

Kahlo, Frida, 80
Kant, Immanuel, 172–73, 184–85
Kayle Hilliard. *See* Davis, Vaginal
Khanna, Neetu, 47–48
King, Martin Luther, Jr., 66
King, Rodney, 152–53
Kitchen Table Press, 84–86
*The Knife* (Aguilar), 35, 156–59, 178
knowledge, 79–86, 116–17, 173; epistemology of, 15–16
Kubler, George, 124

Lacan, Jacques, 14, 22–25, 159, 219n27, 225n14
Lace Gallery, 1–2
LACMA. *See* Los Angeles County Museum of Art
Latina politics, 169–70, 173
latinidad, 15, 35, 96, 159–63, 174, 197–200, 230n81
Latinos. *See specific topics*
Latino studies, 11–16, 33, 52–53, 192, 197–98, 206. *See also specific topics*
LAWVC. *See* Los Angeles Women's Video Center
Laycock, Ross, 166–68, *167*, 170–71
*Leave It to Beaver* (TV show), 154
Leonard, Zoe, 220n33
León-Portillo, Miguel, 66
"Letting Go" (Cuadros), 13, 135–39, 149

"Like a Prayer" (song), 125
"Like a Prayer" (video), 125, *126*
Limón, José, 8–9, 10
Lipsitz, George, 102
live representation, of Chicanos, 59–66, *65*, *66*
*The Living End* (Araki), 176, 177
Livingston, Jennie, 176
lo-fi: aesthetic, 82–83; feminist print culture and, 75–79; knowledge sharing, 79–86; nausea and, 175; performance, 90–93; Shaviro and, 179–82, *182*, 187–89, *188*; style, 33, 35, 76–77, 100–102, *103*, 104–9
*The Long Weekend (O' Despair)* (Araki), 177
López, Marissa K., 134
Lorde, Audre, 54, 115
*Los Angeles*, 37, 42
Los Angeles (LA): AIDS in, 131, 133–34, 141–44; art scene in, 10–11; Brown Power movement in, 101; Chicanos in, 32–33, 155, 195–200, *196*, *199*; culture of, 6–9, 76–77; East, 1–4, 7–9, 52–57, 60–64, 68, 90; Falcon Cable Television in, 73; gangs in, 55–59, *56*; Hag Gallery in, 81; Hong Kong Café in, 75–76; identity and, 187; The Masque in, 9, 38, 90; Mexico and, 134; Mexico City and, 12; minorities in, 54; Museum of Contemporary Art, 170; in photography, 67–68; postmodernity in, 35; punk rock in, 8, 12, 38, 46–47, 52, 86–89, 152; queer Chicanos in, 181–82, *182*; queer counterculture in, 187–88; queers in, 148; Reagan for, 41–42; reputation of, 55; riots, 152–53; *Spray Paint LACMA*, 63–65, *65*; style in, 29; utopianism in, 40; Vietnam War and, 111–12; X in, 34. *See also specific topics*
"Los Angeles," 42
Los Angeles County Museum of Art (LACMA), 32–33, 53–54, 63–64

Los Angeles Women's Video Center (LAWVC), 1–2, *5*
*Lowrider* (magazine), 100–102, *103*
lowrider cars, 101–2
Lucretius Carus, Titus, 94, 99–100, 109, 217n48
Lugones, María, 115–16

makeshift presses, 79–86
"Make Your Own Press Pass" (flier), 125, *126*, 127
malaise: aesthetics of, 35, 151–56; ambivalence and, 33, 35; Araki and, 177–81, *182*, 188–92; ennui and, 52; latinidad and, 159–63; politics of, 42–43; psychoanalysis and, 225n14; Shaviro and, 193; stylized, 224n10. *See also Totally F\*\*\*ed Up*
de Man, Paul, 189
Mango Publications, 84
*Mapping Another L.A.* (Pacific Standard Time), 32–33
Marazzi, Christian, 43, 57–58, 212n49
Marcuse, Herbert, 75, 99, 114–17, 145–46
marginal communities, 44–45, 85–86
Martínez, Ernesto Javier, 113–14
Marx, Karl, 23–24, 47, 146–47, 208n48, 208n52
Marxism, 8–11, 14, 43, 116–17, 227n47
*Marxism and Literature* (Williams), 26
*Masculin Féminin* (Godard), 178
The Masque, 9, 38, 90
mass shootings, 198–200, *199*
materialism, 47, 116–17
*Maurice Blanchot* (Foucault), 151
McCaughan, Edward J., 11–12, 52–53
McGowan, Todd, 25
McMillan, Uri, 224n10
Medina, Rudy, 100. *See also* The Brat
Medina, Sidney, 100. *See also* The Brat
"Melanie Klein and the Difference Affect Makes" (Sedgwick), 118–19
memory, 111–12, 164, 166, 229n70

Mercer, Kobena, 61–62, 70
Mercury, Freddie, 90
Merleau-Ponty, Maurice, 37, 41
*Methodology of the Oppressed* (Sandoval, C.), 168
Mexican Americans, 8–9, 55–57, 56, 66, 83. *See also* Chicanos
Mexico, 8, 12, 33, 60, 66, 134
*Migrant Souls* (Islas), 207n31
Miller, D. A., 51
Miller, Judith, 22–23
Mills, C. Wright, 66
Minich, Julie, 133–34
minoritarian: acculturation of, 8; aesthetics, 4, 7; Chicanos as, 60–61, 91–92; in East Los Angeles, 52–57; identity, 131–32; in marginal communities, 44–45; oppression of, 35; Reagan and, 46; scholarship on, 61–62; writing and, 84–85. *See also specific minorities*
*The Miracle of Analogy* (Silverman), 197
mis-en-scène, 183
misogyny, 105–6
modernism, 7, 45, 57–58; popular, 4, 6, 77, 82, 106; postmodernism, 12, 35, 61, 83, 153–54, 207n40
the Modern Lovers, 1–2
"Mommie's Chest," 2
Montaigne, Michel de, 107–8
Moraga, Cherríe, 9
Moran, James M., 185–86
Morgan, Robin, 66
Morrisroe, Mark, 71
Moten, Fred, 32
*Mourning Sickness* (Comay), 21
Moya, Paula, 116
MTV, 125, 127, 182
Mullen, Brendan, 38, 39, 40, 43, 99
Muñoz, José Esteban, 13, 31, 61, 72, 117–18; influence of, 14, 190, 214n12; scholarship from, 207n31, 214n14, 227n47; on X, 42
Museum of Contemporary Art, 170

music recording, 19–20
Musser, Amber, 15–16, 147, 223n72
"My Aztlán" (Cuadros), 13, 132, 137–38, 141–43
"My Sex," 3–4, 6

Nancy, Jean-Luc, 94–95, 185, 228n66
National Guard, 8
nausea, 58, 175; in culture, 33–34, 46–47; psychoanalysis and, 45–46, 69; style politics of, 28–29, 37–38, 39, 40–48, 67–74, 68. *See also* Sartre
"Nausea," 37, 42, 45, 71
*La Nausée* (Sartre), 34, 44, 47–52, 211n37
Navarro, Patricia, 127–28, 128, 143–45
Navarro, Ray, 11, 34, 143–44, 191, 220n33; Cuadros and, 111, 113–14, 123, 139, 145–50, 155; in Gay Latino studies, 124–25, 126, 127–31, 128
Nazism, 93, 107
negative aesthetics, 18–19
neoliberalism, 40–41
*Nervous Gender*, 1–4, 3, 5, 6, 6–7, 91
New Queer Cinema (NQC), 175–79, 186–92
New York City, 124–25, 127
*Next of Kin* (Rodríguez, R.), 70
Ngai, Sianne, 45–46, 61
Nicandro, Glugio Gronk, 52, 55–56, 64–65, 67, 69, 90. *See also* Asco
Nietzsche, Friedrich, 111, 118, 149
*A Nightmare before Christmas* (film), 148
1968: dissatisfaction with, 7, 118, 154; post-, 8, 33, 35, 40, 56, 162, 174, 187; spirit of, 23, 31
"1990: L.A." (Gonzalez-Torres), 151
Nixon, Richard, 56
*No Mag* (magazine), 93
*Non-Work* (Gonzalez-Torres), 163–64, 165, 166
Noriega, Chon, 63–64
normative Chicano culture, 100–101
normative culture, 74

*Nowhere* (Araki), 177
NQC. *See* New Queer Cinema
Nyong'o, Tavia, 19

*Object Lessons* (Wiegman), 191–92
Ochoa, Michael, 1–2, 4. *See also* Nervous Gender
Oedipal narratives, 127–28, 137–39
*One Dimensional Man* (Marcuse), 75
"On the Beach at Night Alone" (Whitman), 231n9
*On the Nature of Things* (Lucretius), 94
Ontiveros, Randy, 65–66
ontology, 20, 43–44, 149, 160–61; of Being, 49, 147, 197–98
oppression, 23, 35, 112–13, 168
*The Origins of German Tragic Drama* (Benjamin), 31
the Other, 22–23, 28, 31
Otis Art Institute of Parsons School of Design, 124

Pacific Standard Time, 32–33
paraesthetics, 18
*Paris Is Burning* (Livingston), 176
Parker, Dorothy, 81
passionate sensuousness, 145–50
"Past Imperfecto" (Gamboa, Jr.), 69–70
patriarchy, 70–71, 74, 84–85
Pellegrini, Ann, 31
people of color, 115, 131–32
Pérez, Emma, 9
Pérez, Roy, 206n21
Pérez-Torres, Rafael, 133–34
performance studies: artists, 54; barrios in, 63–64; Chicanos in, 15–16; desire in, 85–86; disinformation in, 71–72; Latino studies and, 11, 13; lo-fi performance, 90–93; methodology in, 31–35; ontology in, 20; performativity, 14, 19–20, 23–24, 31–32, 46, 60–61, 130, 134–35; photography in, 55–59, 56, 57–58; queers in, 41–42

Les Petites Bon-Bons, 90
Phelan, Peggy, 31
phenomenology, 37, 41, 43–44, 48, 229n74
*The Phenomenology of Perception* (Merleau-Ponty), 37
philosophy: aesthetics, 206n20; art and, 163–64, *165*, 166–75, *167*, *169*, *171*; from Bernstein, 184–85; culture and, 120–21; of Foucault, 151; *Unbehagen*, 159–63
photography. *See specific photographs*
Phranc, 1–3
*Pipe Bomb for the Soul* (Bag), 91, 216n32
"Plastic Bag," 96–98
Plato, 94
the Plugz, 1–2
political imaginary, 161
*The Political Unconscious* (Jameson), 153–54
politics: aesthetics and, 134–35; of AIDS, 154; of Asco, 32–34, 48; in California, 113; of capitalism, 23–24; Chicano nationalism, 46–47; of Chicanos, 8, 44, 50, 91, 102, 104; counter-culture, 9, 40; cultural, 58–66, *65*, *66*, 69–70; culture and, 16–17; decolonization, 47–48; of difference, 54, 64; of gay liberation, 9–10; of government, 216n40; identity, 91–92, 117–22; Jameson on, 153–54; Latina, 169–70, 173; latinidad, 174; of Los Angeles County Museum of Art, 63–64; of loss, 13–14; of malaise, 42–43; neoliberalism, 40–41; populism, 42, 72; queer, 17, 41; queer Chicano, 17–18, 174; of Reagan, 162–63; of scholarship, 16; social, 102, 104; of social difference, 55; of Styrene, 97–98; subcultural, 10–11; of television-guerrilla-activism, 11; in US, 34–35. *See also* style politics
popular modernism, 4, 6, 77, 82, 106
populism, 42, 72
postmodernism, 12, 35, 61, 83, 153–54, 207n40
postpositivist realism, 116–17

post-punk rock, 15, 82, 96
*Pour Lucrè* (Giroudaux), 189
power, 28–30, 54
pragmatism, 16–17
press passes, 125, *126*, 127
psychoanalysis, 47–48; of AIDS, 135–40, 221n42; alienation, 101–2, 104; attitude, 100–102, *103*, 104–9; *autopia*, 40, 42; Being and, 49; culture and, 2–3; depressive anxiety, 149; of desire, 22–25, 29, 73–74, 76; feminism and, 118–20, 213n1; from Freud, 31, 158–59; of malaise, 225n14; Marxism and, 14; of nausea, 45–46, 69; resentment, 118; of satisfaction, 25; *Unbehagen*, 159–63
punk rock: attitude, 100–102, *103*, 104–9; Bag for, 90–93; Chicanismo and, 77; for Chicanos, 11, 41–42, 111–14; DIY aesthetics in, 81; in documentaries, 37–38, *39*, 40, 72; feminism and, 74, 104; filmmaking, 34–35; history of, 1–2; in LA, 8, 12, 38, 46–47, 52, 86–89, 152; negative aesthetics and, 19; Nervous Gender for, 2–3; post-punk rock, 15, 82, 96; queer, 32–33, 79–86; queer Chicanos and, 1–4, 2, 9, 19–20, 186–87; queers and, 12; racism in, 93; scholarship on, 216n32; in US, 6–7; women of color in, 75–79, 86–89, *89*; Xerox copy machine for, 79, 81–82, 87; X for, 34, 44. *See also specific topics*
Pyn, Bobby, 98

queer Chicanos: AIDS and, 162–63; Chicano studies and, 132–40; in LA, 181–82, *182*; politics of, 17–18, 174; punk rock and, 1–4, 2, 9, 19–20, 186–87
queer counterculture, 187–88
"Queer Form" (journal), 224n10
queer latinidad, 35, 161–62, 197–200
queer Latino studies, 33, 206, 206n28
queerness, 160
queer phenomenology, 48

queer politics, 17, 41
queer punk rock, 32–33, 79–86
queers: aesthetics and, 220n37; ambivalence and, 114–17, 145–50; feminism for, 71; gay identity and, 17–18; Heidegger and, 229n74; in LA, 148; NQC for, 175–77, 186–92; in performance studies, 41–42; punk rock and, 12; televisual aesthetics of, 124–25, *126*, 127–31, *128*
queer studies, 13, 192, 224n10
queer theory, 24, 129–30, 134–35
"Queer Theory Revisited" (Hames-García), 114–15

race, 16–17, 20, 47, 51, 59, 77, 152–53
*Racial Immanence* (López), 134
racism, 69, 93, 133
radical negativity, 18
Ramos, Iván, 14–15
Rancière, Jacques, 170
"Rapper's Delight," 154
Rauschenberg, Robert, 164, 166
Rayford, Robert, 219n30
Rayns, Tony, 178–79
*Reading Chican@ Like a Queer* (Soto), 17
Reagan, Ronald, 8; AIDS for, 10, 34, 113, 162, 174; Bush and, 153; feminism for, 215n28; for LA, 41–42; in Latina politics, 170; leadership of, 30; minorities and, 46; Muñoz on, 72; neoliberalism and, 40–41; politics of, 162–63; Thatcher and, 86, 96; for US, 11, 23–24, 138, 187
realism, 24–25, 116–17
*Real World* (TV show), 182
Rechniewski, Elizabeth, 49
*Reclaiming Identity* (Games-García and Moya), 116
refinement, 67–74, *68*
religion, 60, 102, 133, 136, 159
*Repo Man* (film), 182
resentment, 117–22

"Reynaldo" (Cuadros), 13
Rich, B. Ruby, 175–77
Rimbaud, Arthur, 222n58
Rivera-Servera, Ramon, 190
"Rock Around the Clock," 154
Rodríguez, Juana Maria, 15, 190
Rodríguez, Richard T., 15, 53, 70, 96
Rollins, Tim, 174–75
Rolls, Alistair, 49
Roman Catholicism, 133
Romanticism, 50, 51–52
Roquentin, Antoine, 50, 51–52. See also *La Nausée*
Roth, Josie, 1
Ruiz, Sandra, 14–16, 196–97

Salazar, Rubén, 8, 91
Saldivar-Hall, Sonia, 9
Sandoval, Chela, 167–68
Sandoval, Humberto, 67, 69–70
"Sanyo," 94–97, 99–100
Sanyo electronics, 75–76
Sartre, Jean Paul, 34, 46–52, 59, 66, 152
*Schein*, 58–59
Scholder, Amy, 220n39, 222n58
Schulman, Sarah, 143–44
Scott, Joan, 78
Screamers, 1
Sedgwick, Eve, 17–18, 51, 118–21, 149, 160, 177–78, 218n8
"7 Deadly Days" (Time), 198
"Sex and Dying in High Society," 42
sexism, 3, 104–5
sexuality, 4, 16–17, 20, 59, 77, 154
Shaviro, Steven, 172–73, 190–93; Araki and, 182–87; lo-fi and, 179–82, *182*, 187–89, *188*
*Shrimp* (magazine), 79–80
"Sight" (Cuadros), 135, 139–41, 147, 149
Silverberg, Ira, 222n58
Silverman, Kaja, 197–98, 231n9
Simpson, O. J., 144
Sinatra, Frank, 75

*Slash* (magazine), 1–2, 86–89, *89*, 106
Smith, Barbara, 84–85
Smith, Patti, 3–4
social change, 38, 40–41, 67–68
society, 26–27, 29–30, 55
sociology, 52–53, 210n9
Soto, Sandra K., 9, 17–18
spacious agnosticism, 177–78
Spengler, Oswald, 93
Spheeris, Penelope, 37–38, *39*, 40, 44, 52, 90–91
Spillers, Hortense, 85
Spitz, Marc, 91–93
*Spray Paint LACMA* (performance piece), 63–65, *65*
Stapleton, Edward, 1–4. See also Nervous Gender
*Strange Weather* (Ahwesh), 180
"structure of feeling" (Williams), 26–28
style: of Asco, 67–74, *68*; in capitalism, 24–25; Chicanos and, 179, 185; consumerism and, 30–31; culture and, 154–55; documentary, 188–89, *189*; etymology of, 21–22; ideology and, 21; in LA, 29; lo-fi, 33, 35, 76–77, 100–102, *103*, 104–9; media and, 20; the Other and, 22–23; questions of, 28, 44; scholarship on, 50–51; singularity and, 26; stylized malaise, 224n10; stylized nausea, 73; writing, 33. See also aesthetics
style politics: in culture, 59–66, *65*, *66*, 161–62; of nausea, 28–29, 37–38, *39*, 40–48, 67–74, *68*
stylized discontent, 7, 18, 20, 21–31, 33–35, 50, 109, 113, 151, 162, 171–73, 185, 192–93; ambivalence as, 121; Araki's, 179; Asco and, 67, 70, 73–74; beauty and, 160; lo-fi as, 76, 78, 105; unbehagen and, 161
Styrene, Poly, 97–98, 108, 152
subcultural artifacts, 18–19, 155
*Subculture* (Hebdige), 10–11
"Suburbia Diptheria," 2
Sugar Hill Gang, 154

Sullivan, Nelson, 214n12
"Survive," 90
*Surviving AIDS* (Callen), 122–23, 131

*Talking about depression* (Aguilar), 35, 156–59
*Talking about depression 2* (Aguilar), 35, 156–59
Taylor, Diana, 31
Taylor, Lawrence P., 216n40
"Teenage Apocalypse Trilogy" (Araki), 177. *See also specific films*
teleology, 92, 94
television-guerrilla-activism, 11
televisual aesthetics, 124–25, *126*, 127–31, *128*, 140
*Tendencies* (Sedgwick), 17
Terada, Rei, 58
Terry, Jennifer, 96
Thatcher, Margaret, 23–24, 86, 96
"That's Life," 75–76
third space, 44–45
*Third Woman* (journal), 82–84
Third Woman Press, 82–84, 86
time, 163–64, *165*, 166–75, *167*, *169*, *171*
*Time* (magazine), 198–99
Tlatelolco Massacre, 8
Tomšič, Samo, 29, 226n18
Tongson, Karen, 96
*Totally F\*\*\*ed Up* (Araki), 35, 156; critical reception of, 179–86; culture and, 177–79; for queers, 186–92

*Ugly Feelings* (Ngai), 45
Ultravox, 3, 6
*Unbehagen*, 159–63
United Kingdom, 23–24, 82, 96–98
United States (US), 82; AIDS in, 111–12, 123–24; capitalism in, 30, 43; Carter for, 42–43; in Cold War, 153; consumerism in, 29–31, 145–46; Cuba and, 162–64, 166, 174–75; imperialism, 18; latinidad in, 96, 230n81; mass shootings in, 198–200, *199*; Mexico and, 66; National Guard, 8; politics in, 34–35; post-punk rock and, 15; punk rock in, 6–7; Reagan for, 11, 23–24, 138, 187; social movements in, 38, 40; third space in, 44–45; Vietnam War, 54, 56–57, 111–12, 153–54
"Unprotected" (Cuadros), 13
*Untitled (Death by Gun)* (Gonzalez-Torres), 198–200, *199*
*Untitled (Orpheus, Twice)* (Gonzalez-Torres), *169*, 169–74, 175–76, 181
*Untitled (Perfect Lovers)* (Gonzalez-Torres), 168
*Untitled (Portrait of Ross in L.A.)* (Gonzalez-Torres), 195–200, *196*
US. *See* United States
utopianism, 14, 40–41

Valdez, Patssi, 52, 60, 64–65, *66*, *67*, *68*, 73. *See also* Asco
Vargas, Deborah, 14–15
Vazquez, Alexandra, 85
Velazquez, Gerardo, 1–2, 4, 6, *6*–7. *See also* Nervous Gender
The Vex, 9
video art. *See specific art*
Viego, Antonio, 13–14, 191–92
Vietnam War, 54, 56–57, 111–12, 153–54
Villa, Raúl Homero, 46, 58–59, 212n52
Villaseñor, Becky, 156
violence, 55–59, *56*, 138–39, 198–200, *199*, 224n5
*Violence Girl* (Bag), 90
*Virgin de Guadalupe* (Valdez), 60
Virgin of Guadalupe imagery, 102

*Walking Mural* (performance piece), 60–62, *64*, *66*
Warhol, Andy, 80, 172, 178, 229n67
Waters, John, 71
*We Got the Neutron Bomb* (Spitz), 91–93
The Weirdos, 90
"We're Desperate," 42

whateverness, 67–74, *68*
*What is Cinema?* (Bazin), 183
Whitehead, Alfred North, 172
"The White Noise Supremacist" (Bangs), 93
Whitman, Walt, 231n9
Wiegman, Robyn, 191–92
Williams, Raymond, 26–28, 208n52
women, 1–3, 5, 82–85, 104–6. *See also* feminism
women of color: Cantú on, 83–84; Chicanos and, 83; desire and, 98–99; feminism and, 13, 78–79; Kitchen Table Press for, 84–85; makeshift presses, 79–86; in punk rock, 75–79, 86–89, *89*; scholarship on, 206n28

"Wounded Attachments" (Brown), 117–22
writing, 27–28, 33, 84–85, 108

X, 34, 37, 38, 42–48, 58, 71–72, 152
Xerox copy machine, 79, 81–82, 87
X-Ray Spex, 75, 96–100

Yapp, Hentyle, 160–61
Yates, Brock, 40
Ybarra-Frausto, Tomás, 78
youth culture, 38
Yum-Yum Donuts, 100–101

Zamora, Ruben, 69–70

ABOUT THE AUTHOR

JOSHUA JAVIER GUZMÁN is Assistant Professor in the Department of Gender Studies at UCLA. His writing has been published in *Women and Performance*, *Social Text*, *English Language Notes*, *AfterImage*, *Psychoanalysis in the Barrios*, and *Axis Mundo: Queer Networks in Chicano L.A.*, and he is a recipient of the Andy Warhol Foundation Arts Writers Grant.

www.ingramcontent.com/pod-product-compliance
Lightning Source LLC
Chambersburg PA
CBHW020403080526
44584CB00014B/1147